Treasures of
Western Oregon

By: William Faubion

Part of the Morgan & Chase "Treasures" Series
www.morganandchasepublishing.com
Published in the U.S.A.

Morgan & Chase
Publishing inc.

Published by:
Morgan & Chase Publishing, Inc.
531 Parsons Drive, Suite 107
Medford, Oregon 97501
888-557-9328
www.morganandchasepublishing.com
www.americastreasures.com

Printed by:
C & C Offset Printing Co., Ltd. - China

First edition 2005

ISBN: 0-9754162-1-9
Editors: Cindy Faubion
          Brenda Rausch
          Genevieve Hartin
Contributing Writers:
          Andrea Adams
          Craig Calloway
          Brent Dahl
          Leslie Fazio
          Tom Higham
          Joy Kieras
          Amy Laier
          Mickie McCormic
          Kathy Reynolds
          Don Rickel
          Ron Turpen
          Susan Vaughn
Story Coordinators:
          Wendy Gay
Graphic Design:
          ProVisual Design, Inc.
Custom Digital Artwork for Division Pages:
          Waterpainter.com

Special Recognition to:
Jobie Grether, Leonard Griffie, Adam Nolte, Janna Sample, Nola Shaw, Craig Tansley, Mel Winkelman

Dedication

This book is dedicated to the hard working people of Western Oregon.

Table of Contents

Forward

Welcome to the "Treasures of Western Oregon," where the end of the Oregon Trail is the beginning of a personal adventure. Oregon is still a place where people know and care about each other and those qualities make Western Oregon a wonderful place to visit and to live. The beautiful rivers, tall trees, rolling hills, majestic mountains and verdant valleys provide an exquisite environment for the friendly and caring people you'll meet here.

The city of Portland combines big city ambience with small town friendliness. It boasts world-class cuisine, cultural events, artistic enclaves, professional sport teams, citywide celebrations such as the Rose Festival, scenic parks and breathtaking vistas. Yes, the city has it all and it's all good! In smaller cities and towns, Western Oregon has a sense of neighborliness and pioneer spirit. Each community has a rich history and strives to create a vibrant future. Like a sparkling gem, each town and each business is unique and fascinating.

The businesses that you'll find inside the book know that the secret to success is personal care and exceptional service and that's what they provide. No business can buy space in the "Treasures of Western Oregon" book. Each listing was personally selected by secret shoppers, writers, and publisher's representatives. Only after the business was chosen, was the business invited to participate. That is why "Treasures of Western Oregon" is such fun to read and the places featured in the book are such pleasures to visit. The publisher is confident that each time you step into a "Treasure" you'll be pampered by a specially selected business that represents the best of Western Oregon.

How To Use This Book

This book is divided by geographic areas and type of business.

The primary divisions are Mt Hood and the Columbia River Gorge,
Portland Metro, Willamette Valley, Umpqua Valley and Southern Oregon.
The types of businesses include accommodations, attractions,
coffee and sweet shops, galleries, gardens and markets, gifts, health
and beauty, museums, restaurants, retirement centers and wineries.

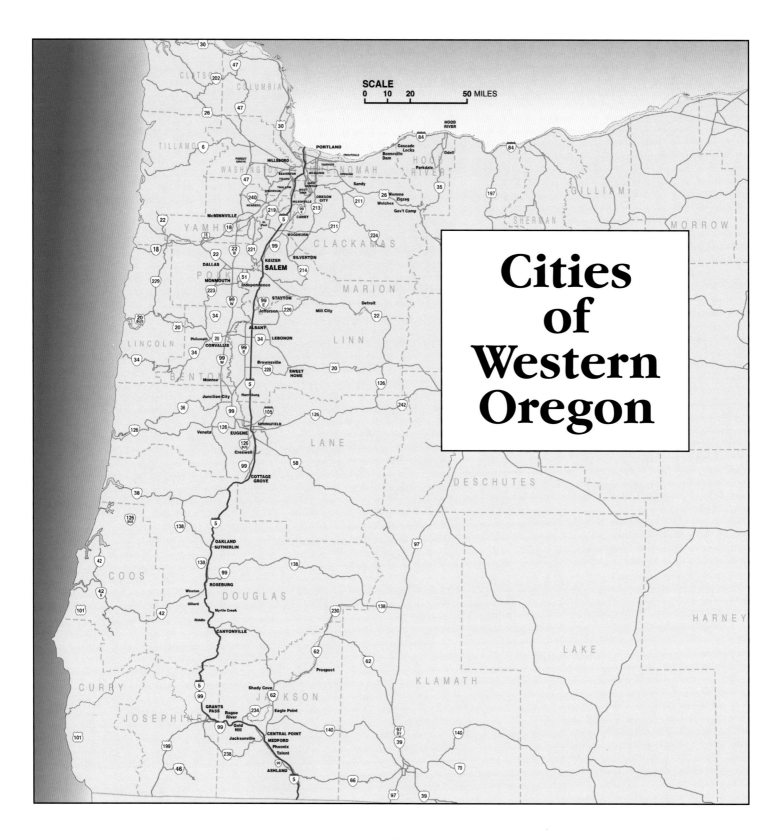

Cities of Western Oregon

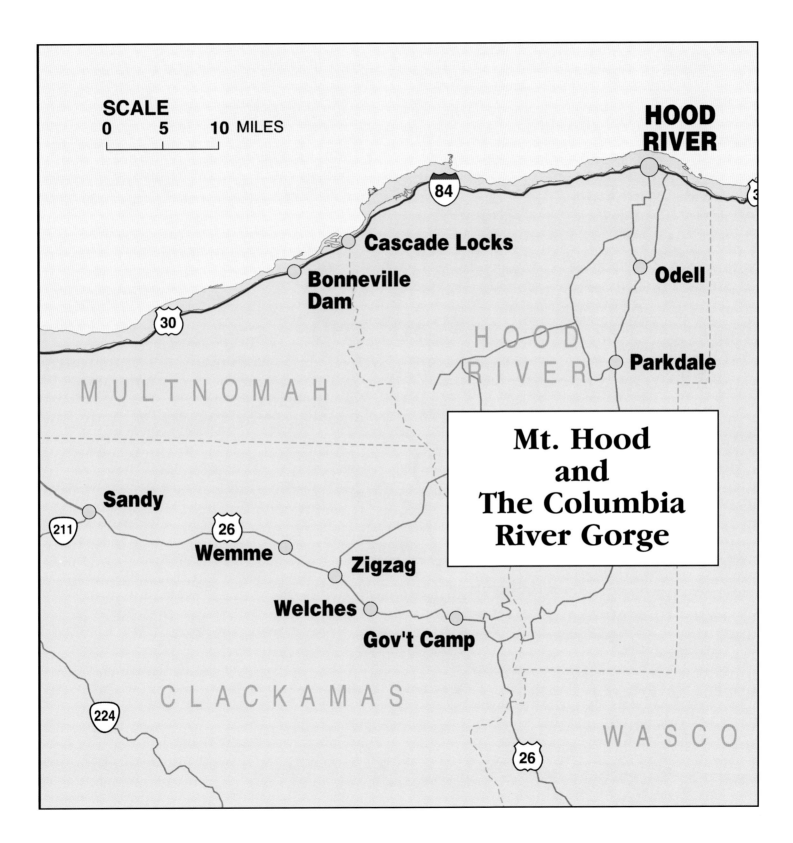

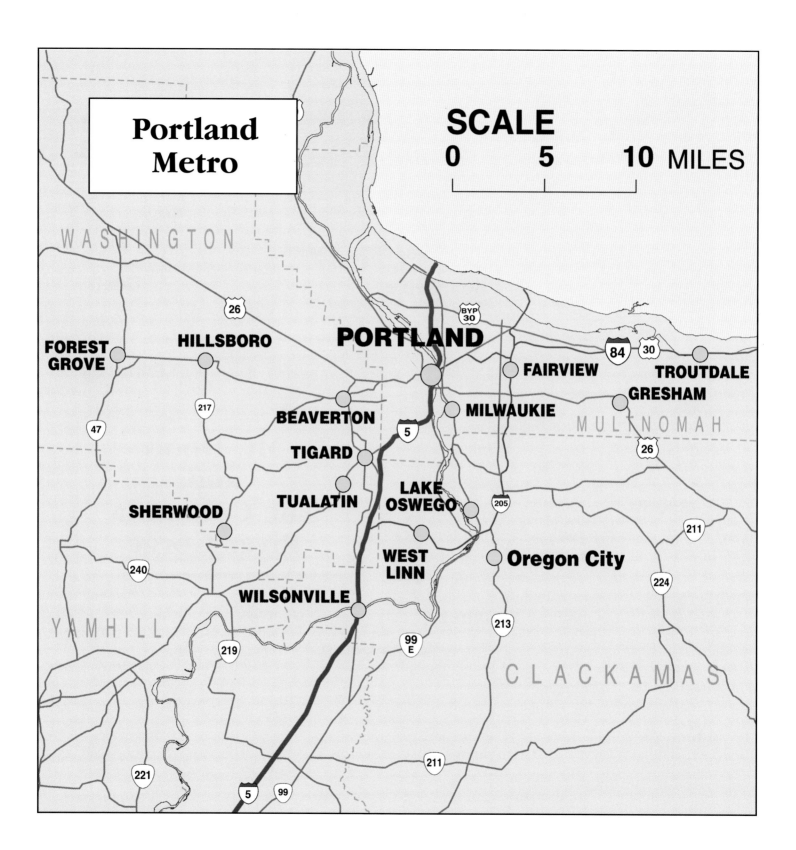

Portland Metro

SCALE
0   5   10 MILES

WASHINGTON

26

FOREST GROVE

HILLSBORO

PORTLAND

BYP 30

84   30

FAIRVIEW

TROUTDALE

GRESHAM

217

47

BEAVERTON

MILWAUKIE

MULTNOMAH

26

TIGARD

5

SHERWOOD

TUALATIN

LAKE OSWEGO

205

WEST LINN

Oregon City

211

240

213

224

WILSONVILLE

YAMHILL

219

99 E

CLACKAMAS

221

211

5   99

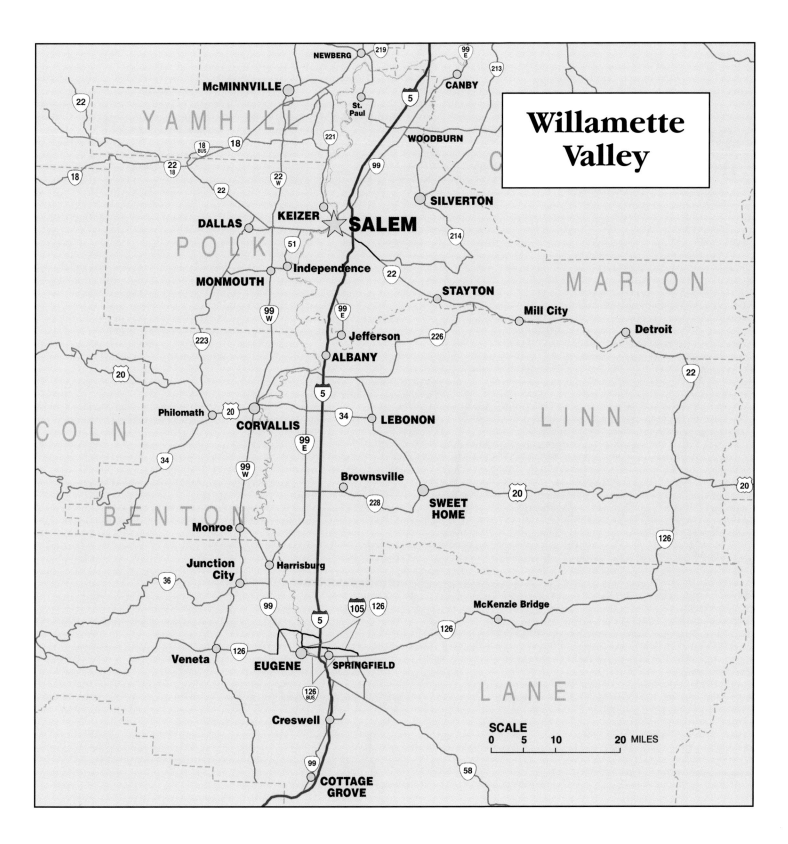

Willamette Valley

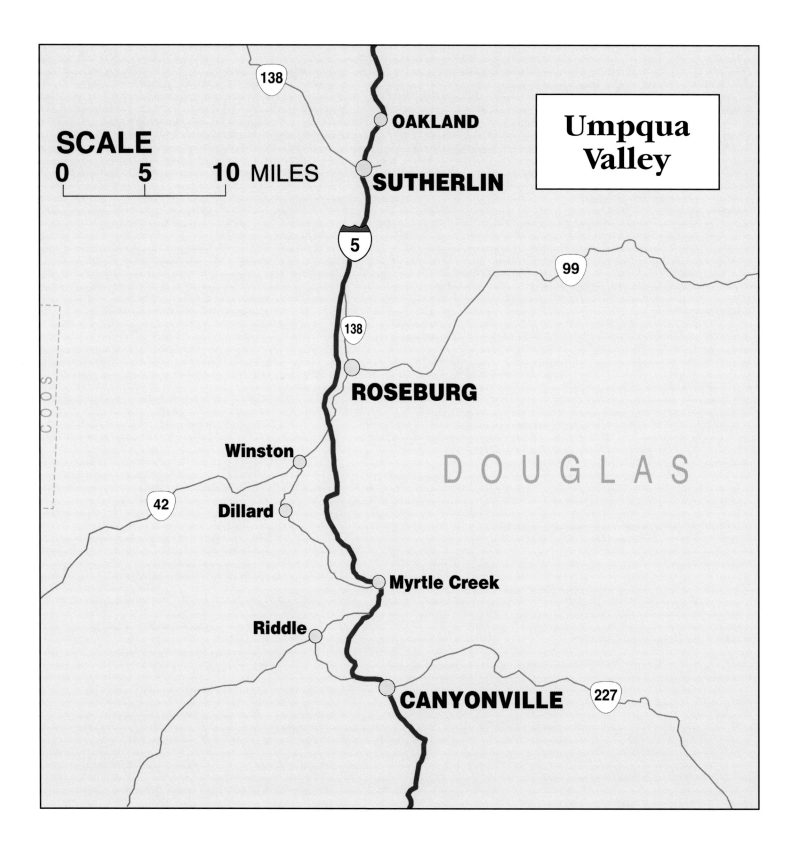

SCALE

0   5   10 MILES

138

OAKLAND

SUTHERLIN

5

99

138

ROSEBURG

Winston

42

Dillard

DOUGLAS

Myrtle Creek

Riddle

CANYONVILLE

227

COOS

Umpqua Valley

Southern Oregon

DOUGLAS

JACKSON

JOSEPHINE

Prospect

Shady Cove

Eagle Point

GRANTS PASS

Rogue River

Gold Hill

CENTRAL POINT

MEDFORD

JACKSONVILLE

Phoenix

Talent

CAVE JUNCTION

ASHLAND

SCALE

0   5   10   20 MILES

CALIFORNIA

Accommodations

Mt. Hood Village Resort

Okay, you're somewhere in Northwest Oregon in your RV and wondering where to stay for a few days. Does a place with a 27-hole golf course sound good? How about over 700 groomed hiking trails, rock climbing, bird watching, mountain biking, miniature golf, fishing, lakes and streams to explore? Interested yet? Then head for the Mt. Hood Village Resort in Welches. The resort has 442 RV sites, 277 of them with full hookups. You say you don't own an RV, but like the sound of the resort? Fine; the resort offers fully furnished cottages, many of which have hot tubs. If you're more adventurous, cabin suites are available, equipped with mini kitchens, showers, toilets, and four bunk beds. If you really want "rustic," ask about a rustic cabin with bunk beds; you use the comfort station across the road for showering, and you cook on an outdoor BBQ. Bring your own sleeping bags to the rustic cabins. The list of activities at or near the resort is incredible. For example, the famous Timberline Lodge is just 20 miles away, and is the only location in the U.S. that offers year-round skiing and snowboarding. Snowtubeing, snowshoeing, snowmobiling, cross-country trails and snowball fights fill the winter season. The town of Welches boasts more than 25 restaurants, from fine dining to pizza delivery, gift shops, antique stores, a post office, doctor, dentist, and terrific massage therapists! While at the Mt. Hood Village Resort, be sure to have a meal at the Wildwood Cafe, where owner/chef Brigette Romeo, a graduate of the Horst Magers Culinary Institute, serves you Northwest cuisine such as Mt. Hood's famous Chantrelle mushrooms and desserts made from fresh-picked huckleberries. Mt. Hood Village Resort is 40 miles east of Portland, at 65000 E. Hwy. 26, Welches, OR 97067. Call (503) 622-4011 or (800) 255-3069 toll-free. Visit the website at www.mthoodvillage.com. For the Wildwood Cafe and Catering, call (503) 622-0298.

Sakura Ridge Farm & Lodge

Sakura Ridge Bed & Breakfast offers a world class mountain view, as well as, "all the benefits of farm life with none of the hassle." Organic asparagus, 80 tons of cherries fresh from the trees, heirloom tomatoes, just picked berries and gourmet varieties of pears make for a breakfast that is truly "fresh from the farm". This is not all Sakura Ridge offers guests. Sakura means cherry blossom and in spring all 30 acres of the 6,000 fruit trees are blanketed in bloom. Lambs accompanied by geese are grazing in the pasture and Mt Hood is covered with snow. The kitchen gardens are filled with herbs, flowers, vegetables, and berries. Sakura Lodge is a very private, casual log lodge with upgraded amenities. The interior is artist designed. Cozy rooms are complete with down comforters and Hudson Bay or Pendleton blankets. All rooms have private baths, some with claw foot soaking tubs. In the summer you can relax in rockers on the wraparound decks, in winter snuggle up to the fire with one of the many regionally inspired books scattered throughout the Lodge. The Lodge is situated in the heart of the Columbia River Gorge. Sakura Ridge is minutes away from an array of natural and recreational offerings. Nearby activities include: golf, water sports, snow sports, hiking, biking, fishing, birding, tennis, and more. Visit the area's many wineries and museums, stroll the streets of Hood River, drive Hood River's famous Fruit Loop or simply spend a day on the farm at Sakura Ridge. Relax in a rocker or join in on the farm activities, picking up a garden tool, bucket or the irrigation wrench. Owners, John and Deanna Joyer, will warmly welcome you to Sakura Ridge at 5601 York Hill Drive in Hood River, Oregon. John is the agriculturist, Deanna, the artist and chef. For reservations visit their website at www.sakuraridge.com (877) 4-SAKURA (72-5872) or (541) 386-2636.

Resort At The Mountain

The luxuriously appointed Resort at The Mountain, located in the western Highlands of Mt Hood, is just an hour east of Portland. Here you will find a wealth of gorgeous rooms and stunning views. Centrally located within a few minutes of the Mount Hood National Forest you can enjoy a multitude of outdoor activities including downhill and cross-country skiing, wildlife viewing, hiking, mountain biking and fly fishing. Within the Resort you will enjoy some of the finest golfing Oregon has to offer. Understanding that golf was created in Scotland, the Resort has worked hard to present tastes of Scotland in everything they do. From Scottish style bunkers and Scottie dog tees to the Tartans Pub and Steakhouse and Highlands Restaurant. Further outdoor offerings include a heated pool and Jacuzzi, four tennis courts, two full-sized croquet courts and lawn bowling greens. The Resort provides equipment rentals for tennis, biking, volleyball, badminton, croquet and lawn bowling. They can help organize group recreational activities or help you find local excursions. Each year The Resort at The Mountain presents several events including the Wild About Game Cook-Off and the Wine and Art Festival. With so much to do and see it is a great getaway for families and companies. The Resort at The Mountain is located at the western base of Mt. Hood, just one-half mile off of Highway 26 in Welches at 68010 East Fairway Avenue. You can reach them at (503) 622-3101 or (800) 669-7666. Check out their website at www.theresort.com.

Columbia Gorge Hotel

Developed in 1904, the site of the Columbia Gorge Hotel was originally owned by Bobby Rand, a Hood River pioneer. He named his hotel the Waw Gwin Gwin (Rushing Water) for the Native American name of the 208' waterfall located on the grounds. The property was later purchased by Simon Benson whose goal was the creation of an opulent hotel at the end of the newly completed Columbia Gorge Scenic Highway. It quickly became a destination for the rich and famous. After several changes in ownership, current Owner, Boyd Graves, bought the property in 1981 and restored it to a thoughtful elegance. Today the Gorge Hotel has 40 rooms: 39 with private baths, 2 with fireplaces and 3 with conference rooms. The Hotel is surrounded by 11 acres of beautifully landscaped gardens, stone bridges, and a babbling brook overlooking the Columbia River. The Gorge Hotel features a restaurant, bar and lounge with live entertainment and an outdoor dining terrace. In 2004, the Hotel was named the Most Romantic Hotel in America. The Columbia Gorge Hotel is located at 4000 Westcliff Drive in Hood River. For more information visit their website www.ColumbiaGorgeHotel.com or call (800) 345-1924 or (800) 345-0931.

Columbia River Gorge

Historic Broetje House
Bed & Breakfast

In 1889, a magnificent Victorian house was commissioned by noted Floriculturist, John F. Broetje on his Milwaukie estate. His passion for flowers resulted in an establishment that has been a Bed & Breakfast like no other for the past seventeen years. The House is the centerpiece, and it is surrounded by stately, one hundred year old sequoias, the first ever planted in the Portland area. There are lovely gazebos, countless flowers and shrubs, and a water tower built in 1909. All this in over an acre of private grounds that provide pastoral comfort and luxury just minutes away from the urban clamor of Portland. Guests may stay in the spacious Queen Anne Room or the smaller but no less lovely Country Charm or Gazebo Garden Rooms. With all of its charm and elegance, it was impossible to keep Broetje House a secret. Prospective guests should make reservations as far in advance as possible. In addition to the amenities provided by a bed and breakfast, Broetje House also has a banquet room, just a short walk from the house through a lovely glass breezeway which overlooks the gardens. Capable of accommodating up to 150 guests, the Banquet Room is a favorite place for parties and wedding celebrations. It's also available for corporate retreats, family reunions or other special occasions. The Broetje House's skilled chef provides full catering for all events. The Broetje House is located at 3101 SE Courtney Road in Milwaukie, Oregon. InnKeepers, Lorraine Hubbard and Lois Bain, will specially design your event to meet your needs, and they are always happy to talk with you. For information, call (503) 659-8860 or visit their website at www.thebroetjehouse.com, where you will find sample catering menus and driving directions to this one-of-a-kind Bed & Breakfast.

Heron Haus

For 20 years Julie Keppeler has provided guests with a luxurious home away from home. At the Heron Haus Bed and Breakfast Inn attentive service and bright airy spaces will greet you. The three-story English Tudor home was built in 1904 and has a casual elegance and beauty that is serene and carefully appointed. Every detail has been anticipated and provides for your comfort. Your bed features over-stuffed pillows and soft throws. There are cozy nooks where you can curl up and enjoy any number of books from their well-stocked mahogany library. Outside you will find a peaceful sitting area and private trail leading to a secluded orchard. With six equally enticing rooms to choose from, you can be assured that all rooms are excellent. At Heron Haus every room has a private bath that is spacious and carefully prepared to include all of the luxuries a home should have. Additionally, for those chilly nights there are fireplaces in each private room and in most common areas. Each room has a DSL hookup and a private phone. Ask about the rooms with a deep, spacious and rejuvenating spa. The continental breakfast served in the dining room includes a pastry basket, cut fresh fruit, cereal, coffee and tea. With the stunning panoramic views that include Mt. Hood, Mt. St. Helens and Mt. Rainier and the twinkling city lights at night there is no question Heron Haus is a Bed and Breakfast experience you'll long remember. Heron Haus Bed and Breakfast Inn is located at 2545 NW Westover Road in Portland. Please call (503) 274-1846, or visit their website at www.heronhaus.com, for reservations or further information.

Portland's White House

Portland's White House was the most splendid home in its district in the early 1900s. It is a Greek Revival Mansion built by a wealthy lumber baron and it looks a great deal like its namesake in Washington, DC, with its 14 massive columns, circular drive and fountain. But just wait until you see the gorgeous interior. Thanks to modern technology you can do just that from your home computer. Portland's White House has a first-rate website that allows you to view every room, as well as the façade and its setting, as though you were standing right there and slowly turning around to see every rich detail. "Using 360-degree digital photos, this tour allows you to explore every aspect of our rooms and suites." There is a formal dining room and large parlor complete with grand piano, the sweeping staircase, magnificent leaded-glass windows, gilt-gold ceilings, and the Grand Ballroom. The five guest rooms in the main house and three guest rooms in the Carriage House are also elegantly appointed with antiques, paintings and porcelains. They have king or queen feather beds, feather pillows and fine linens that will guarantee a wonderful sleep. All this luxury is situated in Portland's Northeast Historic Irvington District where you can enjoy being close to fabulous boutiques, the Lloyd Center, the Pearl District, NW 23rd Avenue Shops, The International Rose Test Gardens, Japanese gardens, Portland Art Museum, Classical Chinese Gardens, Pittock Mansion, and Washington Park only minutes away. Grandeur isn't too big a word to describe Portland's White House furnishings. See it all for yourself at www.portlandswhitehouse.com. PORTLAND'S WHITE HOUSE is located at 1914 NE 22nd Ave. You can check availability of the luxury suites and rooms online or call the friendly hosts at (800) 272-7131.

Century Hotel

Located on the south shore of Tualatin's serene Lake of the Commons is the Century Hotel. Designed as an executive hotel for the 21st century, you will find more than a home away from home here. Each of their seventy rooms is equipped with in-room coffee and coffee maker, personal microwave and refrigerator, iron and ironing board and hairdryer. Additionally, guests can expect attentive friendly service, a complimentary full hot breakfast selection and complimentary newspaper each day. Take advantage of their indoor swimming pool, hot tub and Universal Gym exercise room or even select the private deluxe spa room with Jacuzzi tub in the room. Relaxing views are available from rooms or while enjoying a meal at Hayden's Lakefront Bar and Grill. With menu selections specially prepared by Executive Chef, Mark Bernetich, you will find options that vary from Deep Southern flavors to Italian, Southwestern, Asian and of course Great Northwest favorites. For a sample of his unique menu try the Drunken Spicy Shrimp appetizer, the rich Northwest Chowder of razor clams, Dungeness crab and Smoked Salmon, Charlie's Chop Saltimbocca Double Cut Pork Chop with Maple Glaze and Candied Pecans, and for dessert try the Panna Cotta Baked Cream with Berry Compote. Stroll the nearby parks and shopping districts or take advantage of special guest privileges at nearby golf and athletic clubs. The Century Hotel is located at 8185 SW Tualatin-Sherwood Road, simply take exit 289 from I-5. For more information, call (503) 692-3600. You can also visit their website at www.thecenturyhotel.com.

MacMaster House
Bed & Breakfast Inn

Innkeepers, Louise and Skip Haley, are the gracious hosts at the MacMaster House Bed and Breakfast Inn. As the caretakers of this magnificent historic mansion in the heart of Portland (listed on the National Register of Historic Places), they provide their guests with a homelike ambiance with special touches like breakfast on English Minton china, and music and wine in the evening. Because of its great location, close to the Japanese and Rose gardens, this is the perfect place to stay in Portland, with or without a car. City Center is minutes away by front-door bus service, while the celebrated 23rd Street with blocks of boutiques, restaurants and art galleries is an easy stroll on foot. Take a look at the MacMaster House website (www.macmaster.com) and you will find a virtual tour of the rooms, allowing you to see one of the unique features of this Bed & Breakfast,

gorgeous murals by local Artist, Myrna Anderson. It's a really nice special touch that personalizes each spacious bedroom. The guest rooms are also handsomely appointed with European antiques and bed linens, down comforters, lush pillows, desks or dressing tables, and reading chairs. This cozy sanctuary with seven guest rooms is very well suited for groups as well as the individual traveler. This was one of the first homes to be built on prestigious King's Hill in the heart of Portland in the 19th century. Family notes about the MacMaster family, who built the home, cites one of their daughters attended private school in New York with the Duchess of Windsor, and all of the daughters were debutantes in Portland's society. The room now known as the Artist's Suite was once the MacMaster girls' playroom, tucked up under the 3rd floor dormers. This building is truly a part of the 'living history' of Portland, as well as an ideal place to stay while exploring the city's many attractions. To speak with the Haleys, call (503) 223-7362.

Forest Springs Bed & Breakfast

The Forest Springs Bed and Breakfast at Historic Heiney House is your rural oasis nestled within extinct volcanoes, abundant wildlife preserves and lovely views of Mt Hood's surrounding areas. The early 1900's English style cottage offers five diverse rooms with several styles to choose from. The Parisian, decorated in mid-century Parisian Nouveau style, is the largest and most luxurious room offered and has a large private bath. The Barcelona has a built-in queen sized bed that boasts the best night's sleep in the house. The Sun Room is a salon with a quiet reading and writing area that is shared by the guests of the Parisian and Barcelona, but if both rooms are booked together the Sun Room can accommodate an additional two guests. The San Francisco Room is located on the main floor with a queen-sized bed and bright sunny décor, and the Mount Hood Room is the most lodge-like style of the rooms. For larger groups the entire Bed and Breakfast can be rented to accommodate up to ten guests. Start your day with a breakfast always served with abundant fruit and then head out to see some of the lovely sights and activities. Nearby you will find extensive hiking and biking trails in the Springwater Corridor, expansive farmlands, Multnomah Falls and Mt. Hood. Your Innkeeper, Patrick Arbuckle, also wants you to know that they have an ideal setting for the more personal and smaller scale wedding. They can accommodate a wedding party of up to 75 people. The Forest Springs Bed and Breakfast is located at 3680 SW Towle Avenue in Gresham. Outside of Oregon call toll free (877) 674-9282 or you can reach them at (503) 674-8992. Check out their website at www.forestspring.com.

Inn at Northrup Station

"In the middle but on the edge," Portland's only all-suites hotel is a magical creation whose kaleidoscopic design pays tribute to the great boutique hotels of San Francisco while having a uniquely local feel. The artistic vibrancy and Bohemian ambience of Northwest Portland is the inspiration of the Inn at Northrup Station. From the thirty-foot palm trees ringing the hotel to the hot pink check-in desk and fused glass menagerie on display in the two-story lobby, you'll know as soon as you arrive that this is no ordinary place to stay. The suites feature private decks, full granite and maple kitchens (including restaurant-quality aluminum cookware), data ports with Internet access, and luxurious marble bathrooms. Originally built in 1970, the Inn was transformed into its present state by architect, Steve Routon, a local resident who collaborated with others from the Portland area, including interior designers, Jim Yockey and Pieter H. Reed, and artists Rachel Arnold, Effrain Gonzales, Bob Nadeau and Gayle Forsberg, to create the unique style. All of the furniture at the Inn was created by local artisans. The headboards of the beds are hand-forged metal sculptures produced by Rick North of Renaissance Furniture. The style and artwork on display may make the Inn look like an exclusive resort, but its friendly and casual atmosphere is remarkably welcoming, and the prices are pleasantly affordable. Accessibility is another key to the Inn's success. It is located along Portland's famous streetcar line (at Northrup Station, in fact), so the Inn is easy to get to. Its location in the heart of the "Trendy-Third" fashion district (also known as Nob Hill) makes it convenient to a variety of restaurants, shops and entertainment venues. The galleries of the Pearl District are just a few steps away, though the Inn has so much to offer, from the breakfast bar in the lobby to the rooftop garden that you may not want to leave. The Inn is located at 2025 NW Northrup. Call toll-free, (800) 224-1180, for reservations. Visit the website at northrupstation.com for more information.

Oxford Suites

The Baney family of Bend, Oregon has been in the hospitality business since 1955. In 1988 they developed Oxford Suites, and the concept has spread across the Pacific Northwest, California, and will soon be in Idaho. The model is simple and very appealing. Provide guests with a home away from home while treating them like part of the family. The family focus includes a complimentary Hot Country Breakfast Buffet and evening reception with hors d'oeuvres and beverages daily. An indoor pool, hot tub and fitness center provide everyone the opportunity to relax and have fun. Added conveniences in each suite include a refrigerator, microwave, VCR, a sleeper sofa and accommodations to suit the entire familiy. There are also seasonal packages available including the Portland Shopping Package (to take advantage of Oregon's famous tax-free shopping), the Romance Package (for that special getaway), and the Family Fun Package with something for everyone. Oxford Suites offers two locations in the Portland area. Located on Hayden Island, the Oxford Suites at Jantzen Beach allows you to enjoy scenic views of Mt. Hood while strolling along the Columbia River. Just off of Interstate 5, this convenient location is only minutes from the Portland International Airport and provides easy access to Portland's many attractions. The Oxford Suites in Gladstone sits on the banks of the beautiful Clackamas River where you can enjoy swimming, fishing and natural scenery. This oasis in the midst of the city provides private balconies with breathtaking views. Visit the Oxford Suites at www.oxfordsuites.com or call toll-free, (800) 548-7848, to book the finest in service and hospitality and to find your home away from home.

The Mark Spencer Hotel

A beloved landmark in Portland's Theatre District, The Mark Spencer Hotel has been providing its guests with Continental style, old-fashioned courtesy, and hospitality since 1907. Visiting performers still make The Mark Spencer their home away from home, just as they have in decades past. A visitor couldn't do any better either. Originally called the Nortonia, the twin, six-story buildings were renamed the Mark Spencer in 1966, and the Hotel is now owned by a Portland family. The Hotel maintains its commitment to elegance and customer satisfaction. Eighteen different floor plans characterize the 102 rooms, presenting an exceptional variety of choices. Guests receive a free Continental breakfast, and The Mark Spencer serves tea every afternoon from 3pm to 6pm in the library. You will also find cable TV, voicemail, data ports, high speed wireless access, and fully-equipped kitchens in the rooms. The Mark Spencer features the best of the past and the present. Friendly staff will be glad to help you find interesting new places to visit nearby, or you can simply kick back and relax in the rooftop garden area. Parking is available and the location at 409 SW 11th Avenue is also convenient for public transportation. The Mark Spencer is just a few minutes' walk from the Pearl District's galleries, Powell's City of Books, PGE Park, and the thriving nightlife of downtown Portland. For reservations, call toll-free, (800) 548-3934. Meeting room services for conferences, seminars, and receptions are also available. To find out more go to www.markspencer.com.

Hotel Mallory

The Hotel Mallory in Portland, Oregon offers guests the comfort and charm of European ambiance. Built in 1912, the Hotel is only a short walk from the trendy Pearl District, urban Northwest Portland and the center of downtown. With eight floors and 130 guest rooms, the Hotel offers high-speed wireless Internet access, a 24-hour fitness center, valet parking, and 24-hour room service. Its Honeymoon Suite features crystal chandeliers and an eight-foot circular bed resting atop a velvety red carpet. The Mallory Dining Room, with its green velvet chairs and gold-leafed high ceilings, has an incredibly helpful and dedicated staff. And for meetings and events, the hotel has ample function space to meet the needs of any social or business gathering. The Hotel Mallory is a great place to rest amongst the opulence of timeless charm and modern conveniences. The Hotel Mallory is located at 729 SW 15th Avenue in Portland, Oregon 97205. For reservations or questions, call (800) 228-8657 or (503) 223-6311. For more information you can also visit Hotel Mallory's website at www.hotelmallory.com.

The Benson Hotel

Return visits to Portland along with any first-time trip must include a stop at the venerable Benson Hotel, currently listed on the National Register of Historic Places. A landmark for nine decades and a timeless tribute to its founder and designer, this stately 287 room hotel retains the opulence for which it is world-famous. A.E. Doyle's architectural talent, reflective of a golden era, combined with Simon Benson's tenacity, business savvy and impeccable taste, live on as the foundation of an American classic. Located at 309 Southwest Broadway, guests often stand in awe of the palatial lobby featuring Austrian-crystal chandeliers, Circassian walnut walls, columns and Italian marble floors. Lounging by the lobby fireplace during winter months often leads to celebrity sightings. Twenty-four hour room service, the acclaimed Les Clef D'Or Concierge Services, and the most chivalrous and polite doormen complete the Benson's reputation for excellence. Modern luxury is on display in the Grand Suite with a baby grand piano, fireplace and Jacuzzi, and it continues through each of the panoramic view penthouses and Junior Suites. Deserving of unending AAA Four Diamond ratings, all guest room amenities include two phone lines and dataport, plush terry cloth bathrobes, honor bar, iron and ironing board, and hair dryer. Guests also enjoy a comfortable chair and ottoman, armoire with television, games and movies. Décor throughout is a traditional style with velvet throw pillows on the beds, taupe and black checkered window treatments, brass lamps and a writing desk. Elegant décor and soft lighting create an intimate dining ambience for hotel guests and locals alike at the London Grill, a well-known fixture in the Northwest's restaurant scene. Using only the finest ingredients, the menu features both traditional favorites and bold, innovative creations. The London Grill also boasts one of the most extensive wine lists in the Northwest, with more than 10,000 bottles. Table-side dining and numerous specialty dishes await, including Dungeness Crab Cakes with Roasted Red Pepper Sauce and Cilantro, Dill-cured Salmon served with Cucumber and Red Onion Salad, Roasted Rack of Lamb, and the local breakfast favorite, Eggs Benedict. For reservations, call toll free (888) 523-6766 and to learn more information about the Hotel's rich history check their website at www.bensonhotel.com.

RiverPlace Hotel

A landmark presence on the waterfront, RiverPlace Hotel is Portland's premier upscale hotel on the banks of the Willamette River. RiverPlace is a haven of warmth and tranquility, serenely removed from the noise of the city, yet only a few blocks from the heart of downtown. The Hotel's staff provides a comfortable, inviting refuge where you'll be treated with a level of care not often experienced. And RiverPlace has exciting news for visitors. A four million dollar renovation has just been completed. The new lobby welcomes guests with a warm ambience of Northwest craftsman style detailing, a comfortable lobby library and a complimentary full service business center complete with high-speed Internet access. The Hotel offers a variety of accommodations from oversized deluxe guest rooms to FirePlace Suites with beautiful views and RiverFront Residential Suites, which are the finest riverfront accommodations in the Northwest. Each room and suite features the new FeatherBorne Bed, the finest in sleep comfort, DVD player and personal refrigerator.

As part of the renovation, a new restaurant and bar, Three Degrees, was opened. "Meet, Greet, Eat" is the philosophy of Portland's newest river view restaurant and bar. The menu features many Northwest favorites prepared with the finest fresh, local ingredients. A unique feature of the Bar is the outside deck that offers a wonderful river view, teak rocking chairs and heat lamps for year-round use. The RiverPlace has earned AAA's 4 Diamond rating for 19 consecutive years. With the recent renovations, RiverPlace will continue to be considered one of the finest hotels in the Northwest. RiverPlace Hotel and Three Degrees are located at 1510 SW Harbor Way in Portland, Oregon. For reservations, call toll free (800) 227-1333, or visit their website at www.riverplacehotel.com.

5th Avenue Suites Hotel

The 5th Avenue Suites Hotel opened its doors and welcomed people to stay in May 1996, after an extensive renovation to the 1912 building that once housed the Lipman Wolfe Department Store. The historic building is now home to a 221-room boutique hotel, with suites and deluxe guest rooms that feel like the guest room in a friend's home. But there's more to this Hotel than luxury accommodations. With everything from an on-site business center and wireless Internet access, to the Aveda Environmental Lifestyle Spa, 5th Avenue Suites has what you need, whether you're traveling for business or leisure. It's also a patron of the arts. The Hotel's living room houses a permanent collection of paintings, prints and drawings by local artists, and every month the work of two other local artists is displayed in the Hotel. Guests are invited to draw and paint at the evening wine reception, and every month a lucky guest's artwork is put on display and the guest stays for free! 5th Avenue Suites care about Portland's traditions too. During the heyday of the Lipman Wolfe store, children flocked to the store to meet the

"Cinnamon Bear," whose adventures were broadcast on local radio. When you check into your suite, you'll find a plush Cinnamon Bear nestled on the bed (you can take him home with you for a minimal fee). 5th Avenue Suites Hotel is located at 506 Southwest Washington Street at Fifth Avenue. For reservations, call toll-free (800) 711-2971, or you can visit their website at www.5thavenuesuites.com.

Rivershore Hotel

At the actual end of the Oregon Trail, in historic Oregon City, you will find the Rivershore Hotel. This 114 room hotel overlooks the Willamette River Recreation Area and is just yards downriver from the famous Willamette Falls. After a comfortable night's rest, step out onto the balcony of one of the river view rooms to enjoy the spectacular panorama of Oregon's most historic river and the rare wildlife living along the shore. Hungry? Then head to the adjacent Rivershore Grill for a delicious breakfast. It's the perfect way to start your day. Whether you're in town for business or pleasure, the Rivershore is designed to please. The second floor is specifically planned for the family with extra seating and easy access to fitness, laundry, spa and pool facilities. The third floor is the corporate floor, with executive kings and suites, along with meeting facilities. The Rivershore Hotel offers amenities including a year round outdoor pool (heated for comfort), a fitness/weight center, cable TV, and wireless DSL. Full catering facilities are available for special events such as weddings, meetings and reunions.

There's plenty to do in the area. From an excursion on the river on the Belle of the Falls from the public 320 foot dock, and tax-free shopping at Clackamas Town Center, to visiting the many museums, art galleries and historic homes, the Rivershore Hotel is in the heart of it all! The Rivershore Hotel is located at 1900 Clackamette Drive in Oregon City, just off of I-205, minutes from the Portland International Airport. For reservations and additional information, call (503) 655-7141. Visit their website for a full listing of their extensive services www.rivershorehotel.com.

Belknap Hot Springs Lodge & Gardens

The perfect getaway can be found in McKenzie Bridge, Oregon, at the Belknap Hotsprings and Gardens. With its beautiful gardens, luxurious rooms and suites, and soothing hot springs, this is truly an Oregon Treasure. Belknap Hotsprings and Gardens offers 18 spacious lodge rooms, some with relaxing Jacuzzi tubs. The views from the rooms are breathtaking, with a choice of the mighty McKenzie River or the lush Belknap woods. Rooms are available with either one or two king or queen size beds; some also offer hide-a-beds. For more privacy, stay in one of the seven rustic cabins that range in price from $55 to $400 dollars a night. These come fully furnished and are the perfect spot for a romantic getaway or a family vacation. Pets are even welcome in two of the cabins. Those wishing to camp in the beautiful outdoors will be happy to know that Belknap Hotsprings and Gardens offers 42 RV sites, some with full hook-up, and 18 tent sites. The 45 acres of manicured gardens provide a wonderful spot to relax. The green lawns, beautiful flowers, and soothing sounds of water will still your mind and ease your worries. Take long walks through on the spectacular trails or sit under a tree and enjoy a picnic lunch with loved ones. Be on the lookout for osprey, deer, elk and other wildlife. Taking a dip in the hot springs is an unforgettable experience. The source of the hot mineral water ranges from 185 to 195 degrees Fahrenheit. Soaking in the riverside hot springs pools, where the average temperature is 104 degrees Fahrenheit, is a proven way to forget about life's worries and stresses. Norm McDougal and family of Springfield, Oregon, purchased the Belknap Hotsprings and Gardens in 1995 and invite you to visit their wonderful paradise located at 59296 Belknap Springs Road in McKenzie Bridge, Oregon. From Eugene, travel 60 miles east on Highway 126. The Hotsprings are located nine miles east of McKenzie Bridge. For more information, call (541) 822-3512 or visit their website at www.belknaphotsprings.com.

The Hanson Country Inn

In 1928, J. A. Hanson, a poultry breeder who achieved fame and fortune through white leghorn chickens, built a magnificent 7,100 square foot mansion just west of Corvallis. It is situated on a knoll as the centerpiece of a five-acre estate. Now that architectural masterpiece, lovingly restored by the Covey family, has been transformed into an inn that ranks among the finest in the Pacific Northwest. Set amidst tranquil wooded surroundings, yet within walking distance of Oregon State University and downtown Corvallis, the Hanson Country Inn truly enjoys the best of both worlds. "Civilized accommodations in a sylvan setting." The rooms at the Hanson Country Inn feature many original furnishings and antiques, where guests enjoy full gourmet breakfasts in the sun-filled dining room. After dining, guests can relax on private decks overlooking the well-manicured garden or browse through the offerings in the Library, which have books from the Hansons' original collection. The rooms include private baths, telephones, cable television, and wireless Internet access. Bird watching is a popular pastime at the Inn, and guests are often delighted to see deer wander across the grounds. In addition to guest rooms, the Inn also offers a matchless location for weddings, receptions, parties, business meetings, family reunions and other group events. Special needs are accommodated down to the last detail. The Hanson Country Inn is located at 795 S. W. Hanson Street, just off of West Hills Road. To make reservations, call (541) 752-2919. Be sure to allow plenty of lead time because their rooms are in great demand. For more information, visit their website at www.hcinn.com. The website has lovely pictures of the accommodations (you will be charmed by the library in particular). And you will see a quote from Bill Bryson of Bon Appétit magazine, "To my mind, however, the main attraction in Corvallis is the delectable Hanson Country Inn...."

Valley River Inn

There are lush gardens along a river bank, wineries and golf courses close by. There's a first-class restaurant with innovative Northwest cuisine, invitingly comfortable guest rooms including high tech extras. Within a tranquil setting just five minutes from downtown Eugene, you'll find ballrooms and boardrooms for special events. You'll find all of this and more at the Valley River Inn, a resort-style hotel, convention center, and fine restaurant on the banks of the scenic Willamette River. The Valley River Inn is close to the University of Oregon and downtown Eugene, and is a pet-friendly, kid-friendly hotel. The 257 deluxe guest rooms have all the amenities you would expect in a first-class hotel including: hair dryers, coffee makers, irons and ironing boards, speaker phones, turn-down service (upon request), morning newspapers and European soaps and toiletries to name just a few. Go to their website at www.valleyriverinn.com to see pictures of the rooms, and detailed descriptions of the many suites and their special features. (You can also check out recipes from the restaurant there, and much more.) Sweetwaters Restaurant and Lounge features live entertainment as well as fine dining. It is Eugene's premier lounge, where you can listen to jazz or dance the night away. The Restaurant and Executive Chef, Michael Thieme, have been featured in the pages of Bon Appetit, NW Palate, and Simply Seafood for their Pan Pacific Northwest cuisine that focuses on North American game, Pacific seafoods, and locally gathered organic produce. The Valley River Inn is the perfect location for business or leisure. Unsurpassed comfort and service are what you will find there. Your special event, from an intimate reception to a major convention, will become an absolute success when you have it at the Valley River Inn. Look at their website for details, or contact them by calling (541) 687-0123.

Harrison House

"Located between the Pacific Ocean and the Cascades, life is good in Corvallis. The winters are mild, the flowers are brilliant and the town is comfortable and relaxed. You can savor the flowers and relax in our English Cottage Garden. Rain is a rumor, although we have a supply of umbrellas, just in case." This is a quote from the Harrison House's Website, where you can get details about its comfortable bed and breakfast accommodations and gracious hospitality. Your hosts at Harrison House, the Tomlinson family, moved to Corvallis after living and working in the metropolitan New York City area. They describe their roles, "Maria is the President and Innkeeper, Charlie is the employee (aka House Boy) - as it should be." As part of a stay at Harrison House, a beautifully renovated historic house, you will enjoy a memorable choice of breakfasts. The Breakfast Lite of fruit, fresh-baked scones or muffins will get you on your way to an early meeting. But if you have the time, the Breakfast Robust starts with a fruit course and concludes with either Eggs Benedict, stuffed crepes or other home-cooked favorites. (They are happy to accommodate most dietary restrictions.) Maria says, "At breakfast, you might dine with a guest from one of seventy countries, a Nobel laureate, or a recently published author. If you prefer true haute cuisine, you can enjoy dry cereal and milk with Charlie." Some of the amenities at this bed and breakfast include fresh flowers, a bottle of Harrison House Spring Water, Oregon hazelnuts, locally made chocolate truffles, mints, and the Bedside Reader. Harrison House Bed and Breakfast is a member of the Oregon Bed and Breakfast Guild, guaranteeing high-quality, inspected accommodations. They are also members of Distinctive Inns of Oregon, a group of premier inns. Harrison House is located three blocks from the OSU campus and within easy walking distance to shopping and dining. You can print out a brochure about Harrison House, complete with color, from the Website www.corvallis-lodging.com . And you can call the amiable hosts at (800) 233-6248.

Log Cabin Inn

Established in 1906, the Log Cabin Inn is a real piece of Oregon history where guests today can enjoy the same rustic charm as visitors did a century ago. Actually, the original Log Cabin Inn was completed in the Spring of 1886, with travelers from as far as Europe coming to visit the new resort on the McKenzie River. In August of 1906 the old Inn burned to the ground and except for minor changes the Inn looks much the same today as when it was rebuilt that year. The principal cedar panelings are virtually unchanged. New furnishings and a second cedar-paneled dining room were added later. Innkeepers, Diane and David Rae, and their family cordially invite you to make yourself at home whenever you visit "the Cabin". They have an array of pictures on their website at www.logcabininn.com, where you can see the beautiful setting for a memorable meal or stay in one of their river front log cabins. One of the highlights of a visit is the chance to eat in The Log Cabin Inn's restaurant. The Restaurant specializes in salmon, baby-back ribs, and steaks. In fact many of the menu items are the same as they were in 1906. Venison Game Stew, Beer Cheese Soup served with French bread, and their famous Marionberry Cobbler are local favorites. They also serve delicious, up-to-the-minute dishes like frittatas, vegetarian entrees, and daily specials. On Sundays the Restaurant features a wonderful Country Brunch. The Log Cabin Inn also has facilities to host unforgettable weddings, golf banquets, family get-togethers or other special events. Gift certificates to The Log Cabin Inn are available for dining and lodging. The Inn is located just an hour from Eugene, but you will never find a destination that feels more like a trip to Oregon's historic past. Combine this ambiance with the comforts The Log Cabin Inn can offer and you'll have a wonderful time in store. For more information, please call (800) 355-3432.

Hilton Garden Inn Corvallis

On the campus of Oregon State University there is a hotel with one of the most prestigious names in the industry – the Hilton Garden Inn. A full-service hotel with 128 guest rooms (including four suites), it features all of the luxury guests have come to expect from the Hilton name, at a price that's surprisingly affordable. The Hilton Garden Inn is the wise business traveler's choice. Rooms feature complimentary high-speed Internet access and secure remote printing facilities, dual-line telephones with voice mail and data ports, work desks with desk level outlets and ergonomic chairs – giving the Garden Inn an unbeatable edge. In town to see the Beavers take on the Ducks? The Inn's right next to Reser Stadium. Comfort goes hand-in-hand with cutting-edge electronic connectivity here. From the in-room hospitality centers with refrigerator, microwave oven and coffee maker to the heated indoor pool, spa and fitness center, the Hilton Garden Inn provides everything you need to take it easy or get down to business. Dine at the Stadium Grill Restaurant or pick up food to go at the Pavilion Pantry. Whatever your needs, you can get it. Planning an event? The Hilton Garden Inn has a 1,000-square-foot University Club Event and Game Room, and an executive boardroom that seats twelve. The Business Center has copier, computer, and fax service, and is open twenty-four hours a day. The Inn is also very easy to get to, just ten miles from I-5. It's an hour away from the coast and ninety minutes from Portland. For more information, or to make online reservations, visit their website at www.hiltongardeninn.com. From out of state, you can call toll-free (877) STAY-HGI (782-9444) to make reservations. The Hotel's direct line is (541) 752-5000.

Hilton Eugene & Conference Center

When traveling for either business or pleasure, stay at the Hilton Eugene & Conference Center for the finest accommodations. Located in the heart of downtown Eugene, the Hilton is close to the University of Oregon, Autzen Stadium, the Hult Center for the Performing Arts, and the 5th Street Marketplace. Each of the 272 guest rooms and suites have been redesigned for the utmost in comfort. Choose from standard guest rooms or suites and relax in comfortable surroundings. Standard rooms come with queen or king-size beds and feature such amenities as private mini balconies, premium television channels, wireless Internet access, iron and ironing boards, complimentary coffee and tea with in-room coffee makers, and a free weekday USA Today newspaper. Suites are available, featuring a parlor complete with overstuffed furniture, armoire, and an oak table that can accommodate up to eight people. The Hilton also caters to the executive with nightly turndown service and access to the private concierge club room for continental breakfast or nightly hors d'oeuvres and drinks. The Big River Grille is onsite and features delicious Pacific Northwest cuisine. Guests can also relax in the Lobby Bar and sip a cocktail or local micro-brew after a long day. Other hotel amenities include a barber shop, beauty salon, indoor pool, Jacuzzi, and fitness center. Complimentary parking and airport shuttle is provided. The Hilton is the premier place to hold a meeting or event in Eugene. This hotel has a well-trained banquet and catering staff to help make the most of your special day and boasts over 30,000 feet of conference space. Banquet rooms located on the top floor of the Hilton, feature floor-to-ceiling windows and create a breathtaking backdrop for weddings and other special events. The Hilton Eugene & Conference Center is located at 66 East 6th Avenue in Eugene, Oregon. Phone (800) 937-6660 for more information or visit their website at www.eugene.hilton.com.

Yamhill Vineyards Bed & Breakfast

Sue and Ralph Stein have two warm and welcoming guest rooms at Yamhill Vineyards Bed and Breakfast. The comfy Grape and Garden Rooms feature queen beds, vaulted ceilings, private baths, handmade quilts and antiques that make for a friendly coziness that soothes away everyday stresses for visitors. Their vineyard and bed and breakfast have spectacular views. A splendid assortment of wildlife can be watched from the deck. Deer, finches, quail, red winged black birds and hummingbirds are found in abundance. A stay at the Yamhill Vineyards Bed and Breakfast is a peaceful experience where you can enjoy a magnificent sweep of stars in the wine country's night sky. Of course, there is also a wealth of things to do during the day, from visiting nearby wineries and antique shops to enjoying the indoor spa. (There are 35 wineries within 30 minutes of the B&B and the Oregon coast is just an hour away.) They have vineyard-designated wines and Sue is known for her exciting recipes. Blackberry French toast is a favorite, along with her hazelnut granola pear bread. Another special treat is grape juice made from the wine grapes grown in their vineyard. Sue is also happy to accommodate special food requests because of allergies, if you let her know ahead of time. The Steins characterize their B&B as "truly an indoor and outdoor country garden spa!" Their hospitality includes their Great Room with its spectacular views, a spiral staircase, vaulted ceilings and a rock alcove with a wood stove. If you visit from May through July, you will be able to delight in the blooming of their Foxtail Lilies. This specialty flower is cultivated and sold throughout the U.S. as a cut flower. Yamhill Vineyards Bed and Breakfast is located at 7950 N.E. Cooper Lane in Yamhill. Their website is www.yamhillvineyardsbb.com or call them at (503) 622-3840.

The Campbell House

In 1993, Myra Plant realized her dream when she opened the Campbell House Inn. She transformed the beautiful 1892 Victorian mansion built by gold miner, John Cogswell, into a nineteen-room inn of unparalleled elegance. Twelve guest rooms, six suites and a cottage welcome guests seeking comfort and hospitality in the heart of Oregon. Wireless Internet access, spa tubs, and in-room massage are just a few of the amenities available. Within walking distance of downtown Eugene, the Inn's bucolic setting is a welcome oasis in the midst of the bustling city. More than comfort awaits the Campbell House guest. Complimentary full breakfasts have been a feature of the Inn since it opened, and now guests can enjoy dinner there as well. Wednesdays through Saturdays, the Dining Room serves a Table D'hote style menu. Guests can choose anything from soup and salad to a full five-course meal. The menu changes daily and Chef, Matthew Calzia, uses the finest possible local organic ingredients to prepare a superb culinary experience you won't want to miss. The Campbell House is a place for gatherings, offering a perfect space for wedding receptions, family reunions, and holiday parties. Special holiday events include the Victorian Christmas Tea and the Mother's Day Tea. Small business meetings are also welcome. There are two meeting rooms that can accommodate up to eighteen people conference-style (around a single table), and twenty-four theater-style. Off-street parking for up to nineteen vehicles is available. What better place could there be for a corporate retreat? Recipient of AAA's coveted Four Diamond rating, the Campbell House is located at 252 Pearl Street, at lovely Skinner's Butte. For directions, historical information and sample menus be sure to visit the website at www.campbellhouse.com For reservations, call toll-free, (800) 264-2519 or e-mail campbellhouse@campbellhouse.com. It's an experience you'll never forget!

Scappoose Creek Inn

Set in the grandeur of the Pacific Northwest, Scappoose Creek Inn in Scappoose, Oregon is the perfect setting for a romantic getaway, country wedding reception or base for exploring the numerous sites of the Northwest. Opened in 1996, the Inn is housed in two beautifully restored early 1900's farmhouses at the historic Scappoose Creek Dairy which is nestled on four lush acres. During Prohibition, the original dairy barn was the setting for one of the largest bootlegging "busts," and struggled to stay afloat during the Great Depression, sometimes only making money from the return deposit on the milk bottles. Eventually, the failed dairy was confiscated by the IRS and 60 years later converted into a Bed and Breakfast. Each of the ten guest rooms has its own unique theme, such as Pilot's Paradise, featuring a romantic double Jacuzzi situated under a skylight, or the Americana Room, a salute to the American Flag. Josephine's serves delicious lunches daily, dinner on weekends, and offers a fine selection of wines. Indulge in the charm of an era gone by, with the elegant surroundings and old-fashioned hospitality at the Scappoose Creek Inn, truly an Oregon treasure. Owners, Renee and Duane, will welcome you home at the Scappoose Creek Inn. The Inn is located at 53758 West Lane Road in Scappoose, Oregon 97056. For reservations or information, call (503) 543-2740 or (888) 875-1670. You can also visit their charming website at www.scappoosecreekinn.com.

Kelty Estate B&B

Ron and Jo Ann Ross are justly proud of their charming bed & breakfast in Lafayette, Oregon. While their historic home (listed on the Register of Historic Places) remains basically unchanged since 1934, their painstaking restoration has resulted in a fresh, bright interior with graceful architectural details and selected antiques that recall another era. The Rosses describe their bed and breakfast as, "A gracious way-station for travelers who appreciate a warm welcome and immaculate accommodations." The House was built in 1872 by James Monroe Kelty, who married Sarah Maria Scott, a woman who came from an Oregon Trail pioneer family. Her brother was Harvey W Scott, distinguished early editor of the Portland Oregonian. Although the house was sold in the late 1800s, their son Paul R Kelty bought his boyhood home back in 1934, converting the old farmhouse into an elegant manor, which visitors can now enjoy as beautifully managed by the Rosses. Following in the family footsteps and also becoming well known as the editor of the Oregonian, he retired in 1939 to live in the home that has now been transformed into the Kelty Estate Bed & Breakfast. The delightful white house with its fascinating history is surrounded by lawns and gardens and shaded by two-hundred-year-old trees. Guests can gather around the living room fireplace or on the front porch, where an old-fashioned swing awaits their pleasure. After enjoying a full breakfast featuring Oregon-grown produce, or Afternoon Tea, guests have just a short stroll to browse for antiques. They can easily visit the Yamhill County Museum, see the Spruce Goose or simply enjoy relaxing in a quiet garden nook at the Kelty Estate B&B. You can see their accomplishments for yourself in the photographs of the rooms and grounds posted on their website, www.keltyestatebb.com.   Ron and Jo Anne Ross can be reached at (800)-867-3740.

Macleay Country Inn

In Macleay, Oregon, Dan and Jerry Miller are proud to be the fifth generation to work the Miller Brothers' Ranch and to be the hosts of the Macleay Country Inn. The Inn is a great place to stop for lunch or dinner on your way to the Oregon Gardens and Silver Falls State Park. After eating there the first time, you'll likely decide the Inn is worth a trip all by itself.

The Millers and General Manager, Chris Bryant, invite you to try a selection from their newspaper-sized menu, but point especially to these "signature" items. For an Hors d'Oeuvre, try the Shrimp Cocktail, with your choice of cocktail sauce or the Inn's famous garlic sauce. If you're looking for a hamburger, try the Rancher. It's a half pound of ground beef topped with cheddar cheese served on a French roll. Or perhaps the Hustler. A full pound of ground beef on a French roll, with a choice of cheddar or Swiss cheese. Other signature sandwiches include the Big Reuben, with corned beef, 1,000 Island dressing, sauerkraut and Swiss, served on rye bread. And the Macleay Club: it has ham, turkey, bacon and cheddar cheese on a sesame seed bun. (Bring an empty stomach for this one, it's huge!) At dinnertime, eaters recommend the Prime Rib, stuffed with garlic and slow-cooked to perfection (Friday and Saturday only). Or perhaps the 20-ounce Porterhouse or 12-ounce Ribeye Steak. If steak isn't what you want today, try the Chicken Macleay with breaded chicken breast patties covered in Swiss cheese, lean ham and a secret sauce. Or the Spud Fish, cod with a crunchy potato coating. When you're ready for a beverage, the extensive menu lists no fewer than 20 micro and specialty beers alone. The Macleay Country Inn is located at 8362 Macleay Road SE in Salem, Oregon 97301. To learn more, call (503) 362-4225. The Inn takes reservations for groups of six or more people. Visit their website at www.macleayinn.com.

Flying M Ranch

The site of the Flying M Ranch was once the first "Travelers Home" for stagecoach passengers bound for the Oregon Coast and the City of Tillamook. In fact, the road you take to the ranch today is almost the same one the stagecoach took 145 years ago. The Flying M Ranch offers accommodations for a variety of purposes from pure pleasure to productive business meetings in their rustic and charming facilities along the North Yamhill River. Hosts, Bryce and Barbara Mitchell, foster a comfortable and exciting atmosphere (or relaxing, if you prefer) for Ranch visitors. This is a family-oriented vacation spot and guests of all ages will feel welcome here. The Mitchells' hospitality is genuine and your enjoyment is their true goal. The spectacular log Lodge houses the conference center, dining room and the Sawtooth Lounge. Nestled in the woods, a short distance from the Lodge, are the cabins and a 24-unit bunkhouse motel with western theme rooms. Each room has two queen beds and a private bath, but there are no telephones or televisions to intrude on the country peace and quiet. Separate from the Lodge, the Motel has a deck that overlooks the Yamhill River on one side and the mountains on the other. The private cabins have intriguing western-themed names like: Wortman, Wrangler, Honeymoon, Mountain House, Royal, Hunters Hideaway and Rustlers Roost. The Flying M Ranch is off the beaten path, midway between Portland and the Oregon Coast. Your visit will be filled with fun. In the main Lodge, they offer fireside checkers and other activities for the younger visitors. There are outside volleyball nets, tennis courts, horseshoe pits, trails to walk or mountain bike along, and a swimming pond the size of a city block.

The Mitchells invite you to "Come relax in the sun, take in the game of your choice or go for a horseback ride!" The ranch is open year round and they look forward to your visit. Read more about the Flying M Ranch at their website, www.flying-m-ranch.com. You'll see great color pictures of the facilities. Contact the Flying M Ranch by phone at (503) 662-3222 or (503) 662-3611.

Holiday Inn Express

Whether you're in Roseburg to work or play, you won't want to leave the Holiday Inn Express after just one night. Take the time to breathe in the clean air and savor the beauty of the South Umpqua River from your balcony. With its strategic location at the riverside gazebo, the spa is sure to be the perfect setting for a romantic evening or just the right place to unwind from a busy day. If you're looking for entertainment, Wildlife Safari, golfing and gaming are all within a few minutes of the Holiday Inn Express. There are also countless scenic byways, excellent fishing locations and historic, covered bridges in the surrounding area.

If you're in the mood for just an afternoon of shopping, you'll enjoy browsing the shops located in an historic church building downtown and lunching at a nearby restaurant. Whatever your reason for stopping in Roseburg, the Holiday Inn Express at 375 W. Harvard Boulevard, Roseburg OR 97470, will be your favorite second home. Call toll free (800) 898-7666.

Roseburg Sleep Inn

One of the newest hotels in the Umpqua Valley, Roseburg Sleep Inn & Suites combines all of the personal and business amenities you'll ever need at affordable prices. Enjoy the modern convenience of in-room modem access. You could choose to reinvigorate your mind and body in the fitness room, indoor pool, or you could pamper yourself by relaxing in the spa. Innkeeper Greg Buono grew up in the hotel industry and truly knows how to treat his guests. At Roseburg Sleep Inn & Suites the friendly front desk clerks are eager to help you find whatever you need in town or from the surrounding area. You can always expect a complimentary breakfast at Sleep Inn and you'll also be pleased by a dinner at the restaurant conveniently located across the way. For a comfortable and luxurious stay, Roseburg Sleep Inn & Suites located at 2855 NW Edenbower Blvd. in Roseburg, Oregon is sure to offer you a good night's sleep. For reservations call (541) 464-8338 or visit their website at sleepinroseburg.com.

Delfino Vineyards
Bed & Breakfast

The Delfino Vineyards Bed and Breakfast in Roseburg, Oregon is a cozy wine-country style cottage nestled in the midst of 160 acres of ranch and vineyard. Owners, Terri and Jim Delfino planted their first 15 acres of vineyard in the spring of 2002, including Tempranillo, Syrah, Merlot, Dolcetto, and Cabernet Sauvignon. The Umpqua Valley is quickly becoming known for its ability to produce excellent wines, and the Bed and Breakfast offers guests the opportunity to visit and enjoy the splendor of Oregon's wine country. This air-conditioned, one-bedroom guest cottage boasts a luxurious queen-size bed, full bath, living room and separate queen-size sofa bed to comfortably sleep four adults. A full Continental breakfast including delicious home-baked cranberry scones is served daily, and a pool and hot tub are available for additional relaxation. The Cottage's location is ideal for wine tasting at any of the twelve Umpqua Valley wineries, and fly-fishing on the world-famous Umpqua River is only 30 minutes away. The beautiful Oregon Coast and Crater Lake National Park are easy day trips. Whether you wish to visit and sample wines or escape to a tranquil setting for a weekend respite, Delfino Vineyards Bed and Breakfast is an ideal getaway. Delfino Vineyards Bed and Breakfast is located at 3829 Colonial Road in Roseburg, Oregon 97470. For reservations or information, call (541) 673-7575 or visit their website at www.DelfinoVineyards.com.

Lake of the Woods, Rogue Valley

Edgewater Inn

Since 1999, The Edgewater Inn of Shady Cove, Oregon has been providing a relaxing environment for its guests. Nestled on the banks of the Rogue River, this is where elegance meets the splendor of the outdoors. The Edgewater Inn is owned by Greg Joelson, Actor and former '49er. Greg and his attentive staff cater to the specific needs of their visitors. The Inn can provide massages, rafting, fishing, golfing, and dining for the convenience of its guests. Visitors can enjoy the river from their room, walk on the boardwalk, fish from the banks, or use the boat ramp for their needs. The Inn has many amenities such as a pool/Jacuzzi, weight room, sauna, business center with high speed Internet, and conference room for events. The Edgewater Inn of Shady Cove is a gateway to Crater Lake, offering sightseeing and hiking along with many other local attractions. At the Edgewater Inn you can come rest and rejuvenate yourself on the river. The friendly staff's goal is to ensure their guests feel good and that happy memories are created. The Edgewater Inn is the perfect place to stay and dine the next time you are in Shady Cove. The Edgewater Inn is located at 7800 Rogue River Drive in Shady Cove, Oregon 97539. For information or to make reservations, call (888) 811-3171. You can also visit the Edgewater's interesting website at www.edgewater-inns.com.

Out 'n' About Treehouse Resort

Out 'n' About Treesort & Treehouse Institute of Arts & Culture in Takilma, Oregon is a truly unique, exciting and educational vacation destination. Located in the picturesque valley of Takilma, nestled between the Siskiyou Mountains just below the headwaters of the east fork of the Illinois River, Out 'n' About was the dream of Owner, Michael Garnier and his wife Peggy Malone. After an eight-year battle with Josephine County officials, during which they were ordered to shut down several times, the County at last recognized them as a safe and licensed Bed & Breakfast. Internationally famous for their tree house guest suites, they offer nine elevated cabins. The cabins include the Swiss Family Complex and the Treezebo, and one ground-level Cabintree for those less inclined to spend the night perched high above in the branches of an oak grove. Their Treehouse Institute, established in the summer of 1996, offers avocational instruction in basic engineering, design and construction methods for building treehouses. In addition, they offer horseback riding, rafting, rope courses, guided tours, and local craft workshops. Out 'n' About Treesort is a remarkable and thrilling resort and it will leave an indelibly fond mark on the memories of all who visit. Out 'n' About Treesort is located at 300 Page Creek Road in Cave Junction, Oregon 97523. For more information, call (541) 592-2208 or visit their website at www.treehouses.com.

Ashland Springs Hotel

Ashland Springs Hotel nestled in the beautiful Rogue River Valley of Southern Oregon harkens back to a simpler time. This beautifully restored landmark hotel is on the National Register of Historic Places and is located in downtown Ashland, just steps from the renowned Oregon Shakespeare Festival. Other attractions include: Oregon Cabaret Theatre, Lithia Park, wine tasting and gallery tours, skiing, golf, fishing, river-rafting, tax-free shopping, dining and pampering at the nearby Blue Giraffe Spa. A two-year restoration project has transformed this historic beauty into a haven of taste and elegance reminiscent of small European hotels. Today this nine-story boutique hotel offers first-class hospitality to those who are drawn by business, the arts or the area's natural beauty. An oasis of gentility and charm, this lovely hotel offers seventy tastefully appointed, non-smoking guest rooms. Guests are pampered with superb service and luxurious surroundings. Amenities are many and they include: spa services, high-speed wireless Internet connection, complimentary light breakfast served on the Mezzanine, and complimentary parking. For celebrations, weddings and corporate functions the Grand Ballroom with an adjoining Conservatory and adjacent English garden is an ideal location. Sunday Afternoon Tea is served seasonally on the mezzanine overlooking the grand two-story palm-filled lobby. The Hotel's restaurant marries the magic of Ashland's natural surroundings with the food and wines of the Northwest, creating dishes from the freshest local ingredients which are sure to seduce your palate. For more information, photos and a downloadable brochure, visit the Ashland Springs Hotel website at www.ashlandspringshotel.com or call (888) 795-4545.

The Lodge at Riverside

Located on the spectacular Rogue River in Grants Pass, Oregon, The Lodge at Riverside is a luxurious and relaxing retreat offering four-star service and thirty-two elegantly appointed rooms. With private patios and balconies boasting unparalleled river views, a lushly landscaped pool and spa area, the Lodge offers guests the feeling of removed serenity only minutes from downtown shopping and restaurants. The Lodge's adjacent Conference Center provides meeting and banquet facilities, and their skilled staff will ensure that your event runs smoothly. Hellgate Jet Boat Excursions depart directly from the Lodge's dock, and fishing and rafting trips can also be arranged with pick-up directly at the Lodge. If you're feeling hungry, their Rafters Bar and Grill serves up delicious food with exceptionally friendly service. Experience Southern Oregon at its finest while staying at The Lodge at Riverside, and learn why so many people never wish to leave. The Lodge at Riverside is located at 955 SE 7th Street in Grants Pass, Oregon. For reservations or questions, call (541) 955-0600 or visit their website at: www.thelodgeatriverside.com.

Weasku Inn

Since 1924, the Weasku Inn in Grants Pass, Oregon has been providing a comfortable and relaxing environment for its guests, including notables such as President Herbert Hoover, Zane Grey, Walt Disney, Clark Gable and Carole Lombard. Since being purchased in 1993 by Country House Inns, the Inn has added 12 cabins, and a new meeting room and freestanding boardroom was added in 2004. This historic lodge, hailed by Travel & Leisure as "one of the country's top 25 greatest inns," is situated on ten forested acres resting along the scenic Rogue River. Its log exterior blends perfectly with its uniquely decorated Pacific Northwest interior and the vaulted ceilings and exposed beams add a rustic touch. Enjoy a complimentary continental breakfast or an evening of wine and cheese while viewing the spectacular waterfall and pond from the outdoor deck. With accommodations including twelve river cabins and five lodge rooms, and a beautifully peaceful setting that only Southern Oregon can provide, your stay at the Weasku Inn will be memorably enjoyable. The Weasku Inn is located at 5560 Rogue River Highway in Grants Pass, Oregon 97527. For reservations and inquiries, call (541) 471-8000 or visit their website at www.weasku.com.

Morrison's Rogue River Lodge

Morrison's Rogue River Lodge is an authentic log lodge you will find half hidden by groves of evergreens, maple, and oak. The Lodge is sixteen miles downstream from Grants Pass along the banks of its namesake river. The Lodge and its individual cottages attract all kinds of outdoor enthusiasts including fishermen who come to fish the legendary fishery for steelhead and salmon, whitewater rafters tackling one of the first commercially-rafted rivers in the country, as well as hikers, birdwatchers, families, romantics and all who enjoy being immersed in the sights and sounds of the wilderness. River Guide and lumber mill worker, Lloyd Morrison built the lodge in 1945 as a fishing lodge. B.A. and Elaine Hanten bought the property in 1964. Their first year was greeted with disaster in the form of the 1964 flood. The cottages were swept away by the rampaging river. The main building survived, and the Hantens were able to rebuild. Despite this early setback, the Hantens created a thriving business. In 1967 B.A. pioneered guided whitewater raft trips down the wild section of the Rogue starting their own rafting company, Rogue River Raft Trips, Inc. Today you can take 3-day rafting adventures with overnights at remote lodges along the way. Morrison's became an Orvis Endorsed Fly Fishing Lodge in the late 1980's and remains one of the best destinations for Steelhead and Salmon fishing on the West Coast. As Chef, Elaine created a reputation for providing outstanding gourmet cuisine that remains with the lodge today. It is still a family business with second generation family member, Michelle, managing operations. Lodge amenities include a heated swimming pool, two tennis courts, putting green, volleyball, horseshoes and all manner of lawn games. Additional services accommodate small business meetings, family reunions and weddings. Morrison's is located at 8500 Galice Road in Merlin. Take Exit 61 off I-5 and go west for twelve miles along the Merlin-Galice Road. For more information, call (800) 826-1963, or visit their website, www.morrisonslodge.com.

The Chateau at the Oregon Caves

The Chateau at the Oregon Caves National Monument in Cave Junction, Oregon provides a host of attractions, including a gift gallery featuring works by many Illinois Valley artists, a coffee shop and fine dining, overnight accommodations, area hiking and your ticket to exploring the Oregon Caves. Nestled in the midst of the old growth forest atop the Siskiyou Mountains, the Chateau offers cozy rooms, from modestly economical, to large, two-room family suites. Their 1930's style coffee shop and soda fountain serves an appetizing selection of homemade soups, salads and sandwiches. The chefs at The Chateau at the Oregon Caves combine the freshest local ingredients with flavors from the Pacific Northwest and Asia to create delicious dishes you can enjoy in the dining room while overlooking the wooded ravine. Four hiking trail loops spreading out in all directions offer a range of hiking opportunities, and the 90-minute guided tour of the marble caves is truly remarkable and wondrous. The Chateau at the Oregon Caves is a landmark worth visiting, and will leave you eager to return. The Chateau at the Oregon Caves is located at 2000 Caves Highway in Cave Junction, Oregon 97523. For inquiries, call (541) 592-3400 or visit their website at www.oregoncavesoutfitters.com.

Chanticleer Inn B&B

How's this for a comment from departing B&B guests? "Our only regret is that our stay in your gracious home was so brief. May we come again?" The guests were writing about the Chanticleer Inn in Ashland, Oregon, "everything an Ashland B&B should be." Ashland's oldest continuing bed and breakfast opened its doors in 1981. Here Innkeepers, Ellen Campbell and Howie Wilcox, warmly welcome you to an elegant, newly renovated 1920 Craftsman style home in Ashland's historic neighborhood. A stroll away from the Oregon Shakespeare Festival, restaurants, galleries, and Lithia Park, the Inn offers comfortable quiet rooms, full gourmet breakfasts, and stunning views of the Cascade Mountains. You can relax in secluded gardens with a pond, waterfall and hammock, rock gently in a porch swing, enjoy the butterfly garden, or sample the fresh cookies with a book or the New York Times by the fire. Breakfast includes seasonal fruits and pastries made fresh daily. One of Ellen's signature dishes is Almond Pear Clafouti, a delicious cross between a cake and custard. Ellen continues to expand her repertoire of specialty recipes since she and Howie departed their high tech careers. There are six guest rooms, five with queen beds and one with a king. The rooms are quiet, each with a private bathroom, individually controlled heat and air conditioning, bathrobes, hair dryers, reading lamps, telephones, and TVs with DVDs. Wireless-connection Internet access is available also. The Chanticleer Inn is located at 120 Gresham Street in Ashland, Oregon 97520. You can call them toll free (800) 898-1950, or visit their website at www.ashlandbnb.com.

Jacksonville's Magnolia Inn

Jacksonville is renowned for comfortable, luxurious lodgings, but even here the excellence of the Magnolia Inn distinguishes it as a cut above. The newest and most spacious bed and breakfast establishment in this historic, perennially popular village, the Magnolia Inn combines the most appealing elements of a country inn with the amenities found in the most fashionable boutique hotels. In the three years since it opened, the Magnolia Inn has attracted clientele from as far away as Sweden and the Philippines, as well as having a strong local following. The Inn has also earned AAA's prestigious Triple Diamond rating, and was featured in the December 2004 issue of Sunset magazine. Nine beautiful rooms, all with private baths, invite you to rest and relax. A refreshing night's sleep leads to the inviting smell of freshly brewed gourmet coffee and tempting pastries from local bakeries. During the day you can take a leisurely stroll through Jacksonville's downtown. Once there, you can take in the fascinating history of this former gold rush boom town or go shopping in one of the many delightful specialty stores that line the main street. But you don't need to go out; you can read a book, sip wine on Magnolia Inn's spacious outdoor veranda, or just watch the sights unfold. In the evening, dinner awaits you in any one of a number of award-winning restaurants. All are within easy walking distance. From herbal wraps to dinner reservations to a surprise in-room bouquet, the Magnolia Inn's owners, Frank and Cheryl Behnke, make sure that guests feel welcomed and pampered. No wonder so many guests return year after year. Jacksonville's Magnolia Inn is located at 245 North Fifth Street in the heart of Jacksonville. For reservations, call toll-free, (866) 899-0255, or for more information, visit their website at www.magnolia-inn.com.

The deLaunay House

Nestled near Ashland's Historic Railroad District, the deLaunay House provides the perfect home away from home for travelers and tourists. Since 2002, Owner, Deborah deLaunay has run this guest house. Its suites feature onsite laundry, fully equipped kitchens and kitchenettes, cable television, and wireless Internet access. This beautifully renovated 1909 Craftsman-style home is just a few blocks from Ashland's famous Shakespeare Festival, Lithia Park's beautiful foliage, walking trails, and a tantalizing selection of restaurants and cafes. Decorated with heirloom antiques and original works of art, the deLaunay House's lush interior lends an air of sophisticated comfort. Relax on their lovely front porch and soak up the gorgeous mountain views. Whether it's hiking the countless wooded trails or skiing at nearby Mt. Ashland, the deLaunay House's prime location and luxury suites will leave you eager to return once again and enjoy all that they have to offer. The deLaunay House is located at 185 N. Pioneer Street in Ashland, Oregon 97520. For more information, call (541) 488-5692. You can also view a video showing the attributes of the deLaunay House at www.southernoregontravelogue.com, or you can visit them at www.delaunayhouse.com.

Jacksonville Inn

In rustic Jacksonville, Oregon, the Jacksonville Inn stands as a National Historic Landmark known throughout the West for its elegance and superb service. A recent visitor said, "Superior! Never seen better. This is the most elegant and beautiful place I ever saw." Housed in one of Jacksonville's early permanent buildings, the Inn, built in 1861, perpetuates the nostalgic romances of the gold-rush era. The walls of the dining area and lounge are built of locally quarried sandstone where specks of gold are still visible in the mortar. Hosts, Jerry and Linda Evans and Mike and Jennifer Higgins, offer you eight beautifully decorated hotel rooms plus four luxurious honeymoon cottages. One of the hotel rooms has a whirlpool tub, another offers a steam shower. The beds are queen-sized and some are canopied. All rooms are equipped with laptop computer connections. One of the cottages is now known as the Presidential Cottage, following an overnight stay by President George W. and Laura Bush. The Inn's wine and gift shop offers over 2,000 wines, making it the largest retail wine collection in the area. The Wine Spectator bestowed its "Best of Award of Excellence" on the Inn for its comprehensive wine list. Connoisseurs can look for special hard-to-find vintages dating back to 1811, or shop for everyday bargains. Redmen's Hall, the Inn's banquet facility, provides a charming atmosphere that enhances private meetings, weddings, and receptions. The Jacksonville Inn is located at 175 E. California Street in picturesque Jacksonville, Oregon 97530. Jacksonville is located in the Rogue River Valley, just five miles west of Interstate-5 and the city of Medford. Call (541) 899-1900 or (800) 321-9344 toll-free. Visit their charming website at www.jacksonvilleinn.com. You can also see the separate listing in this book for the Jacksonville Inn Restaurant.

Applegate River Lodge

The Applegate River Lodge and Restaurant is the perfect place for a romantic getaway or family event in Southern Oregon. With its beautiful surroundings and spectacular view of the Applegate River, this is truly an Oregon Treasure. The Applegate River Lodge consists of seven large rooms, each with its own unique theme. Themes range from a rustic Gold Miner's Cabin to an elegant Honeymoon Suite. All rooms have Jacuzzi tubs big enough for two and private decks overlooking the majestic Applegate River. This is the perfect getaway; the lodge has no telephones or televisions so guests can relax and enjoy the beautiful setting and impeccable service. The focal point of the lodge's great room is a beautiful river rock fireplace where guests congregate on cold evenings. The sitting area is a wonderful spot to relax with a great book or play a board game with friends and family. Continental breakfast is served here. The Applegate Restaurant is located next to the Lodge. This casual yet elegant restaurant offers gourmet dinners that are unforgettable. Guests can sit on the deck during the summer and listen to the rushing water of the Applegate River as they sip wine from one of the local wineries. Listen to live music on the deck on Wednesday and Sunday evenings during the summer months and on Wednesdays during winter. The Applegate River Lodge and Restaurant is a popular wedding destination. The beautiful grounds and stunning river backdrop coupled with delicious food and service make this an ideal spot to start a new life together. Couples can rent the entire Lodge for their weddings. Owners, Joanna and Richard Davis opened the Restaurant in 1992. The Lodge was completed in 1997. The Lodge is located between Medford and Grants Pass on Highway 238. The Lodge is open year-round and the Restaurant is open Wednesday thru Sunday from 5:00pm until 9:00pm. For more information or reservations, call (541) 846-6690 or visit their exciting website at www.applegateriverlodge.com.

Lake of the Woods Mountain Lodge and Resort

"Rekindling the spirit and tradition of the Great Northwest," Lake of the Woods Mountain Lodge and Resort is a gem set on the shore of one of the most beautiful natural mountain lakes in the Cascades. Situated near lovely Mount McLaughlin, the Lodge and cabins offer visitors a breathtaking view. Originally built as a 1920's lodge and fishing retreat, the Resort has been restored to its authentic charm. It combines the spirit of the wilderness with casual elegance and comfort. The Resort's 26 distinctive brown clapboard cabins pamper guests with fresh linens and Pendleton blankets, kitchens and some hot tubs. You can also bring your own lodging; full and partial RV hook up sites are available year round. And of course everyone loves the lake! The fishing is excellent and the sailing, swimming, boating, canoeing and waterskiing make for great times. During the summer you can order a picnic lunch at the Marina Grill, dine at the Lodge Restaurant, or stock up at the General Store and prepare an intimate or family dinner in your own cabin. During the winter the Marina transforms into the Nordic center where snowmobiling and cross-country skiing become the favorite pastimes. Whether it is adventure, romance or just the desire to step back into a simpler time, Lake of the Woods is a place you can enjoy with your family and friends for four seasons of fun! It is the kind of place you might remember from your childhood, a description in a favorite book or an old movie, but it is here for you today. In June 2003 Sunset Magazine called it "an irresistible alternative to Crater Lake Lodge," and went on to say, "The lodge and cabins at Lake of

the Woods Resort installed a rustic charm surpassing that of the original." The resort is also a perfect setting for corporate retreats. You will find Lake of the Woods Mountain Lodge and Resort at 950 Harriman Route, 20 minutes from Klamath Falls and 45 minutes from Medford and Ashland. For more information, a downloadable brochure, photos and rates, you can visit their website at www.lakeofthewoodsresort.com, or call them at (866) 201-4194.

McCall House B&B

Visitors to Ashland can't miss the McCall House, it's an eye-catching Victorian masterwork on Oak Street with elaborately decorated two-story bay windows. The Mansion was originally built in 1883 for Captain John McCall (who founded the Ashland newspaper, library, bank, and the Ashland Woolen Mill). It was converted into a bed and breakfast in 1981 by Shakespearean actress Phyllis Courtney. In 2003 the current owners, the McLaughlins, completed an extensive restoration, making this National Historic Landmark shine. Converting McCall's mansion into a haven for travelers was in keeping with its history. In this lovely home, McCall and his wife, Lizzie, hosted such distinguished guests as General Sherman, William Jennings Bryan, and President Rutherford B. Hayes. Hayes' visit is commemorated in the President Hayes Guestroom, one of the ten luxuriously appointed rooms. All rooms feature private baths, antique furnishings, delightfully comfortable beds, and many also have fireplaces. A sumptuous gourmet breakfast is included. If you're in the mood for romance, spend a little extra for the Romantic Getaway Package. With this package, upon your arrival you'll be presented with chilled champagne, chocolates and fruit, roses, and a cozy fire. Superb service is a hallmark of the McCall House. If you're in need of rejuvenation, just let your host know and you'll be scheduled for a relaxing visit to the Blue Giraffe Day Spa, just one block away. The McCall House is located at 153 Oak Street, one block from the Oregon Shakespeare Festival and close to many unique shops, galleries, and restaurants of downtown Ashland, Oregon. For reservations, call toll free, (800) 808-9749. You can visit their website at www.mccallhouse.com for a virtual tour, video footage of the 2003 Open House, and much more.

Rogue Regency Inn

Anticipating your arrival, Rogue Regency Inn is the place to stay in Medford. Whether you're just visiting or planning to spend a life-time, this full-service hotel has everything to make your stay comfortable and enjoyable. As always, you can expect the best room service or you can enjoy a meal at Chadwicks, the Regency's own Pub and full Sports Bar. If you choose to stay in for the night, you may want to reserve a suite with a hot tub so you can truly relax and unwind. Conveniently located in the heart of Southern Oregon's Rogue River Valley, the Rogue Regency Inn is just off Interstate 5 near the Jackson County Airport. For reservations, phone (800) 535-5805, or simply drop in at 2300 Biddle Road in Medford.

Albion Inn

Experience the serenity and quiet comfort of the Albion Inn, located within the tranquil setting of Ashland's historic Hargadine District. Owner and Innkeeper, Nancy Morgan, and her partner Suzanne Badoux, have created an environment guests refer to as "more than a bed-and-breakfast; a retreat." Four level blocks from the Oregon Shakespeare Festival and one block from downtown Ashland, the Albion Inn puts you within easy walking, biking, and hiking distance to all that Ashland offers, yet also tempts you to relax and replenish yourself during your stay. The Inn's sweet farmhouse exterior invites you into spacious, book-filled rooms, inviting common areas, and lush rose, wisteria and lavender gardens. The Inn's organic vegetable and herb beds bestow their riches throughout the summer and fall, and gourmet breakfasts are as bountiful as they are beautiful (Nancy has catered and served as a cooking instructor, and both Nancy and Suzanne are Master Gardeners). The Inn's five rooms are air conditioned, have private baths, and each one has its own distinctive appeal.

There are as many guests who choose "their" same room year after year as there are guests who choose to experience a different room each year. The Inn offers wireless remote access, onsite Internet/e-mail and fax services, and a wealth of written material on Ashland and the surrounding areas. Says Nancy, "Reading through these chronicles, one learns that this valley has long held the power to transform and illuminate both the heart and the mind." The Albion Inn, featured in Arrington's 2004 Book of Lists, is located at 34 Union Street in Ashland, Oregon 97520. Call (541) 488-3905 or (866) 933-5688 toll-free. You can also visit their website at www.albion-inn.com.

The Creekside Cottage

The Creekside Cottage in Grants Pass offers a peaceful and relaxing place to get away from the stresses of everyday life. The quaint, one unit cottage is owned by Keith and Donna Barnes, and is located on the Barnes' twenty-acre private residence. The refurbished cabin is warm and inviting, with rustic lighting and a casual country décor. With a kitchenette and VCR/DVD, leaving the cabin for fishing or rafting on the mighty Rogue River is only an option. Your day will be off to an amazing start with a gourmet breakfast prepared by your host and hostess. Whatever your agenda is, either a day trip to the Oregon Caves or curling up with a good book, your personal preferences will be catered to at this deliciously cozy cottage. Creekside Cottage is located at 390 Grays Creek Road in Grants Pass, Oregon 97527. For reservation information, call (541) 862-8607 or visit them on the web at: www.creeksidecottagebb.com.

Attractions

Timberline Lodge

"Everyone's Mountain Home" is one description of Timberline Lodge, located at 6,000 feet on Mt. Hood, 60 miles east of Portland. This beautiful piece of history is owned by the National Forest Service, so everyone is welcome to come up, relax by the fire, and take pleasure in its outstanding views and unique architecture. Timberline is many things. It's a ski resort, a first-class restaurant, a hotel with wonderful accommodations and service, but most of all it is a public building of extraordinary historical and artistic interest that you are invited to visit. Jon Tullis, Director of Public Affairs, says many people come just for a day trip to enjoy the Lodge, emphasizing that "Timberline is not an exclusive resort," but instead "Everyone's Mountain Home." Created at the height of the Depression, Timberline Lodge was built entirely by hand, inside and out, by unemployed craftspeople hired by The Federal Works Projects Administration. From the initial survey in 114 feet of snow during the spring of 1936 to its completion in 1937, the working conditions were difficult, but the WPA workers were paid well, the food was good and the morale was high. All felt they were involved in something unusual and important. The building they created reflects the best of the WPA's goals to produce works of art with indigenous materials and to employ skilled masters alongside inexperienced workers. The result was one of those rare, happy achievements, a masterpiece in a glorious setting that is unique to the Pacific Northwest. Timberline Lodge was closed during World War 2 and, while it's hard to imagine now, it almost didn't make it through the following years. It went to the brink of demolition in 1978. Timberline's Curator, Linny Adamson, has spent the past 30 years overseeing the re-creation of fabrics and furnishing that are replicas of the originals made with handmade techniques. Artwork abounds throughout the Lodge in paintings, wood carvings, mosaics, wrought iron and stonework. The guest rooms are furnished with such items as original watercolors, hand appliquéd draperies and bedspreads, hand hooked rugs, hand carved furniture and hand forged lamps. A nonprofit organization, The Friends of the Timberline, was formed to allow the public to support the ongoing effort to preserve this architectural and artistic treasure. As a ski resort, Timberline has the longest season in North America, with skiing and snowboarding every month of the year when weather permits. Due to its unique location, that allows for summer skiing on the Palmer Snowfield. With 3,590 vertical feet of winter terrain, Timberline has the most vertical feet of skiing in the entire Pacific Northwest during the winter when the Palmer chairlift is operating. Enhance your skiing experience with instruction from the Timberline Snowboard and Ski School. Non-skiers can take the Magic Mile Sky Ride year-round (weather permitting) up to 7,000 feet. Gaze through a telescope or explore the Silcox Hut, then ride or hike back down to the Lodge, if the snow has cleared on the trails. You can even hook up with the Pacific Crest Trail (maps are available at the front desk) or you can enjoy one of the other hikes near the Lodge. Other amenities include a year-round outdoor heated pool and whirlpool, several restaurants including the Cascade Dining Room which serves gourmet Pacific Northwest cuisine, the magnificent fireplace lobby with a splendid view to the summit of Mt. Hood, and the opportunity to pet Bruno and Heidi, the two St. Bernard mascots in residence. The Forest Service offers historical tours of the Lodge during the summer. There is also a self-starting movie on the history of Timberline available year-round. Visiting Timberline's website at www.timberlinelodge.com, will entice you with 360° panoramic views and allow you to learn more about the 32 miles of trails, ski and snowboarding classes, special events and accommodations. Timberline can be reached by phone at (503) 622-7979. Come visit this authentic jewel and icon of the Northwest! Timberline Lodge is absolutely a one-of-a-kind Oregon Treasure.

Sternwheeler Columbia Gorge And Marine Park

Step aboard the Sternwheeler Columbia Gorge and experience history, legend and riverboat hospitality along the Columbia River Gorge on an authentic triple-deck paddle wheeler. The historical narration of Lewis and Clark's adventures, the Oregon Trail, Bridge of the Gods, and riverboats accentuate the relaxing river cruise and stunning sights. Starting from Marine Park at Cascade Locks, in the heart of the Columbia River Gorge National Scenic Area, you may enjoy watching Native American tribes fish from their legendary platforms as they have done for centuries and will take in many stunning and fascinating sights along the two hour cruise. For something extra special consider one of the Sunset Dinner Cruises for a fine meal and romantic experience or start the day off with a Sunday Brunch Cruise. From there seek out the Cascade Locks Museum, located in the lovely Marine Park, where you'll find more information on waterways, transportation, fishwheels and indigenous history. Open May through September from noon until five. Next, don't miss the adjacent Thunder Island and its scenic beauty. Owned and operated by the Port of Cascade Locks, the 23-acre park and private 3-acre island can be your solution to planning your next event. Sailing competitions sponsored by the Columbia Gorge Racing Association occur March through September and windsurfing occurs year round. Visit the association's website at www.gorgesailing.org for scheduled events. To visit the Sternwheeler Columbia Gorge, take I-84 E to exit # 44 about 45 minutes east of Portland, across the river from Stevenson, WA and Skamania Lodge. You can reach them at (800) 643-1354 or check out their website at www.sternwheeler.com.

Bonneville Lock and Dam

Bonneville Lock and Dam, located just 40 miles east of Portland in the Columbia Gorge National Scenic Area, was built through a public works project in 1937. Utilizing hydropower production, since 1938 it has supplied the area with inexpensive electrical power. Today it can provide the power needs for 500,000 Northwest homes. The locks that traverse the Columbia-Snake waterway allow vessels to commute over four hundred miles from the Pacific Ocean to Lewiston, Idaho. Bonneville Lock and Dam is also committed to fish and wildlife protection. Educational displays and materials from the Army Corps of Engineers supplement the experience. The Dam provides one of the largest public viewing facilities available as well. Here you can view inside the impressive and substantial powerhouses, see migrating salmon as they swim the fish ladder in Spring, Summer and Fall and watch an underwater display of sturgeon. Educational centers provide films and displays about hydropower, river navigation, history and salmon. On the Washington side approximately one mile west of the second powerhouse is the Fort Cascades Trail, a one and a half-mile trail to some of the loveliest views in the area. Bonneville Lock and Dam, near the Cascade Locks, can be reached by taking Interstate 84 from Portland to exit 40 or Washington State Highway 14 to milepost 40. The Bridge of the Gods, located about 2 miles upstream from the dam, links Oregon and Washington. You can reach them at (541) 374-8820 or check out their website at www.nwp.usace.army.mil/op/b/home.asp.

Friends of Vista House

Since 1918, the Vista House at Crown Point State Park has been a memorial to Oregon's pioneers. It serves as a beacon of resilience while resting high above the Gorge of the Columbia River at Crown Point. Construction of the Vista House was commissioned in 1916 after completion of the Historic Columbia River Highway. Prominent Portlander, Julius Meier, along with visionary, Samuel Lancaster, voiced the need for a comfort station along this winding section of the highway to the Board of County Commissioners. On May 1, 1918, after nearly two years of construction supervised by wealthy Portland lumberman John B. Yeon, the Vista House was completed. May 5, 1918 marked the opening day dedication ceremony. While the original architectural plans called for a building covering 1810 square feet, the completed structure grew to cover 3318 square feet. The final cost of the building was $99,148.05, an astronomical sum of money during that time, and nearly eight times the original estimated cost. Since its completion, much has happened to the Vista House.

In 1938, Portland and Multnomah County donated the building and its 1.71 acres to the state for a park, the acreage now totals 306.67. In 1971, Crown Point was designated a Natural Landmark with historic significance and it was placed on the National Register of Historic Places in 1974. In 1982, a group of citizens agreed on the potential community use and involvement with the Vista House, and presented a proposal to the Oregon State Parks. The proposal was accepted and Friends of Vista House was born. The current historic restoration, completed in 2005, will allow visitors to once again enjoy the building as it was originally designed with its spectacular panoramic views from the observation deck, feast their eyes on the rare Tokeen Alaskan marble used to surface the floors and stairs in the rotunda, learn of other interesting nearby sites, or visit the Vista House Gallery & Gifts where one can find one-of-a-kind handmade items by local craftspeople and artisans. Friends of Vista House can be contacted at P.O. Box 204 in Corbett, Oregon 97019. To learn more about this breathtaking landmark, call (503) 695-2230 or visit their website at www.vistahouse.com.

Mt. Hood Meadows Ski Resort

Looking for the most spectacular and varied terrain in the Northwest? You can find it at the Mt. Hood Meadows Ski Resort. Mt. Hood Meadows is a full-service winter resort providing everything you need for a refreshing and memorable day on the mountain. Main base facilities are housed in the North and South lodges (which offer easy access to five lifts), but there is also a satellite base lodge and Skier Services Center at Hood River Meadows. You can purchase daily lift tickets and EpiCenter Snow Sports Learning Center sessions in the lift ticket building just off the South Lodge deck. There are always special packages for skiers of all types, including deeply discounted lift tickets when staying at Hood River Lodging Properties. Hood River was recently named among the Top ten Ski Towns in America by SKIING Magazine. The EpiCenter is a snow sports learning center that offers innovative programs including: The Optimizer, Sunday Ladies Day Clinics, Front Line Guide Services, Snow Monsters, Snow Rangers, High Cascade Snowboard Camp, and the NW School of Survival Adventures. Fifteen percent of the terrain at Mt. Hood Meadows is suitable for beginners, fifty percent for intermediate skiers, twenty percent for advanced, and fifteen percent for expert skiers. There are 240 acres available for night skiing. The longest run at the Resort is three miles. The Mt. Hood Meadows Ski Resort is located along Highway 35, 8 miles north of Highway 26 in Mt. Hood, Oregon 97041. To contact the Resort, call (503) 337-2222. To learn more, you can visit their exciting website at www.skihood.com.

Cooper Spur Mountain Resort

For half a century, the Cooper Spur Mountain Resort has been welcoming guests to the north face of Mt. Hood. The staff is committed to providing a warm and welcoming experience and sharing this special place. The Resort is a mountain lodge and meeting center, featuring log cabins, lodge condo suites, hotel rooms, a log home, restaurant, lounge, tennis court, outdoor deck, and three therapeutic hot tubs. The property is located on 775 acres of private forest land surrounded by Mt. Hood National Forest, providing access to recreation year-round. In winter, the resort offers a Nordic Center with cross country and snowshoe trails, and an Alpine ski area for skiing, snowboarding and tubing. Winter guests receive discounted lift tickets to nearby Mt Hood Meadows Ski Resort. The Resort is ideal for catered group functions both large and small, ranging from corporate sessions to family reunions. The combination of privacy and accessibility allows groups to reserve the property for special occasions. The lodge condos, cabins, and lodge rooms offer flexibility for sleeping arrangements. Cooper Spur Mountain Resort is located at 10755 Cooper Spur Road in Mt. Hood, Oregon 97401. It is 23 miles south of Hood River, only 2.5 miles west of Highway 35. Call (541) 352-6692 for lodging reservations and information, or dial (541) 352-7803 for the snow report and information line. You can visit their website at www.cooperspur.com.

Tualatin Island Greens

If you've ever aspired to be the next Tiger Woods or Jack Nicholson, then there's no better place to practice than the Tualatin Island Greens in Tualatin, Oregon. For the past ten years, owners Charles Johnson, Jr. and Charles Thomas III have created an environment that provides their customers with a great experience. The staff offers outstanding customer service, and their trained PGA professionals offer guidance and instruction from which all can improve their game. In addition to a premier practice facility, their Island Grill restaurant serves a great lunch menu, perfect any time. With an eighteen-hole synthetic turf putting course and instructional golf programs for all members of the family, Tualatin Island Greens offers a quality golf experience at a reasonable price. Whether it's your first introduction to the game or you're a true golf fanatic looking for the perfect practice facility, Tualatin Island Greens has something for everyone. It's no wonder for nine consecutive years it has been awarded the "Top 20 Range Award" in America by Golf Range Times. Tualatin Island Greens is located 3 miles west of I-5, 1 mile east of Hwy. 99W, at 20400 SW Cipole Road, Tualatin, OR 97062. Phone: (503) 691-8400, Website: www.tualatinislandgreens.com.

Family Fun Center

The Family Fun Center and Bullwinkle's Restaurant are just a hop, skip and jump away from Portland and are open year round. With six-acres of amusement park to serve you, there is enough fun to entertain you and the kids for days on end. Outdoors you will find a challenging 18-hole miniature golf course next to the pond full of bumper boats with water cannons. There are Go Karts, Batting Cages, a Human Sling Shot Ride and a 28 foot tall climbing tower as well. Inside you will find the virtual reality laser tag: Lazerxtreme, the roller coaster simulator: Cyber Coaster, and the Frog Hopper ride, an arcade with over 100 games and a four level soft play area for those under five feet tall. When hunger beckons the Bullwinkle's Family Restaurant answers the call. Offering kid friendly pizza, burgers, seven sandwiches, wraps, soups, salads, appetizers and drinks, there is something for everyone to enjoy. But this isn't just an amusement park with kids in mind. They believe that adults deserve to have fun too. They offer corporate packages, team building sessions, company picnics and more. On Fridays and Saturdays from 6-10pm they have their Extended Late Nite Birthday Bash package for those 13 years of age or older. The package offers unlimited miniature golf, go-carts, bumper boats, laser tag and one additional attraction ride ticket, plus an "all you can eat" pizza and soda buffet for groups of six or more. When you're looking for some fun, swing on over to the Family Fun Center at 29111 SW Town Center Loop W. in Wilsonville. You can reach them at (503) 685-5000 or check out their website at www.fun-center.com.

Crystal Springs Rhododendron Garden

If you like flowers and birds, and especially if you are looking for a photographer's dream, head to the Crystal Springs Rhododendron Garden near downtown Portland, Oregon. In a few minutes you will find it hard to believe there is a city anywhere nearby. The Garden comprises seven acres and contains an outstanding collection of rare species and hybrid rhododendrons, azaleas and other ericaceous plants, as well as many companion plants and unusual trees. A spring-fed lake surrounds much of the Garden, attracting waterfowl to nest and feed. Ninety-four species of birds have been counted here, including the Great Blue Heron (Portland's official bird), Canadian Geese, Wood Ducks, Mallards, Lesser Scaups, Buffleheads, Ruddy Ducks, and American Coots. The Garden was jointly established in 1950 by the City of Portland Bureau of Parks and Recreation and the Portland Chapter of the American Rhododendron Society. Rhododendron Society members, Master Gardeners and other experts maintain the garden year-round, care for plants, and are available to answer questions about cultivation and pruning. The Crystal Springs Rhododendron Garden is located on SE 28th Avenue in Portland, Oregon, one block north of Woodstock, across from Reed College and adjacent to the Eastmoreland Golf Course. To get there by bus, ride the TriMet Number 19 Woodstock; it stops within a block of the Garden (ask the driver to call the stop for you). The Garden is open 365 days a year from dawn until dusk. Admission is charged between March and Labor Day. Any time of the year is a great time to visit. From March through June the plants are in full bloom. Several special events are held throughout the year, including the annual Mother's Day Rhododendron Show and Plant Sale. For inquiries, call (503) 771-8386. You can also visit their amazing website at www.portlandparks.org and follow the links to the garden.

Portland Rock Gym

Portland Rock Gym provides a remarkable and remarkably convincing simulation of the most exhilarating rock-climbing experiences. Owner, Gary Rall, is a pioneer in the use of nonpermanent modular climbing holds, which allow the climbing routes to be constantly changed, so that gym climbers are always encountering the unexpected, just like climbers on actual rock formations. When the Gym opened in 1988, it was set up only for bouldering and top-rope climbing, featuring the unique hexagonal Metolius tiles that are still in use today. Gary added new features over time, gradually transforming the possibilities. But novice climbers need not worry, there's something for every skill level here. Instruction is offered for everyone, including children. The Gym, the only climbing gym in Portland, has recently added a new feature, "Studioworks," featuring Hatha Yoga and Vinyasa classes. These classes provide an excellent means for climbers to learn body centering and balance techniques. The gym offers day rates, monthly passes, and annual memberships, accommodating tourists and longtime residents equally. The Portland Rock Gym is open seven days a week and is located at 21 NE 12th Avenue. For inquiries, call (503) 232-8310. See their Website at www.portlandrockgym.com for more information.

58

The Berry Botanic Garden

Portland's Berry Botanic Garden, which continues the legacy of pioneering plantswoman, Rae Selling Berry, promotes Northwest native plants, maintains plant collections, conserves endangered plants, and offers educational opportunities. Rae Selling Berry (1881-1976) was well known as "a plantswoman extraordinaire," and the Garden carries on her work in the field, the laboratory, and at home. The Garden nestles near the top of a hill just north of Lake Oswego, on a site chosen for its diverse habitats. Springs and creeks, a ravine, a meadow, and half-century-old second-growth Douglas fir combine to meet a variety of plant needs. Rae Selling Berry liked exceptional plants; the harder it was to grow, the more devoted she was to its cultivation. Today, the Garden staff describes its conservation mission this way: "To provide comprehensible off-site conservation resources in support of habitat-based conservation efforts in the Pacific Northwest, and to use our expertise in support of plant conservation regionally, nationally and globally." As such, the staff contributes through formal scientific presentations, contributions to books, and consultation work. Educational efforts are intended to interpret to all visitors the importance of plants in our lives with emphasis on regional natives, and to promote sustainable gardening practices appropriate to the region. And did you know that, just as there are endangered animals, there are also endangered plants? Actually, there are many. Perhaps you'd like to learn about how to save them for future generations. The Berry Botanic Garden is the place to start your education. The Berry Botanic Garden is located at 11505 SW Summerville Ave., Portland, Oregon 97219. It is open all year, by reservation. Call (503) 636-4112 and visit the Garden's website at www.berrybot.org.

Oregon Zoo

More than a million visitors come to the Oregon Zoo each year to view rare and exotic animals and learn more about the zoo's residents through fun events and exciting educational opportunities. The creative staff of the Oregon Zoo has put together something for everyone; you can enjoy "Breakfast with the Beasts", or take part in the Elephant's Birthday Bash, the Winter "ZooLights" Festival, or the summer concert series. For a complete listing of zoo programs, see the calendar of events on the website at www.oregonzoo.org. Of course the main attraction is the animals themselves. You will find yourself coming back again and again to get to know them. There is even a petting zoo for the young and young at heart, and no visit is complete without a ride on the Washington Park and Zoo Railway. You will always find something wonderful to see and do at the Oregon Zoo. The Zoo's Cascade Grill Restaurant has a spacious dining room with a high, open-beam ceiling arching over cozy wooden booths. Its carpet and metalwork chandeliers are commissioned art pieces reflecting the great Northwest. When the sun is out the large outdoor deck is the place to be; you can look out over alpine rocks and hear the sounds of exotic animals while you eat a wonderful meal. The Restaurant also has a banquet area for large groups and events. Cascade Outfitters, the Zoo's gift shop, is a treat for the discriminating shopper looking for unique and eco-friendly animal-related gifts. Each purchase helps the zoo fund its conservation programs and environmental education efforts. No zoo admission is necessary to shop in this attractive store. The Oregon Zoo is located five minutes west of downtown Portland at 4001 SW Canyon Road, off Highway 26 West. Take exit 72 from the highway and watch for the zoo signs. Experience this Oregon treasure for yourself! (503) 226-1561.

Broadmoor Golf Course

Times have changed a little since the Broadmoor Golf Course opened seventy-nine years ago, when golfers could play nine holes for a thirty-cent fee. But Broadmoor, now a full eighteen-hole course, remains one of the most beautiful and distinguished golf courses in the Pacific Northwest. "The Jewel of Portland" is now a 6,404 yard par 72 course covering over 220 acres of breathtaking landscape (including a view of Mount St. Helens), and interesting hazards, some of them created by the slough of the Columbia River, which happens to run through the Course. Broadmoor Golf Course has developed its own traditions over time, such as the Memorial Day Invitational for the "Old Bums," as the Broadmoor Men's Club has long been known. The Divot Room at Broadmoor is another much-loved feature. It's a bar and restaurant, managed by Diane Fallon. It features fabulous lunch buffets, especially the prime rib buffet on Fridays. Catering for group events is only one of the many amenities the Broadmoor offers its patrons. The Course is open to professionals and duffers alike, and the mood is relaxed and casual. If you're in the mood for golf lessons, you can make an appointment; there's no better place to learn the game. If you're a long-time golfer, check out the Pro Shop at the Moor before you play the Course. The Shop specializes in Callaway products, but they'll be glad to special order almost anything that fits your game needs. A full line of accessories, many featuring Broadmoor's custom logo, are also available. The Pro Shop is also the place to sign up for any of the tournaments held between March and November. The Course entrance is located at 3509 NE Columbia Boulevard. For questions or to set up a tee time, telephone (503) 281-1337, or visit their website, www.broadmoor-1931.com, for more information.

Portland Classical Chinese Garden

In the midst of Portland's urban Northwest streets there is a walled haven, a city block of peace and grace. The Portland Classical Chinese Garden was consciously created to nurture and inspire its visitors. When architects and artisans came from Portland's sister city in China, Suzhou, they built breathtaking effects and symbolic meaning into every part of the Garden. It is home to hundreds of rare and unusual plants. Serpentine walkways, a bridged lake, and open colonnades are all part of the balanced and harmonious design, with seven pavilions offering places to sit and enjoy the views. This is a place that is unchanging in its tranquil beauty and harmony. But it's also a place that changes with every visit. People say it is "never twice the same," because the hundreds of species of plants bloom and reveal themselves throughout the year. The beautifully designed paths made of pebble mosaics take you along walkways that provide cover over 85% of the Garden, creating a truly all-seasons retreat. The very names of the buildings evoke the culture the Garden brings to us. Moon-Locking Pavilion, Hall of Brocade Clouds, Painted Boat in Misty Rain, Half a Window Clustered in Green, Tower of Cosmic Reflections, Flower Bathing in Spring Rain, Reflections in Clear Ripples, and in the middle, Zither Lake. Portland Classical Chinese Garden is a cultural heritage destination, unique in the United States. The Garden is an "authentic Ming Dynasty scholar's garden," reflecting the mood and elegance of a Chinese dynasty that ended 360 years ago and epitomized the height of cultural achievement. As well as beauty and peace in the midst of city life, the Garden offers programs that encourage us to appreciate richly authentic Chinese traditions. The staff at the Garden is proud of the wide and lively range of events, classes, programs, and concerts. You can find a complete list of them at their website, www.portlandchinesegarden.org. The Portland Classical Chinese Garden is open daily, except for Thanksgiving, Christmas and New Year's Day. You can visit them at NW Third and Everett Streets.

Abernethy Center

Abernethy Center in historic downtown Oregon City plays host to all types of events, big and small, casual and formal. Situated at the end of the Oregon Trail, Abernethy Center provides its guests with the highest quality staff, catering and amenities to ensure that each event is an experience to remember. Their award-winning chef creates mouth-watering cuisine, perfect for corporate luncheons or wedding receptions, and their exclusive on-site catering staff exceeds the expectations of even the most discerning palates. Featuring 4,400 square feet of event space, a retractable LCD projector and 9' by 12' screen complete with a Bose Surround-Sound stereo system, Abernethy Center is your last stop when searching for the best event locale. Their gardens provide the ideal setting for wedding ceremonies, and the Ballroom, with its muted color tones and classic chandeliers, creates a warm ambiance suitable for intimate affairs or extravagant galas. From the modest Clackamas Room to their luxurious Ballroom, Abernethy Center's proximity to the airport, hotels and downtown makes it the perfect place to host your next event. Abernethy Center is located at 606 15th Street in Oregon City, Oregon 97045. Call (503) 722-9400 or visit them on their website at www.abernethycenter.com.

Above: Photo by
Freckled Pear Studio

Far Right: Photo by
Studio C Portland

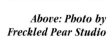

The Oregon Garden

The Oregon Garden in Silverton welcomes you with 20 specialty gardens and thousands of wonders. You'll find waterfalls, quiet ponds, fountains, and beautiful vistas. Its display of dwarf and miniature conifers is one of the largest collections in the country. Visits every few weeks, or even every few days apart, can bring wildly varied discoveries. New blooms and emerging plants abound, and birds and frogs provide background music. Migrating birds especially make each day at The Garden special. Located throughout the Garden, one-of-a-kind works of art blend in with The Garden's living tapestry. You'll want to visit the Signature Oak, an Oregon Heritage Tree more than 400 years old.

Then visit the Rediscovery Forest, a working tree farm that demonstrates forest management practices. Learn how the area's treated water is used in an innovative way to create a thriving wetland habitat for a variety of wildlife and plants. While there, tour the Gordon House, designed by legendary architect Frank Lloyd Wright. It is the only Wright-designed home in the Pacific Northwest that is open to the public. You can wander around the grounds on your own or take a tram tour. If you're there in the summer, look into the Summer Concert Series. Here are just a few of the sites you'll want to experience while at The Garden: The Axis Fountain features a beautiful fountain of Montana stone and a cascading wall of water; Pet Friendly Garden educates visitors as to which plants are pet friendly and which can be toxic; Sensory Garden, a therapeutic garden that features remarkable scents and textures that stretch the imagination. It includes an in-ground compass, a large wood trellis of Port Orford cedar, vertical wall gardens and a rain curtain 20 feet long and eight feet high. The Oregon Garden is located at 879 W. Main St., Silverton, OR. 97381. Call (503) 874-8100 or (877) 674-2733. Visit the website at www.oregongarden.org. The Garden has facilities for meetings, banquets, and receptions. While in the area, visit nearby Silver Falls State Park with its 25 miles of trails and 10 waterfalls. And see the Gallon House Bridge, the oldest covered bridge in Oregon. It's located just north of Silverton, off Highway 214.

Salem Golf Club

The old Salem Golf Club was built on land-grant property in 1927 that skirted the Willamette River and its inlets. Forested with a great variety of old-growth trees, it was a natural setting for something that was to become one of the finest golf facilities anywhere. Open to visitors year round and less than 2 miles from Salem's city center, the Golf Club is particularly unique in having no adjoining or visible development whatever. A round of golf here has been properly described as a "walk in the park." The eighteen hundred surrounding acres house a wildlife refuge and the walking paths of a regional nature setting. The course itself has been rated "Four Star" by Golf Digest magazine. The Salem Golf Club's award winning restaurant is locally famous for wonderful dining and can host functions of all sizes. "Rudy's" is situated in the colonial club house, an exact replica of the old southern plantation which housed General Rosecrans' headquarters during the Civil War battle for Vicksberg. Actually, the old Salem Golf Club has the best of everything for the golfer. A thirty acre driving and practice facility, the most beautifully maintained playing course, and the interesting historical features all combine to make one of Oregon's truly outstanding golf "Treasures". Salem Golf Club is located at 2025 Golf Course Road S., in Salem, Oregon 97302. For more information, call (503) 363-6652 or visit their website at www.Salemgolfclub.com.

McNary Golf Club

McNary Golf Club is a semi-private, member-owned club that encompasses 150 acres of some of the most beautiful meadows to be found in Oregon. The course is open to the public and is one of the most beautiful layouts in the area, featuring lakes as well as impeccable fairways and greens. A small pond fronts the 11th hole, and Claggett Creek enters into play on four holes. Stately oaks, firs, walnuts, redwoods, and pines line the fairways, and McNary is one of the most playable winter courses in the Northwest as well as one of Western Oregon's favorite venues for private tournaments. The signature hole is the 567-yard par-5 18th, voted the best par-5 in the Valley, which winds past slopes toward the lake along the right. With many membership categories available McNary Golf Club has something to please every member of a golfing family, "from the tikes just learning to golf, to Mom and Dad who will find that McNary offers enough challenge and pleasure to fill a lifetime." The Gold, Silver, Bronze and Corporate Memberships give you, your family, or your business associates full access to the 18-hole golf course and club privileges. For a full description of the various rates and benefits, visit the Club's website at www.mcnarygolfclub.com. In addition to having a full-service Pro Shop, McNary's restaurant is an outstanding feature of the Club. It has a peaceful setting with an excellent, full menu and is a great place to have breakfast, lunch or dinner. The Restaurant is a superb choice for hosting your special events like banquets, corporate outings, weddings, and barbeques. Come by for a round of golf and try the best par 5 in the Valley or enjoy a wonderful meal in a beautiful atmosphere. You will enjoy every moment. McNary Golf Club is located at 155 McNary Estates Drive North in Keizer, which is just north of Salem. You can find full directions on their website, or call (503) 393-4653.

Salem's Riverfront Carousel

In a beautiful building on a 15,000-square foot site in Salem's Riverfront Park, the glory days of 19th century amusement parks are recreated in the fantastic Riverfront Carousel. Community artisans created forty-two hand-carved and hand-painted horses in the classic carousel style, plus a mule, a zebra, and two authentically detailed "Oregon Trail" wagons. The Carousel was originally the dream of Hazel Patton of Salem, who was inspired by the carousel she saw on a visit to Missoula, Montana. Hazel saw that the Missoula Carousel had become a focal point for the community and wanted to recreate that in Salem. It took four and a half years and a monumental effort on the part of fundraisers, artisans, engineers, architects, accountants, writers, and many other local supporters, for her dream to become a reality. Since its opening in 2001, the Riverfront Carousel has indeed become a focal point for the community and a source of great pride. Each horse on the carousel was sponsored by a community member, and each horse has an individual personality: Little Joe and Maudie Ann, the ponies who provide toddlers with an easy ride; Francis the Mule; or G.J., the chestnut stallion who represents the State of Oregon. A Carousel ride lasts about three minutes, accompanied by music from an authentic carousel band organ. The Carousel is run by a not-for-profit group, Salem's Riverfront Carousel Inc., and is available for rental. The building housing the Carousel is designed to be the perfect space for birthday parties, wedding receptions, business meetings, family reunions, and any number of other group events. Tour packages that include a visit to the carving studio are also available. Don't forget to stop by the gift shop where they have a wide, wonderful selection of Carousel themed souvenirs and gifts. The Carousel is located at 101 Front Street NE in Salem. To inquire about renting the space or arranging a guided tour, call (503) 540-0374 or fax (503) 763-0630. Be sure to look at the Carousel's website, www.salemcarousel.org, for much more information! This Oregon Treasure is a perfect example of what a community can do when they combine their efforts for a worthwhile cause.

Holiday Farm Resort

If you wonder what paradise looks like, the Holiday Farm Resort at Blue River, Oregon, calls itself "Paradise on the banks of the beautiful McKenzie River." This is a secluded establishment among 92 acres with 800 feet of river frontage. The choices for outdoor activities are limitless. The staff offers private, guided fishing trips in drift boats, rafting trips, or can set up your tee time at the beautiful, nationally recognized Takatee Golf Course a mile away. There are endless back roads and trails in the area for hiking and biking. You can, of course, simply enjoy nature's beauty and relax by the river. Built in 1910, the Resort served for many years as a stage coach stop. President Herbert Hoover came for a visit to fly-fish. In 2000, Closen and Marge Christian bought the Resort and renovated the Farmhouse Restaurant and cottages. Cottages that have individual names: Old Man River - warm and cozy like a late-night fire; Waterwheel – with French doors providing "Mediterranean on the McKenzie"; Lazy Bones - feather bed comfortable; Lookout - perched on the river's edge; Honeymoon - evokes memories of days gone by; and River Apartment - Bright and open with a bird's eye view. Many rooms have refrigerators and microwaves, some have kitchenettes. All rooms are smoke-free. After soaking up a day's activities (or relaxing through it all), try the Restaurant, Lounge and Game Room. The menu in the Restaurant includes Pacific Northwest specialties such as fresh wild salmon, halibut and rainbow trout, filet mignon, broasted chicken, and Porterhouse porkchops. Or you can try the beef brisket, slow-smoked for 12 hours. Ask for the hot BBQ sauce, if you dare! Any item can be taken back to your cottage. The Holiday Farm Resort is located at 54455 McKenzie River Drive in Blue River, Oregon 97413. From I-5, take Exit 194A East to Springfield. This turns into Highway 126 going east toward Bend. Follow the highway to the second stop light. Turn left onto the McKenzie River Highway. Stay on it to the Mile Post 46 marker. Turn right onto McKenzie River Drive. The Holiday Farm is 1-4th of a mile on the left. Call (541) 822-3715 or (800) 823-3715 to find out who is providing current live entertainment in the Lounge. A Banquet Room and Conference Center are available as well. Visit their website at www.holidayfarmresort.com.

Photos by John Andrews, Captured Images

Historic Deepwood Estate

Life goes on at Historic Deepwood Estate. Once a home to three generations of Salem residents, it remains alive as an attraction for guests of all ages. The House, at the heart of the estate, has been described as a work of art. Built in 1894, the striking Salem landmark is one of Oregon's most ornate examples of Queen Anne architecture. It is a grand design with elaborate stained glass windows by Povey Brothers, golden oak woodwork, and a roof line of multiple gables and peaks. A City of Salem Museum and Park, it is managed by the Friends of Deepwood with the help of a multitude of dedicated volunteers. More artistry pleases the eye in the garden rooms, with a year-round wealth of color and greenery. The outdoor rooms were created by the Northwest's first female landscape architectural firm, Lord and Schryver. They include an English tea house garden and an exquisite boxwood garden, connected by hedge-lined corridors that lead under flower covered arches and past ornamental gates and fences. There are five and a half acres of gardens, nature trails, the original carriage house, conservatory and two gazebos, one from the 1905 Lewis and Clark Centennial Exposition. Deepwood Estate is engaging as well as beautiful. Now it's a gathering place for tours, events, classes and Victorian Teas. It's obvious, Deepwood has aged with elegance and style. The craftsmanship and detail of the House are remarkable, the programs are inviting and fun. A wonderful place to visit, Historic Deepwood Estate could be the perfect place for your catered tea, family celebration or business meeting. The well-maintained gardens are a lovely setting for many weddings during the summer. Visit www.deepwood.org and take a virtual tour of the House and gardens. The gardens are open from dawn to dusk, and guided house tours are offered year-round. For more information, call (503) 363-1825.

Photos by Ron Cooper

Vista Balloon Adventures

See an awe-inspiring dawn, views that stretch forever and enliven your senses with an experience you will not soon forget. At Vista Balloon Adventures you can be assured of a lovely getaway that will have you floating on air. Half an hour before dawn you can join Roger Anderson and his crew in preparing your hot air balloon for flight or just sit back and watch as the balloon is laid out and brought to life with industrial sized fans. The propane jets are ignited and your flight begins. Floating ten stories above the earth you will view Yamhill County's stunning wine country just as dawn pinks the sky. For one hour you will take in the fresh morning air, see the valley and enjoy the serenity of early morning. When you touch back to earth you will enjoy a champagne brunch and receive a flight souvenir. Other packages are available for those special occasions as well. Vista Balloon Adventures offers flights for your engagement, wedding, romantic getaway or corporate event. The Romantic Getaway Package includes the Deluxe flight with an overnight stay at one of the local Bed and Breakfasts or McMennamin's Hotel Oregon, plus fine dining at one of several critically acclaimed local restaurants. For an incredible adventure, contact Vista Balloon Adventures at (503) 625-7385 or (800) 662-2309. Flights are launched from Sportsman Air Park in Newberg, OR. To visit them, take the Tualatin exit west to Highway 99W in Sherwood. At 99W., go left (west) over Rex Hill and continue into Newberg. You can also check out their website at www.vistaballoon.com.

Langdon Farms

Just off I-5 in Wilsonville, 20 minutes south of Portland is one of the top ranked "Public Only" resort golf courses in the Northwest, the Langdon Farms Golf Club. Privately owned and maintained by Chris and Tom Maletis, their care and focus shows in every detail. Since 1995 its stunning Willamette Valley countryside setting, inspired architecture and refreshing views have drawn championship and newly inspired golfers alike. Immaculate grounds, peaceful pastoral links and dramatic water features lend to your enjoyment of this championship links-style golf course. With four tee settings all skill levels have an opportunity to play here. For something unique there is a par-4 eighth hole where your golfing skills are further challenged by maneuvering the original 1900's barn which is situated in play down the left side of the hole. Need to polish up those skills? There are 28 stalls, the largest grass practice tee around, two practice greens, as well as lessons for groups or individuals available from their PGA Professionals. When hunger strikes Langdon's Grill in the Big Red Barn serves breakfast, lunch, dinner and can provide banquet or meeting space for your special events year round. For more information contact the Langdon Farms Golf Club at 24377 NE Airport Rd. in Aurora or you can call (503) 678-4653 for tee times or (503) 678-1101 for the restaurant. Please visit their website at www.langdonfarms.com for tournament and calendar listings.

Enchanted Forest

If you're looking for fun and excitement in Oregon, make Enchanted Forest your first stop. Thrills and entertainment for all ages await you. From charming storybook scenes, to the biggest log flume ride in the Northwest, there's something for everyone in your family. Enchanted Forest began as the dream of Roger Tofte. Roger was raising his young family in the Salem area in the 1960's while working as an artist and draftsman for the Oregon State Highway Department. He became frustrated at the lack of family-oriented attractions in the region and decided to do something to remedy the problem. He acquired twenty acres of land near Interstate 5 and began building the park in 1964, "one bag of cement at a time." In 1971, the park was finally ready to open, and it became a hit with local residents and travelers almost immediately. Success allowed the Toftes to expand the park, adding attractions like the Tofteville Western Village, the Comedy Theater, and the Ice Mountain Bobsled Roller Coaster. Expansion continued in the 1990s with the building of the Old Europe Village and the Big Timber Log Ride. New attractions are still being added to this day. Since the park was inspired by Roger's children, it is fitting that several of them now help Roger run it: Susan is the Artistic Director and a Co-Operations Officer, Mary is the Chief Financial Officer and a Co-Operations Officer, and Ken is Head of Attractions Development and Ride Maintenance. Susan choreographed and composed the music for the dazzling Fantasy Fountains Water-Light Show and Ken designed and built the animatronic figures in the Old Europe Village. All of their combined love and dedication makes Enchanted Forest a true family affair. Enchanted Forest is easy to find: just take Exit 248 off Interstate 5, seven miles south of Salem. The park is open daily. For more information, call (503) 363-3060 or (503) 371-4242, or visit the park's website at www.enchantedforest.com.

Cascades Raptor Center

Set on a wooded hillside in Eugene, Oregon, Cascades Raptor Center is a nonprofit nature center and wildlife hospital specializing in birds of prey. Founded in 1987, the Center is dedicated to preserving a healthy and viable population of raptors and other wildlife in their natural habitat through rehabilitation and public education. The raptor family is comprised of eagles, hawks, falcons, owls, osprey and kites . They are all hunting birds with keen eyesight and hearing. They have strong, sharp talons for grasping and killing prey, and curved beaks for ripping up their food. The Center meets the unique needs of these birds and helps humans better understand and appreciate them and their role in the natural order. The dedicated hospital staff care for injured and orphaned raptors using specially designed enclosures, diets, and a diagnostic laboratory. How do raptors wind up there? They collide with vehicles, power lines, windows and fences. They are caught in traps, barbed wire, or fishing line. They are shot, poisoned, or they've had their nest sites destroyed by landscaping, logging, or construction. The Center's goal is to release each bird back to the wild. Unfortunately, in some cases that is not possible, and those who stay give humans a chance to view these magnificent birds in a natural environment. Typically, 50 or so non-releasable permanent resident birds are housed in large outdoor enclosures. They are comprised of more than 28 species, all native to Oregon. The Center is open to the public, as well as for field trips and group tours. Founder and Director, Louise Shimmel, invites you to come experience the artistry of feathers, the adaptation of form to function in the power of beak and talon, the grace of wing and tail shape, the camouflage of shape and color pattern. The Center's Bird Ambassadors provide you the chance to learn about the wild world and the impact human activity can have. Cascades Raptor Center is located at 32275 Fox Hollow Road in Eugene, Oregon 97405. For directions, hours, and admissions, call (541) 485-1320. Visit their website at www.eraptors.org. You can also send e-mail inquiries to Info@eraptors.org.

Hult Center for the Performing arts

Where can you go to experience acrobats or Chopin? Broadway or Brahms? Willie Nelson, jazz, or the Nutcracker Ballet? The answer is the Hult Center for the Performing Arts, and this is just a sample of the wide variety of events in the arts-packed calendar of this Eugene treasure. The Hult Center has been providing wonderful symphony, opera, ballet, modern dance, jazz, musical theater, comedy, rock and roll, and live theatre for 23 years. With 800 performances per year, this is one of the busiest performing arts centers in North America. Eugene can take justifiable pride in having built a top-notch facility entirely with local funds. Resident companies include the Eugene Symphony, the Willamette Repertory Theatre, Dance Theatre of Oregon, Oregon Festival of American Music, Oregon Mozart Players, Eugene Ballet, Oregon Bach Festival, Eugene Concert Choir and Eugene Opera. Widely acknowledged for its outstanding architecture and acoustical achievement, the Hult Center has been called "unquestionably one of the two or three finest performing arts complexes in the world." National and international performers are happy to come to Eugene to play in this "magical facility for the arts." Visual arts have not been forgotten here either. Art has been integrated into every part of the facility, from the hand-painted tiles in the restrooms to the Jacobs Gallery, which features work by regional artists and hosts the annual Mayor's Art Show. For an up-to-the-minute schedule of the Hult's offerings, or to purchase tickets, visit the website at www.hultcenter.org. To make it even easier to be in the know about upcoming adventures in the arts, you can subscribe to the e-Newsletter and receive "fabulous performance deals" such as Wild Card Wednesdays, inside information about performances and free events/lectures, and special offers for e-News subscribers only. The Hult Center for the Performing Arts is in the heart of downtown Eugene, the world's greatest city for the arts and the outdoors! The ticket office can be reached at (541) 682-5000, and 24-hour event information is available by calling (541) 682-5746.

Seven Feathers Hotel & Casino Resort

With year round entertainment and Las Vegas style gaming, Seven Feathers Hotel & Casino Resort is the perfect place to take the entire family. There are fabulous stage shows, professional boxing events, famous performers and plenty of food choices to fit every taste. Seven Feathers houses Kathy's Canyon Café and the Cow Creek Restaurant which have Atkins Diet choices added to their menu. You'll find a great sports bar near the gaming area, a modest convention center and the best staff and service anywhere. Seven Feathers has a huge video arcade, an ice cream store, gift shops, 190-plus RV spaces with hook ups, plus there's even a smoke-free gaming area. Within a short distance of the Casino there's golfing, excellent fishing areas and many other outdoor activities. Seven Feathers Hotel & Casino Resort is the second largest employer in Douglas County and is active in giving back to their community. Seven Feathers is responsible for creating better health and human service opportunities locally, and they are actively involved in creating more career choices for local youth. Seven Feathers is a place you'll come to spend a weekend and end up staying a week. This destination resort has everything you'd ever need to have a great time. Seven Feathers Hotel & Casino Resort is located at 146 Chief Miwaleta Lane in Canyonville. Look for the signs that show where to turn off of Interstate 5. To make reservations, phone (800) 548-8461 or visit their website at sevenfeathers.com.

Douglas County Museum

Remember the curiosity we had about the world around us when we were children? Turn back the hands of time and relive some of those same wonderful experiences by visiting the Douglas County Museum of History and Natural History. There is truly something here for everyone. Around every corner are exhibits that will fascinate you, inspire you and enlighten you. Experience hands on history in the Children's Discovery Room or the rich photographic collection currently on exhibit or also available for viewing in the Research Library. You can request to view a photograph of your ancestors or of area covered bridges. Director, Stacy McLaughlin is proud that the museum also houses one of the state's largest herbariums and has a natural history use collection which is available for biological and scientific research by appointment. The Museum even has one of the largest selections of Northwest books and interesting items available in their gift shop. The Douglas County Museum of History and Natural History is open Monday through Saturday and is located at 123 Museum Drive, Roseburg, Oregon. You can reach them by calling (541) 957-7007 or visit their website at www.co.douglas.or.us/museum.

Myrtle Creek Golf Course

The strikingly beautiful Myrtle Creek Golf Course was voted one of the ten best new affordable golf courses in the nation by Golf Digest. This challenging course blends into the natural landscape while being located only fifteen miles south of Roseburg and only minutes north of Seven Feathers Hotel and Casino. While you're there take a few moments to marvel at the ingeniously designed, oversized undulating greens, the myrtle and oak-lined fairways, the natural water hazards and spectacular views of the surrounding hills. As you casually move through this brilliantly laid out and awe-inspiring course, you're sure to feel like this is what life is really all about. With its elevated tees and convenient location, Myrtle Creek Golf Course is certain to become anyone's favorite place to spend the day. Myrtle Creek Golf Course is located at 1316 Fairway Drive in Myrtle Creek, Oregon. Call (541) 863-4653, toll free at (888) T-Myrtle.

Umpqua Cedar Homes

Nestled in the foothills of the Great Umpqua Valley and centrally located in Douglas County, Roseburg is home to Umpqua Cedar Homes, a local Lindal Cedar Homes distributor. Every day Umpqua Cedar Homes assists families in designing and building their own dream home, a Lindal Cedar Home. Since 1994, Umpqua Cedar Homes and staff have been educating families on the differences between a standard home and a Lindal Cedar Home. With gracious open post-and-beam construction and a lifetime structural warranty, the Lindal difference promises a value, beauty, livability, and low maintenance. For more than half a century Lindal Cedar Homes has been eliminating many of the unknowns that can cost time, money, and headaches during ordinary construction. A Lindal Cedar Home is designed for life, which is evident in our flexible plans and top-quality materials. We've built our reputation on personal service and attention. No matter your budget, timeframe or style, Lindal Cedar Homes has created and built thousands of custom cedar homes. From view-catching, glass-prowed Lindal Classics to warm, woodsy Traditionals and sleek, clean-lined Contemporaries, we have a design for every family and every future Lindal homeowner. Stop by or call our office today. Our doors are open six days a week, Lindal Cedar Homes and Umpqua Cedar Homes, 1638 NW Garden Valley Boulevard in Roseburg, or call (800) 823-3270. You can also visit us on the web at www.umpquacedarhomes.com. Your pleasures. Your priorities. Your personal sense of style. Rise above the rest. Discover your dreams. Lindal Cedar Homes and Umpqua Cedar Homes, prepared to bring your dream home to life.

Oak Hills Golf Club and RV Resort

Both the challenge and beauty of the natural terrain at one of the Umpqua Valley's recently renovated premier public golf courses, Oak Hills Golf Club, will impress you. Head Professional Brad Leiken is there to answer all of your golfing queries and before or after your golf game you can visit with friends as you enjoy breakfast, lunch or dinner in the casual atmosphere of their patio or The Nest Restaurant. The Nest is the only restaurant in the area with such a spectacular view. They serve a locally famous Sunday Brunch and offer distinctive banquet facilities for that "special event". There is even a unique steel dance floor to while away the evening on. There is plenty of room to park your RV and use all the comforts of home in the adjacent Oak Hills RV Resort. There are building sites overlooking the Golf Course that are available within the beautiful Oregon Knolls Estates. For reservations or more information, call (541) 459-2931, toll free (866) 459-4423, or visit the Oak Hills website at www.golfoakhills.com.

Noah's Ark

From the outside this tourist attraction looks just like Noah's Ark. On the inside you'll enjoy exploring their one-of-a-kind restaurant and gift shop. The large, open room allows for a comfortable and relaxed family atmosphere, so it's perfect for the entire family, especially the kids. For a nominal fee there is also a guided tour of a world created directly from the Old Testament perspective. Knowledgable, friendly volunteers bring to life the legendary adventure of Noah's Ark. If you'd like to treat the whole family to a provocative and entertaining experience, then you're sure to love Noah's Ark, located at 411 NW Safari Rd., Winston, OR 97496. Just call (541) 784-1261 or go to our website www.noahsarkwinston.com for more information and directions on how to get there.

Mercy Medical Center

Providing complete, comprehensive care and compassion for nearly 100 years has become Mercy Medical Center's legacy to the Douglas County community. Founded in 1909 by the Sisters of Mercy, Mercy Medical Center continues to serve the Douglas County area with an ever present vision for expansion and improved patient care. Mercy Medical Center offers a full range of health care services, including outpatient rehabilitation services, pediatric services, and a comprehensive cardiac catheterization lab. The health care team at Mercy is dedicated to the "whole person", which means they carefully tend to the physical, emotional, and spiritual needs of each patient. Regardless of economic status, Mercy Medical Center provides quality health services to all people. With a special emphasis on the dignity of all life, the caring people at Mercy Medical Center will provide you with the assurance that when you require their assistance, they will care for you as one of their family. Mercy Medical Center, providing a ministry of healing since 1909, is located at 2700 Stewart Parkway, Roseburg, OR 97470. Call (541) 673-0611.

Wildlife Safari

Located on 600 acres of land in beautiful Southern Oregon, Wildlife Safari is home to animals from around the world. People of all ages can see over 500 native and exotic animals from the comfort of their own vehicle as they take a trip through Africa, Asia and the Americas. You will view animals such as ostriches, rhinos, lions, giraffes, bears, llamas, wild horses, Tibetan yaks, tigers and camels in three large, naturalistic habitats where the animals co-exist. Don't forget to pack your camera for endless photo opportunities around every corner. At the end of your safari, don't miss the Wildlife Safari's signature animal, the cheetah. The park is world renowned for its cheetah breeding program. Amazingly, 35 litters and 143 cheetahs have been born at Wildlife Safari since 1973. After your safari, park your car and tour the Safari Village on foot. Explore the gardens and animal exhibits as you enjoy the singing of white-handed gibbons. Daily animal programs, train rides and elephant rides are available on a seasonal basis. Have you worked up an appetite yet? Enjoy a fantastic lunch in the White Rhino Restaurant with a spectacular view of the lower Safari Village. Snacks are also seasonally available at the Savannah Snack Shack. No visit is complete until you have found the perfect souvenir in the Casbah Gift Shop, featuring gifts from around the world, as well as from local artists in Southern Oregon. Planning your visit at least a week in advance? Call or visit their website to learn about the "Get Inside" events, such as feeding a giraffe or lion, bathing an elephant, walking with cheetahs or spending a half-day with a ranger. Wildlife Safari is a non-profit organization dedicated to the conservation, education and research of endangered animals. The park is open every day of the year except Christmas Day. You will find the Wildlife Safari park south of Roseburg on I-5, exit 119. For more information, including hours and pricing, visit www.wildlifesafari.org or call (541) 679-6761.

Bear Creek Golf

Welcoming visitors year round, this nine hole executive layout is nestled along Bear Creek (thus the name, Bear Creek Golf Course). Two par-4's and seven par-3's plus a beautiful water hazard make this course perfectly suited for all playing abilities. Bear Creek Golf has a full-line pro shop, a covered driving range, practice greens, a snack shop, and golf pro Marla Corbin. Marla not only owns and manages Bear Creek Golf, she's also a certified club fitter and golf instructor. For under $15.00 you can play a round or for under $700.00 a year you can enjoy member privileges while playing every single day if you'd like. Bear Creek Golf is conveniently located on South Pacific Highway just south of downtown Medford. Call (541) 773-1822 to speak with Marla about why you should visit this beautiful course.

Jackson County Airport

Convenient, welcome. Jackson County Airport serves the entire Southern Oregon region. With connecting flights to anywhere in the world, you can probably get in and out of this airport faster than any other in the West. Construction for a new terminal building is scheduled to be completed in 2008. However, the current terminal has everything you need: The Red Barron Restaurant, a snack bar, and a gift shop. And there's only one gate, so you know exactly where to go. When completed, the new two-story terminal will boast six gates and will surely expedite any traveler's wait in line. Phone (541) 776-7222.

Lake of the Woods Mountain Lodge and Resort

Open all year long, Lake of the Woods Mountain Lodge and Resort isn't just where you stay, it's why you came. This is the epitome of the "destination resort," set in the midst of the incomparable majesty of a natural mountain lake, whether you prefer your accommodations to be hearty or hearthside. Distinctive rustically-decorated cozy cabins pamper up to 6 guests with down comforters and gas-view stoves. For a closer experience of nature, reserve an RV or tent site surrounded by swaying emerald pines and visit the General Store, showers, and other amenities. Order a picnic lunch, dine at the lodge restaurant with lakeside seating and bar, or stock up at the General Store and prepare an intimate or family dinner in your own cabin or campsite. A snowmobile guide service, the newly-remodeled marina and boat ramp, and a full range of equipment rentals assure your family will have fun in any season. Ask about corporate retreats and packages for your business. 950 Harriman Route, Klamath Falls, Oregon 97601. (541) 949-8300. www.lakeofthewoodsresort.com.

The Rogue Creamery

Recently, an American-made blue cheese was crowned the "Best Overall Blue" at the World Cheese Awards in London. It was the first American blue cheese to win the world title and it was chosen over the best European cheeses. The following year, the Smokey Blue Cheese won the "Best Cheese in America" award. The maker of those cheeses - the Rogue Creamery in Central Point, Oregon. Thomas Vella opened the Rogue Creamery in 1935. Today, Master Cheese-Maker, Ignazio (Ig) Vella, carries on the tradition. Called the "Godfather of Artisan Cheese," Ig sold the Creamery to David Gremmels and Cary Bryant. Reportedly, when David and Cary approached Ig with an offer to buy, he replied that if they wanted the cheese, "you're going to have to make it yourself," but three weeks later a handshake sealed the deal. Rogue Creamery cheeses reflect both the artistry of the cheese makers and the taste nuances of local products. The milk comes from a single source: a certified organic, sustainably run, local dairy. Each cheese is made by hand in small batches and each stage of production is closely monitored. The result is cheese of the highest quality, rich in flavor and tradition. Says Ig, "Our cheeses have been made with great care and attention, from our artisan creamery to your table." The cheese and gift shop is a delightful place to sample cheese, find gourmet foods and select interesting kitchen items. Rogue Creamery makes many types of cheese and you can purchase small chunks to full wheels of cheese. The Rogue Creamery is located at 311 N. Front Street in Central Point, Oregon 97502. For inquiries, call (541) 665-1155 or (866) 665-1155 toll free. To see some of the delectable products they offer, visit their website at www.roguecreamery.com.

Red Mountain Golf Course

Owned by Brad and Kris Vandehey, this secluded mountainside course is one you can truly appreciate. You also stand a good chance of seeing wildlife that frequents the area. Brad and Kris are only part of the team who keep Red Mountain Golf Course in perfect condition. Their sons, Derekk, Dylan, and daughters, Tristin, Taylor, and their two dogs, Bogie and Phoenix, are all fully involved in the day to day operations of the course. This nine-hole golfer's dream is complete with a snack and pro shop. You can rent everything you need to have a great afternoon of golfing, including renting an electric cart. If you really enjoy the course, you can rent their remodeled cabin that sleeps up to four adults.

Reservations are recommended. Red Mountain Golf Course is located at 324 Mountain Greens Lane in Grants Pass, Oregon. You can phone the Vandehey family at (541) 479-2297 or visit their website at www.redmountaingolf.com.

Oregon Cabaret Theatre

For an unforgettably entertaining experience, don't miss the Oregon Cabaret Theatre, offering the best in musical theatre and comedy since 1986. Imaginative West Coast premieres alternate with innovative productions of nationally-acclaimed musical theatre in a setting you won't find anywhere else in the world. You will be seated at a table on tiered levels or in the balcony in this elegantly renovated church. Feel free to order anything from a beverage or appetizer to a full gourmet dinner or brunch tailored especially to each production by the master chef. For a special treat, order a delectable dessert to be served during the intermission. Laugh until your sides hurt at a hilarious parody or a raucous English Panto. Enjoy a sparkling revue of song and dance. This cabaret is renowned for presenting top quality productions with talented professional performers and superb productions values. You won't find better food, comedy or music anywhere. Shows sell out quickly, so make your reservation, order a season subscription, or call for box office hours or a brochure. Oregon Cabaret Theatre is located at 1st and Hargadine in Ashland, Oregon. For ticket information, call (541) 488-2902, or visit their website at www.oregoncabaret.com.

Photos by
Tom Lavine

Eagle Point Golf

Ranked among the top ten public-access courses of 1996, Eagle Point Golf Course is not only award-winning, but affordable. The Galpin family is known for quality building projects, and Eagle Point Golf Course is one of Southern Oregon's best jewels. The brilliant design, created by Robert Trent Jones, Jr., allows the finest playing conditions year-round. Relax with a cool drink in the comfortable atmosphere of Arthur's restaurant, named after grandpa Galpin, and you'll want to stay to enjoy a tasty appetizer or full-course meal. Tasteful retail shops are in the construction phase, and the Galpin family offers many beautiful homes available for sale just off the golf course. Visit Pro Richard Reiber for group schools or personalized attention adaptable to your needs. Richard has the uncanny ability to "feel into" your swing and use language you can understand to enhance your love of the game. Richard and all the staff at Eagle Point Golf Course are dedicated to providing exceptional service. Call for tee times and clinic schedules. (541) 826-8225 or (541) 261-1911. www.eaglepointgolf.com.

Rogue Klamath River Adventures

Exhilarating welcome. Rogue Klamath River Adventures, the premier rafting company in Southern Oregon, will provide everything you need for an exhilarating experience on breathtakingly beautiful Southern Oregon and Northern California rivers, or even fulfill your wildest dreams on the mysterious Amazon. If you're looking for a fun afternoon for your family or a challenging adventure in Class IV+ whitewater, your professional guide will provide state of the art equipment and exceptional customer service. Their twenty-six years of experience means they've taken care of everything, so you can relax and enjoy the ride. Let them transport you from the Medford/Ashland area for a half day float , or plan a full day including a gourmet meal followed by their famous brownies. In the fall, you may enjoy a longer rafting or fishing excursion with either lodge or camping accommodations. Excursion packages available to Chile, Peru, China and Alaska mean you won't run out of new adventure opportunities. No matter what your skill level or thrill threshold, Rogue Klamath River Adventures has a trip planned with you in mind. Call them toll free at (800) 236-07669, or locally at (541) 779-3708.

Mt. Ashland Ski & Snowboard Resort

Twooshing Greetings. Find exhilarating fun and adventure just six miles inside Oregon's southern border at I-5's milepost 6. In another few minutes you'll be swooshing the slopes at Mt. Ashland Ski & Snowboard Resort. The variety of runs and spectacular views of the rugged Siskiyou Mountain Range will delight even the most experienced skier or 'boarder. The rental shop has everything you could possibly need for the whole family to enjoy a day of cross-country skiing or snowshoeing, or take lessons and experience the thrill of night skiing. Drop into the lodge for a snack, or have a drink in the lounge and let the warm and friendly staff help you find whatever you need. World class accommodations are available at Callahan's, also listed in this book, just minutes from I-5 and Mt. Ashland. You can leave your car at home and get to know the locals on the convenient ski bus from nearby Ashland, Medford, or even as far away as Grants Pass. They'll give you the scoop on the best places to eat and other fun things to do in Southern Oregon. Phone for prices and other information (541) 482-2897.

Alpacas at Lone Ranch

Remember that alpaca sweater you saw in a store a while back? How would you like to have a look at the animals that grew the fleece? Head for Alpacas at Lone Ranch in the scenic Upper Rogue Valley, between Eagle Point and Shady Cove. It's an easy and scenic drive from the Medford area. Owners, Richard and Renate Gyuro, maintain a herd of nearly fifty of these unique animals. For a terrific family outing, you can experience these gentle, mystical animals by walking in their pastures and getting your hands into their fleece. Also, they have the most endearing features, especially their wise and soulful eyes. While at the Ranch, visit the Fiber Nook for alpaca garments and yarn. To learn more about these fascinating animals and the place they live, call (541) 826-7411 or (541) 821-8071. You can arrange for a free tour and ask for directions to the Ranch. Private overnight accommodations are available. To get a better look, you can also visit their website at www.alpacasontheweb.com.

Orange Torpedo Trips

Orange Torpedo Trips is the world's foremost inflatable kayaking outfitter, running trips on 6 different rivers in four states throughout the west. In 1969, local Grants Pass, Oregon banker Jerry Bentley recognized the commercial potential of a guided inflatable kayak company after buying a couple of Sevylor Tahiti inflatable kayaks and running the lower Rogue River Canyon. The Rogue features many Class III rapids and two challenging class IV rapids. Maintaining a guest to guide ratio of three or four to one, Jerry and the successive owners have been able to safely provide first-time paddlers with a safe, scenic and educational river experience. Expanding their repertoire to include many multi-day adventures, Orange Torpedo Trips now offers trips in Idaho, Oregon, California and Arizona. With over 60 employees during the summer, they take approximately 3,000 people down the rivers annually. For an amazing, spectacular and unforgettable adventure take a trip with Orange Torpedo Trips, it'll be the trip of a lifetime! Orange Torpedo Trips' mailing address is P.O. Box 1111, Grants Pass, Oregon 97528. Call for more information on their toll free number (800) 635-2925 or visit their website at www.OrangeTorpedo.com.

Britt Festivals

In 1963 the Northwest's first outdoor music festival was launched on an acoustically resonant hillside estate that once belonged to pioneer photographer Peter Britt. Since then, Britt Festivals has become the premier outdoor summer music festival in the region. Located in the historic 1850's gold rush town of Jacksonville, in Southern Oregon, Britt presents a summer long series of concerts featuring world-renowned artists in jazz, country, dance, folk, pop, world, blues, musical theater and classical music. Past performers include Willie Nelson, Bill Cosby, Ringo Starr, Crosby Stills & Nash, Wynton Marsalis, Vince Gill, Jean Pierre Rampal, Smokey Robinson, Peter Paul & Mary, and the Danish Royal Ballet, to name a few. With a total capacity of 2,200, the natural amphitheater is a venue of unparalleled beauty overlooking the Rogue River Valley. Each summer about 75,000 patrons travel from all over to enjoy Britt's world-class performances, spectacular scenery and relaxing atmosphere. For a concert schedule and more information, call (800) 882-7488 or visit www.brittfest.org.

Oregon Shakespeare Festival

Quick, what's the location of the oldest existing full-scale Elizabethan stage in the Western Hemisphere? If you didn't guess Ashland, Oregon, you haven't visited this picturesque town nestled in the mountains along Interstate-5. It's just a dozen or so miles north of the California border. Ashland is so closely associated with its annual Shakespeare Festival that it's a wonder the town isn't named Williamsburg, or Avon. Established in 1935, the Oregon Shakespeare Festival (OSF) is among the largest and oldest professional regional repertory theatre companies in the U.S. Each year it presents an eight-month season of 11 plays. Three or four are by Shakespeare and seven or eight are by classic and contemporary playwrights. They are performed in rotating repertory in three theatres, one of which is outdoors. OSF employs approximately 450 theatre professionals from all over the country, and has a volunteer staff of nearly 750. The awards won by the festival are legion. One of the most recent being a rating by Time Magazine as among the top five regional theatres in the country. Here is a sample of plays scheduled for production for the year this book was prepared: Shakespeare's "Richard III," George Bernard Shaw's "The Philanderer," John Murray and Allen Boretz' "Room Service," Eduardo DeFilippo's "Napoli Milionaria!," Hannah Cowley's "the Belle's Stratagem," Robert Schenkkan's "By the Waters of Babylon," August Wilson's "Ma Rainey's Black Bottom," Octavio Solis' "Gibraltar," Shakespeare's "Twelfth Night," Christopher Marlowe's "The Tragic History of Doctor Faustus," and Shakespeare's "Love's Labors Lost." The Oregon Shakespeare Festival is headquartered at 15 S. Pioneer in Ashland, OR 97520. Call (541) 482-4331. For information about current productions or to order tickets, visit the OSF website at www.osfashland.org.

Candy, Ice Cream, Bakeries & Coffee

The Oregon Candy Farm

The Oregon Candy Farm has been a favorite candy maker since 1933. Crafted with care, using the finest chocolate available anywhere, their confections include only the finest ingredients. Delicacies include heavy whipping cream, pure dairy butter, wildflower honey, old-fashioned molasses and pure cane sugars. The Oregon Candy Farm is best known for their affordable high quality variety of chocolates, many with house-roasted nuts, including Oregon hazelnuts. Still loyal to traditional candy making methods, they now offer more than 100 confectionery delights. Try the original house-made marshmallows, cooked in a copper kettle over open flame, and their award winning Rocky Road for a memorable treat. On Monday through Friday from 9am to 5pm you can watch the candy makers in action through their kitchen viewing windows. The Shop is also open on weekends from noon until 5pm. You are invited to taste what a difference fresh-made makes. The friendly staff enjoys assisting with and creating special gift and holiday orders. Shipping is available, just let them know what they can do for you. The Oregon Candy Farm is located at 48620 SE Hwy 26, on the way to Mt. Hood, only 5.5 miles east of Sandy. Look carefully for the blue Oregon State directional signs just before milepost 30, and turn up the hill. You can reach The Oregon Candy Farm by calling (503) 668-5066 or email them at TheOrecandyfarm@aol.com.

Lauterell Falls in the Columbia River Gorge

Longbottom Coffee & Tea Inc.

The Longbottom Coffeehouse and Roasting Factory in Hillsboro is more than your average coffee stop. Michael Baccellieri has crafted a warmly designed outlet for his coffee roasting perfection. This extensive factory makes hand crafted blends of prized regional coffees from 100% Arabica beans and can handle coffee bean orders from 1.5 ounces to 1 million pounds. Even though you are at a full functioning factory, the Cafe is relaxed and cheerful, a far cry from the hustle and bustle one might expect. They are also not strictly devoted to serving coffee. They provide excellent accompaniments such as their full cases of hot pastries, muffins and scones, freshly baked each morning. They offer traditional hot breakfasts as well. Check them out for lunch any day but especially on Thursdays and Fridays when they create their succulent signature Traeger Smokehouse Barbecue and offer Slow Smoked Ribs, chicken, roast beef and sirloin. Their use of fresh local ingredients takes their meals up another notch. The enjoyable atmosphere, excellent coffee, friendly service and free wireless Internet access make this a great place to start your day. Longbottom Coffee and Tea is conveniently located at 4893 NW 235th Avenue, just off of US 26 at Shute Road in Hillsboro. You can reach them by phoning (503) 648-1271. You can also check out their website at www.longbottomcoffee.com.

Beaverton Bakery

Since 1925 this third generation full-line bakery has been providing quality ingredients and timeless techniques to their broad array of specialty bakery items, much to the delight of area patrons. Today Beaverton Bakery produces bakery goods for restaurants, grocers and caterers throughout the greater Portland metro area, as well as for sale in their family shop. Here you can enjoy cookies, pastries, doughnuts, breads and pies. All are made with homemade jams, custards and fillings as well as seasonal treats such as raspberry, blueberry, peach and garden cakes that are available only for a limited time each year. They create delectable options with corporate logo cookies, cinema cakes, theme cakes and unforgettable anniversary and wedding cakes. Consult with their wedding specialists in the Wedding Shop to plan your special anniversary or wedding day. With nearly eighty years of experience you will find that every detail has been meticulously planned for you. When you just need a cheerful and pleasant meal you will enjoy the selection of Espresso drinks and lunch items in Shirley's Coffee Shop, located next to the 1887 Robinson House. Beaverton Bakery will also deliver breakfast trays and lunchbox service to you or your business, just call ahead. With over seventy staff, the Beaverton Bakery folks are proud to say that they can handle any special requests no matter how large or small. Located at 12375 SW Broadway in Beaverton, Oregon. You can reach Beaverton Bakery at (503) 646-7136 or visit their website at www.beavertonbakery.com.

JaCiva's

People who have frequently traveled the highway to Mount Hood may remember Heidi's Swiss Village Bakery, a fine pastry shop run by Jack and Iva Elmer. Well, in 1986, Jack and Iva created a new pastry shop right downtown in Portland. The name combines their own names: "JaCiva's," and it is one of Oregon's finest producers of exquisite European chocolate, truffles, candies, tortes, wedding cakes, pastries and surprises. Would you like to get your business logo sculpted in chocolate? This is the place! In addition to their bakery, Jack and Iva's creations may also be found at elegant Portland hotels, fine restaurants, high-end supermarkets and many other fine locations in the metropolitan area. JaCiva's has received many awards over the years, including the United States Pastry Alliance Gold Medal and the Austin Family Business Award. Jack Elmer understands that making great chocolates is an art. When you stop by, you'll discover that the family-oriented atmosphere is the best place to enjoy a treat, be it a piece of chocolate or a magnificent wedding cake. You can also get cakes for other special occasions, or choose from the full line of European pastries and tortes. Try a different confection each time you come in, and when you've tried everything, start over again. JaCiva's is at 4733 Southeast Hawthorne Boulevard in Portland, Oregon. Look for the large burgundy and white awning on the north side of the street. For more information, call toll-free, (866) 522-4827 (JACIVAS) or visit their website at www.jacivas.com.

Upper Crust Bread Co.

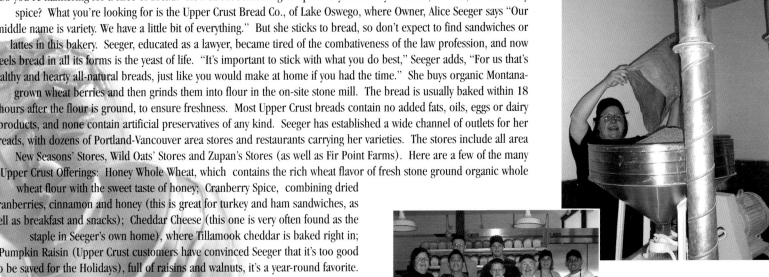

So you're hankering for a slice of bread. How about something unique – say blueberry crumble, challah, or cranberry spice? What you're looking for is the Upper Crust Bread Co., of Lake Oswego, where Owner, Alice Seeger says "Our middle name is variety. We have a little bit of everything." But she sticks to bread, so don't expect to find sandwiches or lattes in this bakery. Seeger, educated as a lawyer, became tired of the combativeness of the law profession, and now feels bread in all its forms is the yeast of life. "It's important to stick with what you do best," Seeger adds, "For us that's healthy and hearty all-natural breads, just like you would make at home if you had the time." She buys organic Montana-grown wheat berries and then grinds them into flour in the on-site stone mill. The bread is usually baked within 18 hours after the flour is ground, to ensure freshness. Most Upper Crust breads contain no added fats, oils, eggs or dairy products, and none contain artificial preservatives of any kind. Seeger has established a wide channel of outlets for her breads, with dozens of Portland-Vancouver area stores and restaurants carrying her varieties. The stores include all area New Seasons' Stores, Wild Oats' Stores and Zupan's Stores (as well as Fir Point Farms). Here are a few of the many Upper Crust Offerings: Honey Whole Wheat, which contains the rich wheat flavor of fresh stone ground organic whole wheat flour with the sweet taste of honey; Cranberry Spice, combining dried cranberries, cinnamon and honey (this is great for turkey and ham sandwiches, as well as breakfast and snacks); Cheddar Cheese (this one is very often found as the staple in Seeger's own home), where Tillamook cheddar is baked right in; Pumpkin Raisin (Upper Crust customers have convinced Seeger that it's too good to be saved for the Holidays), full of raisins and walnuts, it's a year-round favorite. Ready for one more? Try this. Spinach Onion Parmesan, for a great combination of cheese and chopped spinach, with a wisp of onion (it makes an amazing dinner and sandwich bread). That's just a sample of the varieties at The Upper Crust, whose slogan is "A Cut Above the Rest." Try a loaf for yourself and find out. The Upper Crust Bread Co., is located at 31 S. State Street in Lake Oswego. To make inquiries or to order bread, call (503) 697-9747.

Fireside Coffee Lodge

Great coffee 24 hours a day, seven days a week. The Fireside Coffee Lodge is the only 24-hour coffee shop in Portland. They opened with a bang on April 15, 2002 with a Tax Day Party for last minute filers (complete with runners to the Post Office). And they have provided such great service to their customers and the community that they received the "2003 Business of the Year Award" from the Better Business Bureau in the Small Business Category. Owner, Tori Lungren, is very proud of the Fireside Coffee Lodge. The atmosphere is rustic and friendly. She invites you to "Come sit in front of our stone fireplace and surround yourself in our Mountain Lodge atmosphere while enjoying your favorite coffee specialty drink." At Fireside Coffee Lodge "you'll find yourself getting away from the hustle and bustle without ever leaving the city." The Rustic Lodge décor is complete with log furniture, moose, bears, rustic snowshoes and vintage skis. Customers can avail themselves of Internet access-wired and wireless as well as enjoy the Fireside's menu, which offers a wide variety of coffee drinks, both hot and iced, smoothies, Italian sodas, hot and cold sandwiches made to order, salads, soups and home baked bread. Pastries, muffins, coffee cake, biscotti, brownies and other desserts, too. They have everything you could want to go with great coffee. The Fireside Coffee Lodge is deeply involved in the community with ongoing support to Portland non-profits like the Doernbecher Children's Hospital and the Needy Kids' Fund. Fireside also sponsors the "Wakeup Portland" News Trivia Quiz with Paul Linnman on 1190 KEX. This warm, friendly place is terrific for business meetings and social gatherings, as well as a blessing for students and service workers who are taking care of business in the middle of the night. Come in to the Fireside at 1223 S.E. Powell Blvd., in Portland and experience for yourself the comfortable, at home atmosphere. For more information, call (503) 230-8987.

Piece of Cake Catering & Desserts

Where cakes are a work of art – Piece of Cake Catering and Desserts is an award-winning bakery that offers fabulous cakes and desserts. It was established in 1979, when Marilyn DeVault, Food Designer and Founder, first made a cake for her brother's birthday. It was the beginning of "the most passionate cake bakery" in Portland. Through the years customers have made Piece of Cake a family tradition. "We have had doctors mark on their calendars months in advance so that their staff will not forget their birthdays, and it must come from Piece of Cake!" In the past 6 years Piece of Cake has also developed a full range of amazing special dietary needs cakes like vegan, wheat-free, sugar-free, gluten free, soy-free, and our newest formula brownies that have no sugar, no wheat, and no dairy – truly a miracle. "Our secret recipes put the fun in vegan treats without sacrificing your health or taste." At their website, www.pieceofcakebakery.net you will find complete descriptions of their many treats. "We tell our new customers that our cake is 1000% better than the last cake they tasted. If you are planning a wedding, birthday or anniversary, you can come in and sample our cakes. It is fun and you can bring in the decision-making friends and family to be a part of the tasting." On their website you can sign up to receive Piece of Cake's e-mail newsletter, Cake Gossip, where you can get the latest information, special offers and discounts straight from the Shop. But as great as the cake is, Piece of Cake is more than cake. Marilyn DeVault has a flair for the unusual and the elegant – cookies, tortes, cheesecakes. And the staff bakers and decorators are proud to serve up "earthy, 1940s 'comfort' food like grandma used to make." They were voted Best Bakery in Portland and won Best at the Chocolate Safari at the Wildlife Safari. Ask about their full-service catering, or come in to browse their wonderful selection. Piece of Cake Bakery is at the west end of Sellwood in SE Portland, two blocks south of SE Tacoma Street, at 8306 SE 17th. For inquiries or to order your hearts desire, call (503) 234-9445.

Parisi's

You can find Gelato almost anywhere in Italy, but if you're looking for Gelato in Portland, Parisi's is the place to go. Gelato is Italian ice cream and if you have not experienced it, you are in for a treat. What makes Gelato so good? Gelato is made in small batches in a "batch freezer" which produces a much denser product than American ice cream. It has less air whipped in and it is also served at a higher temperature. The creamy richness comes from the density and texture not an added bump of butterfat founding other premium ice cream. Parisi's Gelato is made with fresh true raw ingredients, nothing artificial. To give you an idea of the heavenly indulgence available, one of their best-selling flavors is "French Chocolate Caramel Brandy Fudge." Parisi's Gelato supplier made the "O" List as one of Oprah's favorites in the July, 2004 issue of her magazine. In the short time since Mike and Mary started Parisi's, it has become a popular neighborhood café. Mary's background as a scratch baker has been a valuable asset as they offer more than just Gelato. Mary makes several flavors of fresh fudge on a regular basis as well as homemade cookies from family recipes. Parisi's offers "make our own" Panini sandwiches on rustic artisan bread. Choose a meat, choose a cheese and two spreads and Mike will grill it per your order. Caffe Umbria Italian roast coffee and espresso drinks are also available. Parisi's is located at 4605 NE Fremont Street. From downtown Portland, take I-84 eastbound, exit on 33rd Avenue, left or north on 33rd to Fremont Street and turn right. You will be so glad you did! Telephone (503) 287-7444 for more information.

Photos by Janice Pierce Photography

Original Bavarian Sausage Company

When Michael Neumann and his family moved from Germany to Oregon, they brought with them the gift of delicious German delicacies. The Original Bavarian Sausage Company in Tigard, Oregon carries a wonderful selection of imported German and European deli products, and over 35 different German beers and wines. They also carry a number of gifts, including steins, toys, nutcrackers, books and various candies and other goodies. Most importantly, OBSC sells a large variety of their good German homemade sausages. Enjoy a traditional German breakfast of coffee, a boiled egg, German rolls, butter, cheese, cold cuts and jam in their cozy eating nook. In addition to the Sausage Company, the Neumanns also own and operate Neumann's German Bakery in Portland, offering over 12 varieties of rye breads and rolls, which they ship world-wide. The Bakery also serves up the most delicious cookies, pastries, cakes and special wedding cakes. Though the Bakery has been in existence for 30 years, the Neumanns have garnered acclaim and recognition in the four years since they purchased the OBSC. Visit both the Sausage Company and the Bakery for a devilishly delectable good time. Original Bavarian Sausage Company, located at 8705 SW Locust St., Tigard, Oregon 97223. Call them at (503) 892-5152. Neumann's German Bakery, 10528 NE Sandy Blvd., Portland, OR 97220, phone (503) 252-1881.

Foxfire Teas

A young couple, Quinn and Katherine Losselyong, came west to Oregon to realize their dream of starting a business. It would be a place to sit and enjoy a good cup of tea. The result of that vision is Foxfire Teas. A spacious, airy room with custom decor throughout, Foxfire Teas has a large fireplace, sculptures, and tables that were all designed to the Losselyongs' specifications. Foxfire specializes in bulk, loose-leaf teas, stored in special tins along the west wall, where customers serve themselves. As customers pay for their tea, they can select from the many pastries offered. And there are other drinks besides tea available. If they wish, customers can choose coffee, hot chocolate, Chai, iced tea, or an elixir tonic. There are special tea lattes as well. Foxfire is one of the few tea or coffee places in Portland that offers a children's area with its own chalkboard coloring table, toys and books. This area invites

parents to sit in overstuffed chairs and sip their tea while they watch their children enjoying themselves. The large open interior space was a joint project designed by the Losselyongs and their good friends, whose website you can visit at www.compressedpattern.com. When you walk into Foxfire Teas you will immediately feel a very guest-friendly atmosphere for people of all ages. Foxfire Teas is located in Suite #102 at 4605 NE Fremont Street in Portland Oregon. Call (503) 288-6869 for more information.

La Provence Bakery & Bistro

At La Provence Bakery and Bistro in Lake Oswego, Oregon, you can expect that Owner, Didier Blanc-Gonnet, will serve you breakfast, lunch, or dinner in a warm, social, French-inspired atmosphere. Since its opening in 1996, La Provence has been busy serving regulars and visitors alike. As to decor, the walls are covered with art and photos from the Southern Region of Provence. Customers comfortably dine on classic cakes, breads, pastries, and desserts while the staff provides extremely fast, friendly service. Outdoor seating is available in the summer, with hanging flower baskets and a garden setting. Didier is a member of the Bread Guild of America. He distributes his goods to area coffee houses and retail outlets in the area. As this book is being published, he plans to open another store in Portland in March of 2005. La Provence Bakery & Bistro is located at 15964 SW Boones Ferry Road in Lake Oswego, Oregon 97035. Call (503) 635-4533. A waiting list is common for the Saturday and Sunday breakfasts which are the most popular meals of the week at La Provence.

Van Duyn Chocolates

Since 1927, Van Duyn Chocolates has offered chocolate lovers in the Northwest a rich selection of unique, high-quality, boxed chocolates. Founder, Neuman van Duyn introduced the recipes of his Belgian grandmother, combining classic European chocolates with the very best Northwest ingredients. The staff at Van Duyn Chocolates are guided by five basic principles: value the customer, never compromise quality, strive for chocolate excellence, create a winning team, and make each day a little sweeter. The efficient and dedicated team at Van Duyn are still committed to the Founder's vision of providing the customer with great tasting chocolate with no compromises, period. In keeping with their Northwest tradition, Van Duyn's still use Oregon products including Oregon mint in their Truffle Mint, Hood River cherries in their Cherribon and local nuts in a variety of their candies. Visit Van Duyn's several locations throughout the greater Portland area for a glimpse into the past, present and future of great chocolate. For questions, call (503) 227-1927 or visit their website www.vanduyns.com to find a location near you.

Helen Bernhard Bakery

Remember the wonderful smell of fresh baked pies and breads? You can experience all of that again at the Helen Bernhard Bakery in Portland. Inside you'll find a breathtaking array of delicious goodies that are sure to make your mouth water. The Bakery was established in 1924, and the Bernhard family lived in the house next to the present shop. Helen's earliest recipe book, dated September 1923, was written in heavy pencil, with many smudges and rewrites. As business grew, additions were made and eventually, the former home became devoted to the bakery. In 1939, the present bakery building was erected and three generations of Bernhards worked in it until, in 1988, they sold the bakery to Richard and Mary Laufer, local bakery owners, who have devoted their lives to family and baking. Today their son, Mike, continues the tradition. The bakery has seen many changes over its 70 years of existence, but amid all those changes, the home bakery feeling still remains. Wedding cakes are still one of their specialties.

Visit their website at www.helenbernhardbakery.com where you can marvel over the full list of delicious cake flavors. Bernhard's Bakery will deliver cakes anywhere in the Portland area with flavors ranging from Chocolate, Chocolate Chiffon, White Chocolate, German Chocolate, White (Lady Baltimore), Pink Champagne, Yellow Butter, Banana, Carrot, Poppy Seed, Apple Spice, Sponge, and Pumpkin (October – December). Then there are the fillings! You can pick and choose different styles of wedding cakes or bring your own idea or picture. Beside the Wedding Cakes, they do special cakes like Sacher, Grand Marnier, French Silks, Chocolate Tortes, Black Forest, Crème de Mint, and Cheesecakes. Of course you will find Fruit Flans and Strawberry Tarts in season. Also Donuts, Danishes, Scones, Muffins, Sticky Buns, Strudel, Turnovers, Lady Fingers, Éclairs, and Petitfours. That's just a taste of what you will find. Did we mention 16 kinds of bread and 26 kinds of rolls, as well as pies, and cookies? Come in and experience Helen Bernhard Bakery, a most delightful homestyle bakery, at 1717 NE Broadway in Portland, (503) 287-1251.

The Coffee Cottage

The Coffee Cottage is more than a place to fuel up on caffeine. It's a coffee house in the classic style, a place for live music, spoken-word performances, and literature. Originally operated out of a remodeled garage by Peter and Amy Miller, The Coffee Cottage was revitalized by Dave and Sally Mehler in 1997. The Mehlers made it their mission to be a "cultural light, haven, and gathering place for the community," and they achieved it through their commitment to providing the best products along with giving the best possible customer service. Coffee is the heart of The Coffee Cottage, and the Mehlers have taken great pains to ensure that the quality of their coffee is second to none. In addition to the classic espresso, latte and mocha, their menu features twenty-four unique specialty drinks like the Cinnamon Twist, a Mexican mocha with caramel and cinnamon, and the Lucky Charm, a white chocolate mocha with toasted marshmallow and vanilla flavoring. A recent expansion gave them the opportunity to start roasting their own coffee, much to the

delight of customers who can now take the Cottage's special blends home with them as well as enjoying them on the premises. The Mehlers also restarted the Cottage's bakery, which had fallen into disuse, and their delicious pastries are the perfect complement to the coffee. If you're in the mood for a meal, the Cottage also offers sandwiches, wraps, salads, and soup. Weekends The Coffee Cottage features live music by local performers in an eclectic variety of styles. The Cottage has its own bookstore and local authors sometimes drop by to chat or simply enjoy the atmosphere. Wireless Internet service is available, making the Cottage a cyber-café as well. Small wonder that the Cottage has become the place to be for a wide cross-section of the Newberg community, from business people to students at nearby George Fox University. Dave and Sally also host events on the monthly First Friday Art Walks, including art exhibits and receptions. The Coffee Cottage is located at 808 E. Hancock in downtown Newberg, just off of Highway 99. For more information, call (503) 538-5126.

The Oregon Tea Garden

For a "unique dining experience" featuring teas, scones, bright yellow walls and umbrella chandeliers, visit the Oregon Tea Garden in Silverton. Owned by Michele Thompson and in the same location for over three years, the Garden is known as a special place to relax and enjoy conversation. In addition to the yellow walls and umbrellas, the Tea Garden features white tablecloths, blue and white china, assorted English teacups and antique oak furnishings. There are even costumes on hand, should you want to dress up for your occasion. The menu, which changes daily, features Oregon products and organic produce when available. The desserts are made on the premises. Some customers claim to drive 100 miles just to enjoy Michele's bread pudding. Michele will not reveal her scone recipe, which she proudly says is "the best in the world!" Topped with clotted cream, raspberry-rhubarb-rose jam or lemon curd, the Tea Garden's scones are truly memorable. For real elegance, try the Silver Tea. It begins with a scone and pot of tea, followed by a two-tiered presentation of assorted tea sandwiches, fresh fruit and a generous sampler of the desserts of the day. Dessert selections include a Lemon Tart, Queen of Sheba Cake and a Belgian Chocolate Truffle Cake with strawberry sauce. In addition, a different Soup Du Jour is served each day, and a Quiche of the Day is baked fresh in the kitchen. Sandwiches might include turkey, albacore tuna, or vegetarian. The beverages menu includes sodas and cider as well as the teas, and coffee, espresso, latte or cappuccino is to be had as well. The Gift Shop offers locally made aprons, tea cozies and unique hand-painted tea sets, as well as, of course, a large assortment of fine teas. The Oregon Tea Garden is located at 305 Oak Street in Silverton, Oregon 97381. That's at the corner of First and Oak in Historic Downtown Silverton in the Silverton Realty Office Building. For hours, call (503) 873-1230. Reservations are not required but are recommended. Catering is available and special group menus can be scheduled in advance. Visit their website at www.oregonteagarden.com. "Tea talks" featuring guest speakers, classes, and tea tastings are held during the winter, and are announced on the website.

Cornerstone Coffee Roasters

In a building built in the early 1900's, Cornerstone Coffee Roasters is truly the cornerstone of the community. Long known for being THE meeting place for clubs, regulars, bible study groups, teenagers, and business folks discussing the latest "deal," Cornerstone is where it happens. Whether you're enjoying freshly roasted coffee and delectable pastries, a light lunch with friends, the live musicians on Friday nights, or the monthly displays of local artists' works, Cornerstone can accommodate you. During the warm months, guests can enjoy the patio out back with tables and umbrellas while chatting and enjoying their coffees. The Owners, Dave and Jean Shaffer, have made a traditional European coffeehouse into the local coffee drinker's haven. Some come in the morning to start their day with a light breakfast, an excellent cup of coffee and to see the daily fresh roasting of the coffee beans. After attending a local play or evening function, many drop in for coffee and a wonderful selection of luscious desserts to cap-off their evening. Open for business for 13 years and voted "Best of McMinnville" each year since 1998, Cornerstone Coffee Roasters is truly the "gathering place" and the hub of Historic Downtown McMinnville. Future plans include expanding their mail order and wholesale operations. For those on the go Cornerstone also operates Cornerstone Express, a drive–thru espresso shop at 2nd and Baker in McMinnville. Visit them at 216 NE Third Street in McMinnville, Oregon 97128. You may contact them at (503) 472-6622, or at their website www.cornerstonecoffeeroasters.com.

The Underground Coffee House

Locals know that for a delicious cup of coffee in a vacation-like atmosphere, the place to go is the Underground Coffee House in Newberg, Oregon. The Underground Coffee House serves up a wide selection of premium hot coffee drinks and mocha milkshakes. Their gourmet deli offers custom-made sandwiches, rich soups, and tasty baked goods. This warm and inviting spot is the perfect place to relax with friends or family or just spend the afternoon alone. Once you enter this tropically-themed coffee house and find their Internet access, comfy furniture and friendly, attentive staff, you won't want to leave. On Friday nights, the Underground Coffee House hosts live music. Owned by Jeff Jordan, the Underground Coffee House is an impressive two-story, 2800 square feet establishment. The upstairs is a great place for meetings. Visit the Underground Coffee House at 1002 N. Springbrook Road, Newberg. For more information, phone (503) 554-1843 or check out their website at www.underground-coffeehouse.com.

Let's Do Coffee & More

Opening early and closing late, like a good coffeehouse should, Let's Do Coffee & More has acquired quite a reputation for great coffee and conversation in the year since it opened. Owners and local residents, Brad Davis and Craig Shannon, know the value of a good cup of joe. For their delectable coffee, they carefully chose Caffe Vita Roasting Company from Seattle from among many contenders. Pastries provided by local bakeries are a superb accompaniment to the delicious brew, and for those looking for more substantial fare, Let's Do Coffee & More also offers sandwiches, quiche and salads for lunch or dinner. They have some amazing desserts as well. Where does the "More" in the name come from? From the greeting cards and gifts offered for sale here. You'll find coffee mugs (of course), men's and women's skin care products, candles, gourmet foods, locally-created arts and crafts, pottery, purses, and more. And more! Wireless Internet access is available, and there are two work stations with Internet access that patrons can use free of charge. Let's Do Coffee & More is a local gathering place that is sometimes referred to as "West Linn's Living Room." Unlike national coffee chains, this is a coffeehouse that truly belongs to the community. Brad and Craig are actively involved in local charities and school groups and they support the local arts scene as well. Let's Do Coffee & More is located at 19373 Willamette Drive in West Linn, Oregon. For more information, call (503) 635-4224 or visit their website at www.letsdocoffeellc.com.

Brigittine Monastery

The Brigittine Monks of the Willamette Valley have been skillfully preparing and selling delicious high quality fudges and truffles since the early 1980's. A fully self-supporting monastery, they quietly produce gourmet confections utilizing only the best and freshest ingredients to create delicious packages of pure luxury. Highly acclaimed in gourmet periodicals and top ranked news programs, the chocolate fudges and truffles of the Brigittine are renown. During a visit to their year round gift shop in a serene section of the Willamette Valley, you will enjoy an unhurried and peaceful shopping experience where quality and service are the rule rather than the exception. At the Brigittine Monastery you will find Chocolate Fudge Royale available with or without nuts, in chocolate, amaretto, pecan praline and chocolate cherry nut options. The Truffles Royale are available in chocolate, cherry chocolate amaretto, chocolate cherry, chocolate mint, chocolate maple, chocolate raspberry, chocolate butter rum, and milk chocolate. The Monks use pure chocolate, fresh dairy butter, real cream, the freshest nuts and real flavors. The Brigittine philosophy of silence during the daytime provides the quiet peacefulness that is immediately noticeable upon your arrival, but the monks are permitted to speak when it is useful. You will find the Brigittine Monastery at 23300 Walker Lane in Amity, Oregon. For more information you can reach them at (503) 835-8080 or visit their website at www.brigittine.org.

Pacific Hazelnut Candy Factory

Opened in 1985, Pacific Hazelnut Candy Factory in Aurora is best known for its chocolate coated hazelnuts, fruits, and hazelnut toffee. Along with his daughter Karen Freedman, Owner Ersel Christopherson, runs the candy factory using family recipes first developed and sold from the family farm in 1985 after his wife, Joan (now deceased) began experimenting with toffee and hazelnuts. In addition to their famous hazelnut candies, they also carry milk and dark chocolate, chocolate coated blueberries, razzcherries, and cranberries, chocolate coated coffee beans, dry roasted and seasoned hazelnuts, and a line of sugar free varieties. Their fabulous gift shop also sells linens and teas. The popularity of their candy is far-reaching and both Made In Oregon and Williams & Sonoma carry

their products. Whether you're a purist and prefer straight milk chocolate or are eager to sample their famous hazelnut candies, Pacific Hazelnut Candy Factory is a great place to visit anytime. Located at 14673 Ottaway Avenue in Aurora, Oregon 97002. For more information about their great products, call (503) 678-2755 or (800) 634-7344, or visit their website at www.pacifichazelnut.com.

97

Mellelo Coffee Roasters

In Medford, Sal and Tami Mellelo know very well that coffee sales are based on quality, not price. Their response is to offer a fine Italian coffee that pleases an ever-growing cadre of coffee lovers who find Mellelo distinguished for its quality. Say Sal and Tami, "We roast to order in small batches and hand blend each origin one at a time. This process takes one-third longer, but we don't mind as this is what sets us apart from commercial roasters. Our process of roasting combines Old World quality and artistry with today's technology. It produces a smooth, rich, aromatic espresso and a full-bodied cup of coffee." And not only do customers agree, so does the Specialty Coffee Association of America, which recently awarded Mellelo the winner of its "Tops" award, one of the most coveted awards a coffee roaster/retailer can receive. The "Tops" award is presented on the basis of product quality, service, staff education, training and commitment to service, and retailing reputation. Sal started with a six-foot expresso cart on a downtown Medford street corner, and as of this writing has four locations in Medford. He supplies many fine restaurants, performing arts centers, hotels, and more. He also supplies drive-through locations all over the U.S. Every batch is roasted to order for each customer, using gas-fired German roasters from a company that has been in business for over 160 years and is considered the finest of its type. So try a cup of Colombian Supremo, Costa Rican Terrazu, Panama Lerida Estate, Celebes Kalossi, or any of their other roasts. The friendly and efficient staff at Mellelo Coffee Roasters are all waiting to help you to take that first perfect sip. Mellelo Coffee Roasters are found at these Medford locations: 3651 Lear Way, 229 W. Main Street, 100 E. 6th Street, and in the Jackson County Library building at 205 S. Central. For information, call (541) 779-9884 or you can visit their website at www.mellelo.com.

GoodBean Coffee

In 1990, Michael and Mary Kell founded GoodBean Coffee, right in the heart of the best coffee country in the United States, the Pacific Northwest. At the time, specialty coffee roasting was still a new idea, and GoodBean stood out among the few specialty roasters in Southern Oregon. Now specialty coffee is everywhere and GoodBean's quality still stands out. The Kells take great care to select only the finest beans, and their air-roasting process ensures a higher level of quality than the more common drum-roasting process. With coffee, as with popcorn, air-roasting prevents problems with burning and uneven heating that could ruin the flavor of a batch. GoodBean's fifteen years of success testify to the fact that they're doing it right. GoodBean provides wholesale coffee to hotels and restaurants, retail coffee to home consumers, and the Great Coffee for the Great Office service for small businesses. GoodBean's JavaThru franchise offers budding entrepreneurs the opportunity to set up shop in Southern Oregon's burgeoning drive-through coffee stand business. GoodBean's retail outlet is located at 165 South Oregon Street in the former Table Rock Saloon, a 140-year-old building in historic downtown Jacksonville, Oregon. For more information on their products, services and franchising business, call toll free, (800) 480-4036 or visit their website at www.goodbean.net, where you can also watch a fun Quicktime movie about Jacksonville, the Kells, and their coffee.

Tee Time Coffee Shop

To "taste a slice of life" in downtown Grants Pass, Oregon, try the Tee Time Coffee Shop, where you can build your own breakfast and build your own omelet. This quaint coffee shop with seating downstairs and upstairs in a cozy loft made of logs is open for breakfast and lunch. They set out an array of items you can choose from to create a made-to-order breakfast. Those items include eggs, pancakes, French toast, hash browns, bacon, sausage (links or patty), ham, hamburger patty, biscuits and gravy, toast, juice (orange or cranberry), biscuit, fresh fruit cup, English muffin, oatmeal, and bagel. Egg beaters are available in place of eggs. If you like, there's a similar choice of ingredients from which you can create the perfect omelet. The ingredients include cheese, ham, tomato, bell peppers, Cajun sausage, bacon, sausage, salsa, mushrooms, olives, sprouts, green chilies, guacamole, and onions. At lunch time, hot sandwiches are aplenty, as are hamburgers, deli style sandwiches, wraps, and salads. Customers have responded by voting Tee Time the "Best Breakfast" place locally for six years in a row! Elliott and Daniella Crowder own the establishment and their employees are like family, including some of the prettiest and friendliest waitresses in town! The Restaurant inherited the golf theme decor from a previous owner. Elliott says the surfboards on the wall more accurately reflect his soul. The Tee Time Coffee Shop is located at 117 SW H St., in Grants Pass, Oregon 97526. For take-out orders or to have your meal waiting for you when you arrive, call (541) 476-3346.

Cary's of Oregon

This is one destination you don't want to miss! Cary's of Oregon is a candy manufacturer that specializes in a unique 'soft-crunch' English Toffee. Drop by for a sample. With six flavors to choose from, there is something to delight the candy lover in us all. How about creamy milk chocolate or rich, dark chocolate with toasted almonds or hazelnuts? There are several specialty products; for the coffee lover, there's dark chocolate with an espresso blend, and for the purist, you'll find Toffee Fingers (imagine a light almond brittle). While you're there make sure to try some of their award winning Trail Toffee, finalist at the New York Fancy Foods Show in the Outstanding Snack category. This is a delicious blend of toffee, toasted almonds, raisins and dried cranberries. There is a big viewing window that allows visitors to take in all the action. Cary's of Oregon opened in 2001 and the story behind it is really something of a fairy tale. Founder and president, Cary Cound, originally obtained the recipe from his wife's grandfather. The family had a tradition of making the candy for the holidays and before long, friends insisted on becoming customers. Soon a dream was born. With a background as a mechanical engineer, Cound was able to design and build some of the equipment used in the factory – a regular Willie Wonka. The company has carved an impressive niche for itself in the gourmet food marketplace, selling nationwide through retail outlets, mail order and on their website. Their gift baskets are highly sought after and anyone who has tasted the candy knows it is truly unsurpassed. Located at 1700 Nebraska Ave., in Grants Pass, Oregon 97527. Call toll-free (888) 822-9300 or visit online at www.carysoforegon.com. P.S. We'll let you in on a little secret. Locals can't get enough of the "seconds" put out daily. Just another reason to make Cary's of Oregon one of your stops when visiting Grants Pass.

Galleries

The Caswell Gallery

Located at the gateway to the majestic Columbia River Gorge, The Caswell Gallery, "featuring the Northwest's finest artisans," is home to the largest and finest selection of bronze sculpture in the area. As well as seeing the works of many artists, visitors also have an exceptional opportunity to see how these lasting works of art, from miniature to monumental, are created. Go on a tour into the Cascade Fine Arts Foundry, adjacent to Caswell Gallery, and see how molten bronze is poured, as well as the intricate means by which the molds are created. This is a unique chance to see the workings of a bronze studio and to learn the secrets of this age-old art. The resulting sculptures are signed and numbered editions, and the staff is pleased to answer questions and help you learn about their skills. This is a friendly, relaxed place where visitors can see what art is all about. It is also a place of inspiration. The gallery carries paintings and other mediums, like art glass, pottery, and jewelry, as well as sculpture. The tour directs you back through the gallery, which features a variety of works by local and regional artists, alongside nationally known sculptors, including resident Artist and Owner, Rip Caswell. His specialty is monumental bronze wildlife and figurative sculptures. Caswell also has another major gallery in Jackson Hole, Wyoming. Although his commissions have included prestigious corporate clients and celebrities, Rip is very approachable and very involved in the gallery and the community. The Kidz Art gallery focuses on young artists, and demonstrations are offered in a variety of mediums for all ages. The Caswell Gallery is conveniently located just off I-84 east of Portland at Exit 17, on the west end of historic downtown Troutdale at 201 W. Historic Columbia River Highway. You may then choose to follow the Columbia River Highway as it continues up to the waterfalls and scenic panoramas of the Columbia Gorge. Their website is at www.caswellgallery.com and has an incredible list of artists and events. You can also call them at (503) 492-2473.

Photos by
Timothy J. Park

Laura Russo Gallery

Representing the finest in contemporary Northwest Art, the Laura Russo Gallery includes an impressive selection of artists ranging from those with a major influence in the region to emerging artists. Laura Russo started her Gallery in 1986 and over time has expanded to a large exhibition space in Northwest Portland. The Gallery usually features two artists each month and hosts an annual group show. There are also separate shows for emerging artists and specifically curated exhibitions. Some of the Gallery's well-known artists include Jay Backstrand, Frank Boyden, Michael Brophy, Michael Dailey, Judith Poxson Fawkes, Tom Fawkes, Cie Goulet, Gregory Grenon, Fay Jones, Mary Josephson, Jun Kaneko, Mel Katz, Michihiro Kosuge, Rae Mahaffey Lucinda Parker, Jack Portland, Henk Pander, Rene Rickabaugh, Margot Voorhies Thompson, and Sherrie Wolf. The Gallery also represents the estates of Louis Bunce, Kenneth Callahan, Carl Morris, Hilda Morris and Michele Russo. The Laura Russo Gallery is located at 805 NW 21st Avenue in Portland, Oregon. You can reach them at (503) 226-2754 or visit their website at www.laurarusso.com.

Fireborne...Creations in Glass

This is a gallery that really communicates its owners' passion for their art. Visitors come in to explore and leave saying, "I love this place!" Part gallery and part retail gift shop, Fireborne…Creations in Glass offers customized services to their customers, like complimentary gift wrapping and insured shipment worldwide, with prices that range from ten dollars up to several thousand dollars for collector-quality artwork. But most of all, they offer their enthusiasm and a chance for visitors to see a marvelous range of contemporary art glass made by 100+ Northwest artists. Located in the heart of downtown Portland's restaurant and theater district, Fireborne . . . Creations in Glass was established in 1999 by Lisa Jost and Myrna Fitzpatrick. The owners were former career bankers who "went through one too many bank mergers." They combined their severance pay, strong business backgrounds and their love of art glass, and created a partnership that formed Fireborne.

Now they spend their days running the Gallery, visiting artists' studios, and attending art shows. Their Gallery has a variety of hand-blown, fused, slumped and cast works of glass art. Each piece is individually handmade, and therefore is unique. No two pieces will show the same color, shape or size. On their striking website www.fireborneglass.com, you can find a stunning array of pictures of individual works, including glass vases, bowls, perfume vials, paperweights, sculptures, platters, lamps, and gift items created by dozens of artists. They remind us that while the photos are representative examples of each artist's work, of course no two pieces will be alike. The Gallery's owners invite you to come enjoy the magnificent glass creations at Fireborne...Creations in Glass. Perhaps you will find a treasure to take home. You will definitely find an eye-opening presentation of a brilliant art form. "Our goal is to offer a wide variety of glass art at reasonable prices and to provide superior customer service." Open Monday through Saturday, Fireborne…Creations in Glass is located at 515 SW Broadway, in Portland. For more information, you can call them at (503) 227-6585.

Cargo

Patty Merrill has a passion for culture, travel and fine crafts. That passion led to the creation of Cargo. A place that focuses on one of a kind, new, antique and used furnishings from all over Asia, Africa and Mexico. Patty has built a warm and enticing warehouse of fabulously collectible home decor. She seeks to share her love of this diverse world with you. Her space is filled with special items brought back to the States. These selections change with each incoming shipment. Frequently containers from Indonesia include antique teak benches and dining tables, carved gates, antique saris, rickshaws, Japanese garden walls, masks and ethnic carvings. From Asia are gongs, stone Buddhas, carved screens, Tibetan chests, Russian icons, shrines and altar tables. From Africa you may find tribal rugs, kuba cloths, beads, tribal jewelry and textiles among widely different cultural arts. With over 10,000 square feet of space comfortably filled you are sure to find much to explore that you can't get at your average import shop. Patty has sought to foster business practices that benefit the artists of these fine crafts in rewarding ways. It is through these skillfully maintained relationships that she is able to provide you with items you cannot find elsewhere. Cargo is located at 380 NW 13th in Portland's Pearl District, on the corner of 13th and Flanders. Please give them a call at (503) 209-8349/243-7804 or check out their website at www.cargoinc.com.

Attic Gallery

If you want to see what's new and fresh from local and Northwest contemporary artists, you owe yourself a visit to the nine exhibition rooms of the Attic Gallery in Portland. Mediums include oil and acrylic paintings on canvas, watercolor and pastel paintings on paper, photographs, ceramics, sculpture, glass, and original serigraphs. The Gallery also has a poster pavilion holding hundreds of posters and all major poster catalogs, plus CD ROM catalogs of all major print publishers. Owner, Diana Faville stresses originals and limited-edition prints. She also represents Atlantic Arts, Stevens Fine Art Originals, Phoenix Art Group Originals and Progressive Editions. There is a full-service custom frame shop and design center, with over 2,500 molding samples to choose from. The staff can help you with custom hand-painted frames to match your art or theirs, frame your certificates and diplomas, and provide shadow boxes to house rare collectibles and memorabilia. The Gallery prizes its reputation for showing the work of new artists and exhibitions, encouraging and caring about area artists and helping them gain the attention of the public. The Gallery gets its name from the fact that Faville started the Gallery in an attic in 1973. From that space, she grew into a warehouse in a box plant, which served from 1979 to 1984, when she moved to the present location. As the business has grown, so has involvement of Faville's family. Daughter, Maria, brother, David, sister-in-law, Lilli, and son-in-law, Tommer, are now part of the Attic Gallery staff. The Attic Gallery is located at 205 and 206 SW First Avenue in Portland, Oregon 97204. Keep in mind, a public reception is held the first Thursday of each month, from 6pm to 9pm. You can reach the Gallery at (503) 228-7830, or visit their website at www.atticgallery.com. Each of the dozens of artists whose works are available at the Gallery has his/her own page on the website. Send requests for information to attic-di-faville@uswest.net.

Retrospection Fine Arts & Antiques

Since 1983, Retrospection Fine Arts & Antiques in Portland has established a well-deserved reputation for connoisseurship in its field. The Gallery, which discerning collectors recognize for the significance and range of the items on hand, offers expert advice and information from Owners, Marcella Peterson and Michael Riley. Gallery highlights include silver, porcelain, textiles, and Asian antiques and collectibles. The inventory changes constantly, given Marcella and Michael's expertise and far-ranging contacts. Marcella is widely known for her expertise in antiques, particularly in silver and ladies' accessories. She also writes, lectures, and serves as a consultant to collectors and museums. Marcella is also a recognized expert on chatelaines. Michael has extensive experience in porcelains and textiles and is an internationally renowned authority on Asian antiques and art objects. His specialties include objects from Imperial Chinese and Japanese cultures, along with ivory, lacquerware, scrolls, and paintings. Marcella and Michael are generous in educating and consulting others, sharing their lifetime of scholarship and expertise. They bring to Portland a passion for research, collecting experience, and the personal dedication of true connoisseurs. Said one recent customer who has shopped extensively in New York antique shops and art stores, "The owners of Retrospection know antique silver and exquisite things, and they have fine taste and discretion." Retrospection Fine Arts & Antiques is located on the Light Rail MAX line, in the Fine Arts Building at 1017 SW Morrison Street in downtown Portland, Oregon 97205. For inquiries, call (503) 223-5538. The staff can arrange shipping to anywhere in the world, and of course in Oregon there is no sales tax.

Quintana Galleries

Specializing in the indigenous arts of the Americas, the Quintana Galleries in Portland has the finest representation of Native American art in the Portland region. They have been in business for 33 years, developing a world-class selection of art from the wide range of traditions and craftsmanship of the native cultures of the Northwest Coast, Alaska, the Southwest and Mexico. Pioneers in the Portland art community, Rose and Cecil Quintana recently moved from their landmark location downtown to the 9th Avenue Art Corridor in the Pearl District. Their expertise is highly sought after, and research, consultation, and appraisals of Native American arts are important parts of their business. It is also important to them to share their knowledge, welcoming students as well as collectors to their gallery. They have been active with native communities as well as with the arts community, and you can often find special events such as live carving demonstrations in the Gallery. With one of the most striking websites to be seen, the Quintanas have made a virtual gallery of art objects available online. When you visit the website at www.quintanagalleries.com, you can view selected works by type or by region. Under the heading Northwest Coast for example, you can choose to view masks, totems, panels, boxes, rattles and bowls plus other wood carvings, argillite and prints. The other areas are Arctic and Special Collections, which cover kachinas, baskets, beadwork and pottery. There is also a section on the contemporary art of Native America and Mexico. But viewing a virtual gallery is all just a small taste of what you will find when you visit in person. Nothing can compare with seeing these art objects in person and the Quintanas' friendly, approachable manner makes a visit here a pleasure. This will be a truly memorable encounter with some of the finest indigenous art in the world. Come in to the Gallery at 120 NW 9th Avenue in Portland, Oregon, (503) 223-1729 or (800) 321-1729. You will never forget your visit!

Portland at Night

Lawrence Gallery

The Lawrence Gallery began 28 years ago in what had been the general store in Sheridan, Oregon (a spot with a checkered history during Prohibition, when it served as a brothel before becoming a community hall). What began as an artists' enterprise has grown into three exceptional locations. Gary and Signe Lawrence are the owners, and over the years they have expanded the Gallery's offering to include paintings, glass, jewelry, and sculpture, including their own artwork. According to Artisan NW, the Lawrence Gallery is a "nationally known, highly respected" gallery with a fine service record among collectors around the world. They carry mostly Northwest artists in an inviting mix of works, but also feature world-famous artists such as Picasso, Rembrandt, Chagall, and Miro. Their three locations are in Portland's Pearl District, on the Oregon Coast in The Shops at Salishan, and the original gallery in the heart of wine country between McMinnville and Sheridan, which handle more than $8 million worth of art. They definitely make good on their promise to deliver the very best in artwork in the Northwest from paintings to sculpture, glass, and pottery. In addition to the high caliber art work, the Sheridan gallery features an outstanding eatery called the Fresh Palate Cafe, an outstanding atelier eatery, and Jebidiah's Private Reserve, a wine shop and tasting bar located inside Lawrence Gallery. Spend an afternoon dining on enticing cuisine, tasting award-winning wines and viewing an always impressive display of artwork from over 100 nationally recognized artists." Their website at www.lawrencegallery.net gives us a glimpse of the artists and their artwork, and features the galleries' new events and shows, as well as how to find their three locations.

Lawrence Gallery Sheridan in the Heart of Wine Country Hwy 18 midway between McMinnville and Sheridan (800) 894-4278.
Lawrence Gallery Portland In the Heart of the Pearl 903 NW Davis Street (503) 228-1776.
Lawrence Gallery Salishan On the Oregon Coast The Shops at Salishan, Hwy 101, Gleneden Beach (800) 764-2318.

Ken Scott River Run Gallery

Ken Scott calls himself an initiator and an innovator, and describes his art as finding ways to make something out of nothing. What gives him the greatest pleasure is "to make-do with what is at hand, to find the gold amongst the rubble." His works have evolved in several directions. He makes wall pieces out of steel, using oxygen/acetylene, thermal-arc cutting torches, welding processes and grinders. He does bronze castings, many of Oregon wildlife, as well as making sculptured lighting, and garden art. You may have already seen his work – for example, the bronze sea lions sculpture at the Sea Lion Caves in Florence on the Oregon Coast. Ken says metal sculpting is not a casual experience. Instead, "it is like working in a metal scrap yard with hard hats and torches, you're dodging sparks, and cooling quenched fingers all day long." To succeed you have to stay with it until both the artist and the project reaches a certain standard, a standard that grows as the artist's experience grows. Ken goes on to say that with metals, the sky is the limit. "And whether the design is geometric or organic, it's all possible!" The Ken Scott River Run Gallery is also available for wedding celebrations of up to 100 people, with catering offered. Visit his gallery's website at www.kenscottsculptures.com for a glimpse, but nothing will replace the experience of seeing them in person, as well as enjoying Ken's hospitality and learning about his demanding and rewarding art form. You can see them all at his gallery at 42837 McKenzie Highway in Leaburg, Oregon. For more information, call (541) 896-3774.

Newberg Gallery

The Newberg Gallery, created by Certified Picture Framer Sally Dallas, is committed to creating beauty in your life. With over twenty years of experience in custom framing, Sally can design and frame almost anything. How good is she? Good enough to have won five awards from the Cascade Picture Framers' Guild in the past six years, including First Place awards in 1998 and 2000. Sally's frames are made of the finest materials. The Gallery offers thousands of moldings, mat boards (all of which meet the Library of Congress specifications for conservation quality), and glass types, including museum-quality antireflective glass that blocks 97% of UV light. Sally works with you and your décor to create the best presentation. But even the best frame is only as good as the picture inside it, and the Newberg Gallery has a picture for every frame. Art is displayed in seven rooms, each with a unique style and theme, decorated and accented with art glass (hand-blown and fused), ceramics and home décor items. The work of over eighty artists is featured in a variety of media, including etchings, giclees, oil paintings, lithographs, and photographs. Both national and international artists are represented. Sally is committed not just to her gallery but to the Newberg community, as well. She sits on the board of the Newberg Area Chamber of Commerce and the Newberg Downtown Association, and participates in the First Friday Art Walk; the Gallery's website hosts a special page listing all events for each month's Walk. In 2004, she helped coordinate the Newberg Harvest Festival. The Gallery is located at 115 North College Street in downtown Newberg, on the corner of Hancock Street (Route 99). For more information, call toll-free (877) 351-5987 or visit their website at www.newberggallery.com.

"…let us create beauty in your life."

American Trails

Welcome. Just one look inside American Trails will tell you you're in one of the most intriguing galleries in the world. Located right on the Plaza in the heart of Ashland, you'll want to explore every bit of the unique collection of historical and contemporary Indian art – from the jewelry and masks of the Pacific Northwest to wood carvings and pottery from Mexico. There's so much to see, including an amazing selection of Hopi, Zuni and Navajo jewelry, multi-stone inlay work, fetishes, and fossil and animal totem jewelry. Be sure to see the rare original pine needle baskets, many from local tribes. Traditional designs and techniques are passed down to the members of carefully chosen families who become part of the American Trails family. Whole families of artisans are known to visit the gallery from as far away as South America. Owner David Bobb (a rare and fine art himself) knows history and understands the importance of the works he offers. Gallery Artist Shanna Zeck, a Lakota Indian, will help you choose the perfect gift or a piece for yourself. This is an opportunity unique to Southern Oregon and not to be missed. 27 North Main (on the Plaza), Ashland, Oregon 97520, (541) 488-2731.

Ashland Hardwood Gallery

Since 1999, Ashland Hardwood Gallery in Ashland, Oregon has been showcasing fine works of art by a variety of different artists, a majority of them local. Owner, Aaron Diamond proudly displays finely crafted furniture and sculpture, as well as pine-crafted articles of clothing by Artist, Livio Demarci. Woodcarvings of hats, bras, shoes and the famous "suit seat" are all available for purchase. The Gallery features a most impressive collection of wood art, including Balinese handcrafted sculptures, unique rocking horses by Crayne Hennessy, beautiful breadboard sets by Edward Wohl and heirloom bowls by David Lory. So, whether you're looking for a gorgeous stained glass wall sconce or a unique piece of wooden furniture, Ashland Hardwood Gallery will provide you with a stunning selection of artistic wooden masterpieces. Ashland Hardwood Gallery is located at 17 N. Main in Ashland, Oregon 97520. For questions, call (541) 488-6200 or visit their stunning website at www.hardwoodgallery.com.

Davis & Cline Galleries

Open spaces, beautiful and interesting things to see and experience, and all are in an atmosphere of warmth and comfort. Such is the ambience when you visit the Davis & Cline Galleries in Ashland. The Galleries have been owned and operated by John and Carol Davis since 1998. Davis & Cline's Galleries feature the work of some twenty contemporary West Coast artists and eight sculptors in various media. The Galleries contain three exhibition areas with a separate room for glass art. The focus of the Galleries is to show internationally known artists. Gallery Director, Chandra Holsten, has been instrumental in bringing the country's major glass artists to the Galleries. Represented in glass art are works by Dale Chihuly, Christopher Ries, Steven Weinberg, Benjamin Moore, Latchezar Boyadjiev and Dante Marioni. Josine Ianco-Starrels, former Curator of the Los Angeles Municipal Museum and, now, Guest Curator at Davis & Cline, has been influential in bringing the majority of the well-known artists to Davis & Cline. Davis & Cline Galleries can be found at 525 and 552 "A" Street in Ashland, Oregon 97520. You can reach them at (541) 482-2069 or visit their website at www.davisandcline.com.

"Imperial Yellow Persian with Gloss Black Lip Wraps", 2003, Dale Chihuly, 13x39x24 inches.

Photo by Scott Leen

Photo by Brian Prechtel

Illahe Design Studio and Gallery

Tucked among Ashland's A Street galleries, you will find a treasure trove of ceramic tiles at Illahe Design Studio and Gallery, named for a Chinook Indian word which means "home; place where I live." Susan Springer's ceramic work is the heart and soul of Illahe Tileworks and this charming gallery. Her hand-pressed and hand-painted tiles are made in series, like the Rogue Valley Harvest series reflecting the orchards and vineyards of Southern Oregon. Other series are inspired by sea life, gardens, woodblock prints and local wildlife, and that's just a small sampling of her designs. Susan's tiles are available from selected retailers across North America, but this is the only place to see the full variety of her tiles and ceramic art on display. Visitors are treated to a rich and colorful display of Susan's ceramic wall pieces, including mosaic and ceramic sculpture. Established in 1978, Illahe Tileworks' custom designs adorn many private residences and businesses, and have been featured in Old House Journal. You are invited to commission a special work just for your home, but the services at Illahe encompass even more. They also do restoration and reproduction work on broken and missing tiles, even working from old photographs to color-match vintage tiles. In April 2004, Susan opened Illahe Design Studio and Gallery to showcase her tiles and ceramic art locally, and to feature other regional artists interested in doing custom art for people's homes. The gallery represents a number of artists working in many media including painting, pottery, photography, jewelry, sculpture and more. Come in and enjoy the rich variety! Illahe Design Studio and Gallery is located at 500 A Street, Suite 3, in the historic Railroad District. For more information, call (541) 488-5072 or visit the website to see samples, www.illahetile.com.

JEGA Gallery and Sculpture Garden

JEGA Gallery is on the cutting edge of Ashland's thriving gallery scene. Owner and sculptor, J. Ellen G. Austin (the gallery takes its name from her initials) has created a space that is both a vibrant working gallery and a sculpture studio. She creates sculptures that "combine serious with sensuous, confrontative with humor." JEGA, which recently celebrated its 11th anniversary in Ashland's historic Railroad District, also represents a select group of artists from around the world in a selective variety of media. These artists fit in perfectly with J. Ellen's philosophy and "have the potential to provoke and challenge perspectives of viewing the world." The community looks forward eagerly to JEGA's special events including yearly spring Women's History Month Happening, "Women with Attitude and Men who like Women with Attitude," and an annual summer Jefferson State Sculpture Exhibit. Her mission to combine intellectual social/political challenges with playfulness is reflected in a quadrennial "Send in the Clowns" show, which runs during presidential election years. J. Ellen's commitment to art in the community led her to help found the Ashland Gallery Association. The Arts Council of Southern Oregon has honored her with the Advocate for the Arts Award, given for her leadership in making Ashland a friendly place for contemporary art with an edge. Her accomplishments have also been recognized by the Baldwin School of Bryn Mawr, Pennsylvania, which honored her with a Lifetime Achievement Award last year, and the Bradford College of Bradford, Massachusetts, which gave her a Distinguished Alumni Award. JEGA Gallery is located at 625 A Street on the corner of 5th and A in Ashland, Oregon 97520. Call (541) 488-2474.

Gathering Glass Studio

Gathering Glass Studio, located in Ashland's historic Railroad District, is a must see art destination in a town known for Shakespeare. It is owned and operated by glass artists, Scott Carlson and Steven Cornett, who has previously worked together as members of "Team Chihuly" on projects including the Bellagio Hotel's ceiling installation in Las Vegas. They invite you to come and watch as 25 years of combined glassblowing experience is demonstrated to the public. It is free and fun for all ages. Beautiful blown and sculpted art glass creations are on display in the studio gallery and are available for purchase. Gathering Glass Studio offers classes for learning the art of glassblowing. Once you have completed the intermediate class, you may rent studio time to perfect your glass blowing skills. Custom orders are welcome. Bring your ideas, drawings or special color scheme and Gathering Glass Studio's artists will create a special piece of glass art just for you. To learn more about Gathering Glass Studio, see their website at www.gatheringglass.com, call (541) 488-4738 or, better yet, visit the studio at 322 N. Pioneer Street, Ashland, OR 97520.

Lithia Park, Ashland

113

Gardens, Flowers and Markets

Smith Berry Barn

For over 25 years the Smith Berry Barn has been specializing in quality grown berries. As a small family-owned and operated farm, it has grown over the years to offer much more than just great tasting berries. The 30-acre farm now produces over 25 varieties of apples, pears, heirloom tomatoes, peppers and other gourmet produce. True to its heritage, Smith Berry Barn offers over eight varieties of specialty cane berries, including Golden Raspberry, Loganberry, Blackberry, Boysenberry, and the prized Oregon Marionberry. Housed in an historic barn, Smith Berry Barn has a complete gourmet gift shop. In addition to a wide selection of specialty gourmet foods the shop also features seasonal fresh produce, wonderful jams, syrups and honey made fresh from the farm. The gift shop also has herbal bath products, garden antiques and statuary, books, herb and perennial starts, organic vegetable starts and so much more. On July 4th the annual Berry Festival is a fun filled day of music, wine-tasting, berry desserts and family entertainment. Apple lovers will enjoy the Heirloom Apple Festival, which takes place each weekend in October. The flavors of the season come alive with over 25 varieties of apples, pears, fresh pressed apple cider, and scrumptious apple pie. Kids of all ages love the hayride, pumpkin patch, games, music and tasty BBQ. The Smith Berry Barn is located approximately ten miles from Beaverton, Hillsboro and Newberg at 24500 S.W. Scholls Ferry Road in the historic town of Scholls. You can reach the Farm at (503) 628-2172 or visit their website at www.smithberrybarn.com.

Portland's Saturday Market

Portland's Saturday Market is one of the city's top attractions. In existence for over a quarter of a century, Portland's Saturday Market is the largest outdoor arts and crafts market in continuous operation in the United States. The essence of the Market is that all of its members have 'made it, baked it, or grown it' themselves in the Pacific Northwest. Filled with the colors and flavors of more than 300 artisans of all ages, there is an array of quality arts and crafts, baked goods to take home and 26 food booths in the International Food Court. The Market features a wide variety of original local musical and dance performances on its Main Stage every Saturday and Sunday from 11:30a.m. to 4:00p.m. Styles range from Bluegrass to Jazz, and Rock to ethnic. In addition, the Market hosts many special festivals and events throughout the year. Rain or shine, the Market opens every Saturday and Sunday for shopping and just plain fun from March until Christmas Eve. To keep everyone in the spirit as the holiday shopping crunch begins, the "Festival of Last Minute" starts one week prior to Christmas every year. During this last minute crunch, the Market is open every day. Located underneath the Burnside Bridge in the heart of Portland's Historic Old Town, the Market is between SW Naito Parkway and SW 1st Avenue. The Market is open 10:00a.m. until 5:00p.m. on Saturdays and 11:00a.m. until 4:30p.m. on Sundays. For more information visit the website www.portlandsaturdaymarket.com. Promotions Coordinator, Renee Conlee can be reached at (503) 222-6072 ext. 11 or by e-mail at renee@saturdaymarket.org.

Farmington Gardens

Visit Farmington Gardens for the best that the fertile Willamette Valley has to offer. Established in 1994, this family business has evolved from a roadside stand into a comprehensive garden center with a reputation for high quality plant material and a very knowledgeable staff. You will find a wide range of annuals, perennials, shrubs and trees, and more than that, the friendly expertise you need to make the right plant choices.

Farmington Gardens' website at www.farmingtongardens.com gives you a glimpse of the breadth of their knowledge. In the "gardening reference section" you will find more than sixty topics covered in extensive detail. The website also has excellent directions and maps. And they carry a wide range of supplies for everyone, from the novice home gardener to the experienced professional landscaper.

Their goal is to provide high quality plants at a reasonable price, and make sure that their customers are satisfied with their purchases and educated about them. "We have a deep passion for plants, and it shows!" The Farmington Gardens annual Tomato Tasting Festival has been so successful that it now includes peppers and basil. Check the website for dates for this free event. It features 60+ varieties of tomatoes, and recipes as well as tomato and pepper culture information. Farmington Gardens is a strong supporter of local good works as the sponsor of a charity "Winefest," involving many local businesses and benefiting Willamette West Habitat for Humanity. "We were thrilled to have over 400 guests here to sample wines and munch on tasty hors d'oeuvres, while the White Rhino Marimba Ensemble entertained us throughout the evening with their joyful tunes." And the five homes currently under construction in Washington County will have plants and shrubs ready for them at Farmington Gardens, when the new owners are ready to landscape. Farmington Gardens is open daily year round. Call for hours at (503) 649-4568. Farmington Gardens is located at 21815 SW Farmington Road in Beaverton, Oregon. "We look forward to seeing you!"

Flowers Tommy Luke

Founded in 1907, Flowers Tommy Luke is Portland's oldest florist. You could say we've been patching things up for a very long time. We're dedicated to creating floral arrangements that are personal and unique. So much so in fact, you'll find our arrangements are more like art. And that's exactly the kind of reputation we're after. You won't find beautiful arrangements that light up a room next to the frozen food section at the grocery store or on the Internet. It's our commitment to personal service that makes our work stand out in a crowd. And isn't that what you want from a florist? Whether you need a corsage for the senior prom, flowers for your wedding, arrangements for citywide cultural events or a weekly display of flowers for the office, Flowers Tommy Luke is your florist. After all, it isn't an event until the flowers arrive. Over the years Flowers Tommy Luke has changed owners, but never its commitment to quality and creativity. Anthony Vuky bought the business in 1999 and continues the longstanding tradition of personal service, great on-staff floral designers and a strong commitment to supporting the local community through charity work and buying from local growers. The Shop is located at 2044 NW Pettygrove Street, Portland. To order, call (503) 228-3140 or toll-free (800) 775-3140. To see examples of Flowers Tommy Luke's arrangements log on to www.tommylukeflowers.com.

Gifford's Flowers

Since 1920, the Gifford family has been selling flowers in Portland. Beginning with a flower stall run by Mary Gifford at the Portland Farmers' Market, four generations of Giffords continued to provide their Portland clientele with flowers. Finally Gifford's Flowers arrived at their present home at the corner of Broadway and Jefferson. Upon arrival you're greeted with a beautiful showcase of colorful flowers outside. Their beauty beckons newcomers to step in and discover for themselves why Gifford's is among the finest florists in the area. Mary's grandsons, Bill and Jim, who now run Gifford's, recently welcomed Bill's daughter, Laura, to the family business. Gifford's is known for offering the greatest variety and the highest quality of seasonal flowers, plus superior customer service is provided by a knowledgeable and friendly staff. Special orders are welcome. At Gifford's you can get the perfect floral arrangement for any occasion: birthdays, anniversaries, "get well" and sympathy bouquets, new babies, business meetings, banquets, or holidays. Deliveries are available in the greater Portland area and Vancouver, Washington, and Gifford's ships Christmas wreaths as well. In addition to cut flowers, Gifford's also carries a wide variety of plants for home and garden, including an assortment of breathtakingly beautiful orchids. Accessories such as vases, baskets and planters are also available. Gift-givers can get greeting cards here, as well as balloons, gourmet food and fruit baskets, and exquisite treats from Moonstruck Chocolates. Gifford's Flowers is located at 704 SW Jefferson Street, Portland. For information, call (503) 222-9193, or toll-free, (800) 875-9193. To see their amazing website, go to www.giffordsflowers.com.

Cornell Farm

The present owners of Cornell Farm, Ed Blatter and Deby Barnhart, are the third generation to run this dream come true. After starting as a goat dairy in 1926, the Farm was moved to its present location on Barnes Road, and then became the very successful plant nursery that it is today. Cornell Farm offers over one thousand varieties of annuals and perennials, including shrubs and tropical plants, like orchids. Their tried-and-true top quality nursery stock is carefully cultivated to establish a good root system, which makes it especially popular with customers in the know. Cornell Farm features the cutting edge in container gardening for indoor and outdoor growers, plus gardening accessories, a gift shop, and Christmas tree trimmings. Prior to the nursery many crops were grown here, including strawberries and orchard fruits. The Farm still raises its famed English Holly, the oldest planted English Holly on the West Coast, a perennially popular Christmas specialty shipped to customers on the East Coast. Deby hosts seasonal events and workshops at the Farm, including the fall Pansy Festival with over a hundred varieties of pansies on display. There is even a Scarecrow Auction, where the employees make their own individual scarecrows which are auctioned off for a local charity. Cornell Farm is open seven days a week at 8212 Southwest Barnes Road in Portland, just east of St. Vincent Hospital. For more information, call (503) 292-9895.

Tony's Fish Market & Smokehouse

Located in the heart of Historic Oregon City, Tony's Fish Market and Smokehouse was started in 1936 by Tony Petrich. Tony was a fisherman from Croatia and his wife, Stazie, had grown up on a farm in Sylvania. In the beginning, Tony fished and sold most of his catch to wholesalers. The rest Stazie sold in their fish market. Eventually their son Vincent became manager of the Market, and in 1964 he built the first smokehouses, using his father's family recipe from the old country to smoke the fish. Following what was now a family tradition, Marko, Vincent's middle son, joined the business. In 1986, Vincent and Marko added a processing plant next to the Market and installed electronic smokehouses to meet the increased demand for Tony's popular smoked fish products. Though these products are produced for commercial distribution, Tony's Fish Market continues to carry them, along with fresh seafood year round. Marko and his wife, Penny, now own and operate the business, and their adult children carry on the tradition. Gregory runs the family-owned fish market; Elizabeth and William oversee operations in the processing plant. A fifth generation is waiting in the wings to keep the very best in fresh and smoked seafood available from this true Oregon Treasure. Tony's Fish Market and Smokehouse is located at 1316 Washington Street in Portland, Oregon. For more information, call (503) 656-7512 or visit their website at www.tonyssmokehouse.com.

Willamette Valley Farm Fields

Swan Island Dahlias

Originally located on Swan Island in Portland, the business moved to Canby in the 1940's where it is located today, still under the original name, Swan Island Dahlias. Family owned and operated for over three generations, Swan Island Dahlias has been the Dahlia center of America for over seventy years. As one of the nation's leading hybridizers, Swan Island Dahlias introduces between ten and twenty new varieties each year with an average of four years of development with each new variety. Visit the fields from 8am until 8pm daily beginning August 1st through the end of September to get the incredible view of over forty acres in a rainbow of color. The annual Dahlia Festival runs the last weekend in August and Labor Day weekend, which showcases over 15,000 blooms in over 350 floral arrangements. The Show also features floral arranging and tuber dividing demonstrations, culture talks, as well as refreshments and fresh cut flowers to remember your show experience. A feast for the eyes, this is one event not to be missed. Swan Island Dahlias ships all over the world. Orders can be placed for spring delivery from their online catalog, by phone or from their mail order catalog. Visit Swan Island Dahlias at 995 NW 22nd Avenue in Canby, Oregon. You can also reach them at (503) 266-7711 or check out their website and online ordering at www.dahlias.com.

Harbick's Country Store

"Yes, we have it!" That is Harbick's long-standing motto. In an age when country stores are scaling back or folding, Harbick's Country Store offers an ever-growing list of goods and services. Now Harbick's, on rural Highway 126, is the largest general store between Springfield and Sisters. Owners Darin and Kail Harbick opened the outlet in 1991, a year to the day after its predecessor, Phil's Phine Phoods, was razed by an arson fire. Tradition is what Phil's Phine Phoods was all about and the Harbicks plan to keep it that way. You can walk in and find black jelly beans and chicken on a stick, and everything from hummingbird feeders, kitchen faucets, general hardware, groceries, gifts, gas, propane, fishing tackle and licenses to deli selections, Lotto and garden supplies. They have expanded their hours to accommodate customers and have added features such as an ATM machine, video rentals, and notary service. Summer, especially July and August, is the peak time for their business. More recently, a restaurant opened next door. Open for breakfast, lunch and dinner. Harbick's is located at 91808 Mill Creek Road in Blue River, Oregon. Go east of Eugene on Highway 126 to Mile Post 47.5. You may contact Harbick's by calling (541) 822-3575.

Heirloom Roses

Visitors to Oregon's Willamette Valley should not miss Heirloom Rose Gardens and Nursery. With acres of beautiful roses in a serene setting, the Gardens are the perfect spot to spend a tranquil day. Heirloom Rose Gardens has the largest rose display of any nursery in the country. Over 4000 varieties of roses can be found on five gorgeous acres. The vivid colors of the roses and the fragrant blossoms wafting on the breeze are unforgettable. The Gardens are a popular place to come to relax and reflect. The Tranquility Garden, featuring all white roses and perennials, seems to draw visitors in need of quiet thinking. Visitors are welcome and encouraged to meander throughout the gardens to find the perfect addition to their own gardens or to simply enjoy the roses. People can sit on the benches and let the day slip by or picnic under the lush trees. A small gift shop sells garden items, rose books, calendars, and jellies, as well snacks, water and soft drinks. John and Louise Clements planted the first garden in 1990. Together the Clements have over 60 years of growing experience. They are clearly experts in their field, traveling around the globe in search of new and unique roses. The Clements also breed their own beautiful roses. Each year, 30,000 rose seeds are planted from crossing parent roses. After much evaluation, three to six roses are introduced to the public. Heirloom Rose Gardens also imports a variety of roses from Europe. Heirloom Rose Gardens can ship roses to all fifty states year-round. Heirloom Rose Gardens and Nursery is located at 24062 Riverside Dr. NE in St. Paul, midway between Salem and Portland. From Interstate 5, take exit 278 and travel west seven miles to Highway 219. Turn right and follow the signs to Heirloom Roses. The Gardens are open dawn until dusk from May to October and amazingly, admission is free. For more information, call (503) 538-1576 or visit www.heirloomroses.com.

GloryBee Foods

For the sweetest place on earth, come to GloryBee Foods. Nestled in the beautiful Willamette Valley, GloryBee provides hive products and wholesale and retail honey to customers around the world. Whether you're a baker, a craft maker, a beekeeper, or someone with a sweet tooth, GloryBee has just what you need and want. When you visit GloryBee Foods you'll be amazed at all the wonderful products they offer. Their colorful displays of Aunt Patty's Organic Sweeteners, bee pollen, propolis, royal jelly, beeswax, candies and many different kinds of honey are a testament to the wonderful ways that bees enrich our lives.

GloryBee was founded in 1975 by beekeeper Dick Turanski, and the family-owned business has grown to become the largest honey packer in Oregon. Their organic products are "Certified Organic" by Quality Assurance International and kosher by the Orthodox Union. If you're thinking of producing your own line of candles, candies or health and beauty products, talk to the friendly staff at GloryBee and they'll help you with your selections. In addition to honey they also have beauty products such as avocado butter, grape seeds, and rose hips, plus all the supplies you need to make your own soaps, salves, and lotions. The GloryBee showroom is located at 55 North Seneca Road in Eugene, just off Highway 99, between Roosevelt and West 11th. Visit their website at www.GloryBeeFoods.com or call their toll-free number (800) 456-7923.

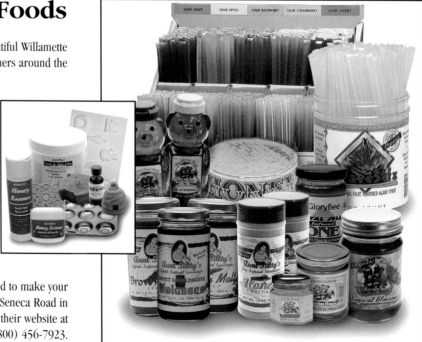

The Flower Farmer

Here is a fabulously fun, entertaining and educational locale the whole family will enjoy. Train lovers will thrill to the narrow gauge Phoenix and Holly Railroad as it meanders through acres of bountiful flower gardens, the European vegetable garden and the animal barn. Each season brings new and fresh events such as the beautiful Christmas Lights Display, the Easter Egg Hunt and the Basil Wine and Art Festival. The Halloween Haunted Train Ride is sure to delight youngsters of all ages. Leo and Louis Garre's Fruit Stand is open from 10am until 6 pm daily from June through October. The displays of fresh, seasonal produce and fragrant flowers are a delight to the senses. As an extra treat, you're welcome to stroll in the flower gardens and pick your own bouquet. The Garres are famous for their wonderful trains, produce, flowers and friendliness. If you'd like a personal-sized train for your home or office, the Garres can assist with planning, engineering and building one of your own. So, spend a day with the Flower Farmer, at 2512 North Holly Street in Canby. For more information, call (503) 266-3581. For calendar listings, fun photos and a map, visit their website at www.flowerfarmer.com.

Al's Garden Center

Al's Garden Center is a perfect example of a true Oregon business, steeped in agriculture and the spirit of entrepreneurship. What Al and Ann Bigej began in 1948 as a roadside fruit stand housed in an unused chicken coop on Hwy 99 E. has evolved into a third generation privately owned-family business. Opening Al's Fruit Stand wasn't an easy feat, but it was their middle son, Jack who is the true entrepreneur with his passion for business and plants. In 1958, Jack at the age of 17 took on more responsibility for the family business. In 1959 Jack decided to expand the business by selling nursery stock. The nursery stock was such a success that by 1961 Jack was brought into his father's business as a partner. In the 1980's, Jack was certain that he could grow a higher quality plant product, and produce it at a lower cost to the customer. He also wanted to be different, having a wider variety of plants than anyone else. Now Al's four growing facilities located throughout Oregon supply over 90% of Al's perennials and annuals, as well as wholesale to many local independent nurseries. With three of Jack's children returning to the business in the 90's, and bringing in one of the nation's best plant producers, Al's Garden Center has grown in leaps and bounds. It is Jack's and his family's innovative ideas and love of plants that have kept Al's successful and growing for over 56 years. You'll hear Jack continually say, "I don't do it because it's work." Al's Garden Center is located at 1220 N. Pacific Highway (99E) in Woodburn, Oregon. Al's is open throughout the year seven days a week. See their website www.als-gardencenter.com or call (503) 981-1245.

The Thyme Garden

"An awesome display of over 700 varieties of herbs!" This is just one of the many attractions you will enjoy with a visit to The Thyme Garden in Alsea, a scenic drive just 19 miles west of Corvallis. This family owned herb farm and nursery hidden in the Coast Range Mountains has one of the largest collections of herbs in the Northwest. Their extensive display gardens, nursery and nature trails are free for public viewing between mid-April and mid-August, 10a.m. to 5p.m. Rolfe and Janet Hagen preside over 80 acres of living treasures including two mountain streams, forests and a collection of herbs from around the world. There is a sunken shade garden with trickling water falls, and a conservatory they call the "Aromatherapy Room" because it is filled with such wonderful scents like the Angel's Trumpet with as many as 200 10" long flowers blooming all at once! Collecting and organically growing herb plants and seeds from around the world for culinary, medicinal and ethno-botanical uses are the Hagens' business and their avocation. The Hagens' interest in herbs began at their country restaurant, which they surrounded with herb gardens. Growing herbs led to selling herb seeds and, in 1989, they decided to embark on a new adventure expanding the seed business and starting a nursery. However, they continued their love for cooking with herbs by offering herbal luncheons including a tour of their gardens (by reservation only). Recognized for quality, service and price, they say "Our quality is a direct result of a superior organic environment, incredible attention to detail, a love for our plants, our people, and our Mother Earth." They host festive events throughout the spring and summer, including a free Mother's Day Celebration that has become the biggest event of the year. The entire Thyme Garden facilities and gardens are rented for unforgettable weddings and special occasions. They will also cater your wedding or event with an amazing feast of herbal delights including a Salmon Bake prepared the traditional way around an alder fire outdoors for your guests to enjoy. A visit to Western Oregon would not be complete without a visit to The Thyme Garden. Visit their website at www.thymegarden.com for details on their unique farm, events and products. You can also call them at (541) 487-8671.

Fir Point Farms

Starting in April of each year you can plan a day at the Farm. Tour a working family farm for quality family fun. Dedicated to including children in the activities and providing education on agriculture, the folks at Fir Point Farms make getting your weekly produce much more valuable than your average grocery trip. Here your children can enjoy pony rides, corn mazes, feed trout in the spring fed pond, feed tree-climbing goats and enjoy storytelling sessions. Each month there are special events to celebrate the season or the latest crops that are starting to ripen and the whole family will enjoy the variety of chickens, rabbit and sheep, hay rides and more. Wide selections of pumpkins, squash, melons, beans, corn and tomatoes are available at the Produce Stand or you can request items picked right then to ensure the freshest of farm produce. You too can pick produce and cut flowers to make your own special bouquets. Don't miss the special events in Fall and of course the pumpkin patch. When you want to start your own garden, Fir Point Farms is a great place to begin. Their huge greenhouse offers starters of many favorite items. With over 35 acres of farmland you can be sure to find something that suits your fresh produce needs and with hundreds of home made jams, jellies, syrups and candies, a log cabin filled with hazelnuts and other regional nuts, there is plenty to fill your pantry as well. Fir Point Farms is located at 14601 Arndt Road in Aurora, Oregon. You can reach them at (503) 678-2455. Fir Point Farms is open from April through December 21st with the exception of July Fourth and Thanksgiving.

EZ Orchards Farm Market

EZ Orchards Farm Market was opened in 1992. They have been farming in the Willamette Valley since 1870. Locally owned and operated, this family farm is dedicated to providing its customers with the very best each season has to offer. Even when shipping products nationally the same great care is applied to their hand picked and hand packed produce. Seasonal fruit, berries and vegetables are brought in daily from the farmer's fields. Included among these delicacies are carefully selected asparagus, peaches, marionberries, raspberries, blueberries, cherries, strawberries, melons, apples, pears, and a vast number of vegetables. With the largest selection of Northwest gourmet foods in the Willamette Valley, you can pick a variety of preserves, baking mixes, mustards, candies and more. When you find the perfect bouquet of fresh cut tulips, daffodils and irises make sure to match them with a hand blown glass vase. EZ Orchards Farm Market has a garden with 75 varieties of lavender on display as well. During the autumn harvest season keep an eye out for their uniquely themed Corn Maze, with a straw mountain slide and Indian tipi, and more. They also provide a petting zoo, pumpkin patch, hay rides, pony rides, pedal tractors, and live blue grass music. EZ Orchards Farm Market is open Monday through Saturday. They are located at 5504 Hazel Green Road NE in Salem. You can reach them at (503) 393-1506. Check out their website at www.ezorchards.com.

Hazelnut Growers of Oregon

At Hazelnut Growers of Oregon, their only business is hazelnuts, an expertise that we can all benefit from as we enjoy the wide and luscious selection of hazelnut products they offer. Ninety-nine percent of all hazelnuts grown in the United States come from the rich soil of the Willamette Valley in Oregon. They explain this as the result of the region's gentle climate and abundant rainfall, which produces larger nuts with an exquisite flavor and freshness. These hazelnuts are widely considered to be the best in the world. And you can visit their website to "learn more about the sweetest hazelnuts in the world." Just a few of the things you will find on the Oregon Orchard site are wonderful recipes for appetizers, breads, pasta, salads, sauces, desserts, and beef or fish and other main courses. They make it easy to shop online for seasoned nuts, toffee coated, dry roasted, in their shells or without, and of course a selection of gift tins from the Hazelnut Six Pack O'Cans to Hazelnut Happiness (featuring four compartments of Mint Chocolate, Dark Chocolate, Chocolate Toffee and their "new" Marionberry, and Raspberry candy-coated hazelnuts) and much, much more. You can also go in to their outlet store, established in 1995, and pick out your personal favorite. The Hazelnut Growers of Oregon ship from this store in Cornelius, Oregon, to customers all over the world, including Japan and many European countries. This is the only hazelnut cooperative in the United States. Founded in 1984, Hazelnut Growers of Oregon has more than 150 growers and more than 10,000 acres. They have a strong commitment to their customers and employees and, as a cooperative, profits are distributed to its grower members. "You can be assured of the consistent high quality and uniformity of our hazelnut products, backed by strict Oregon grade standards and USDA inspections." When you think of hazelnuts, in shell or shelled, natural or dry roasted, sliced, diced, meal, butter or paste, seasoned or candied, think of the hazelnut specialists, Hazelnut Growers of Oregon. Call (800) 923-NUTS, or visit www.oregonorchard.com.

Kruse Farms

In 1923, Don's father, Bert Kruse started with 15 acres of logged-off land. After many years of honest dealings within the community, Kruse Farms became known for growing excellent produce and for being active participants in their community. Your first impression of Don Kruse is that he is a salt-of-the-earth, true Oregonian through and through. His knowledge and skills for farming were passed down the old fashioned way, by his father. It is a lifestyle, a way of life, and Don and his wife Sally's chosen path is to remain close to the soil. He takes great pride in his family's history of four generations being involved in growing the best possible fruit and vegetables for their neighbors. The Kruse family continues serving Roseburg area residents with their fine produce, and Don's sister is involved too. She is the Head Baker for Kruse Farms Bakery. It is there that you can sample some of the most delectable homemade pies you could ever imagine. Kruse Farms prepares and ships baskets all over the world. You can select from candies, Kruse Farms preserves and syrups to many varieties of dried fruits, nuts, pastas and mixes for your personalized basket. In the fall, there is even a seemingly endless pumpkin patch for the younger members of the community. Don has always found positive ways to be involved in his community, including serving many years on the Roseburg School Board. Don's son, Jeff, followed his example of community service and presently serves in the Oregon Legislature. Kruse Farms, continuing a tradition of excellence, is located at 532 Melrose Road, Roseburg, Oregon, (541) 672-5697.

Market Of Choice

Perfection in shopping. Enter the Market of Choice and you'll immediately be greeted by the delicious aroma of fresh baked breads, desserts and fresh ground coffee. This is not your average trip to the grocery store. Market of Choice offers a step back in time with its service, quality and atmosphere. Local produce, real chefs in the deli, local wines and beers, local cheeses and many different farm products are all a part of what makes this place so special. Market of Choice also has a salad and olive bar where you can create your own favorite dinner salad. All of their products are carefully selected and nearly 40% of the inventory is organic. There's even a wine steward on staff with wine tasting available. For a shopping experience, rather than experiencing a chore, come to the Market of Choice and see what a real grocery store should be like. Visit the Market of Choice at 1475 Siskiyou Blvd. just east of Southern Oregon University in Ashland.

The Majestic Upper Table Rock in Southern Oregon

Valley View Nursery

Celebrating 25 years of excellence, Stranberg's family-owned and operated nursery provides the largest selection of shrubs and trees within 200 miles of the Rogue Valley. The business started out as a love for growing plants. The Stranberg family quickly learned that it takes more than a love of plants; it takes people to grow, sell and buy plants. Valley View Nursery carries everything you might want for your gardening and landscaping needs. They will provide you with information on how to plant, tend and prune your nursery purchases. As you walk through their grounds, you will be able to choose from ornamental maples, shade trees, fruit and nut trees, shrubs, accent and border plants, hedges, ornamental grasses, groundcovers, perennials, annuals, hanging baskets, vegetables and more.

For the finishing touches to your garden, you will want to browse their selection of cast stone fountains and statuary, koi and water garden supplies, patio furniture and unique pottery and planters. Valley View offers free classes on a variety of nursery related topics. The classes are fun and guaranteed to help your garden grow. Paul and his very friendly, knowledgeable Valley View crew are always willing to answer your gardening questions. Drive on out to 1675 N. Valley View Road in Ashland, or 1321 Center Drive in Medford. For further information, call (541) 488-1595 or visit their inspiring website at www.valleyviewnursery.com.

Phoenix Organics Garden & Eco-building Center

In the Rogue Valley of Southern Oregon, there's no better place to find supplies to help you connect to and preserve the earth than Phoenix Organics Garden & Eco-building Center. "Organic gardening and environmentally friendly eco-building products have become very popular among the masses over the last decade," explain owners Steven Jaramillo and Abraham Harris. "By using nontoxic and chemical-free environmentally friendly products, one can keep the environment clean and healthy." To help you in that endeavor, Phoenix Organics carries everything from nontoxic exterior and interior paints, floor finishes, carpets, sustainable floors, natural cotton insulation, strippers, adhesive, and more.

Are you a home gardener or landscaper? Phoenix Organics Garden Center has everything you need to grow 100 percent organically with organic fertilizers, insect-pest-disease control, soil amendments, organic compost, fruit trees, shrubs, vines and native trees. The staff can help you with "edible" landscape design, landscaping you can eat. The store also offers bio-diesel to the public for off-road use. Bio-diesel is a sustainable source of energy. Say Steven and Abraham, "All our products are designed to make Mother Earth a better place." So if you're ready to make a commitment to environmentally sound practices and products, Phoenix Organics is the place to go. Phoenix Organics Garden & Eco-Building Center is located at 4543 S. Pacific Hwy., Phoenix, OR 97535. Call (541) 535-1134 or visit their website at www.phoenixorganics.com.

Gifts

The Real Mother Goose

Professional craft artists have repeatedly acknowledged The Real Mother Goose as the Best American Fine Craft Gallery. For over thirty years this has been the place to find stunning arts and crafts with aesthetic as well as functional use. With three convenient locations in the greater Portland area, over 1000 artists represented and 10,000 square feet of gallery space, it features one of the widest selections of fine crafts and innovative art in the country. With such a large selection there are finds in every price range from $10 on up. Allow time to take in their broad selections of exceptional quality craftsmanship in jewelry, glass, ceramics, exotic woods, furnishings and wearable art, as well as a few specially selected toys for those young at heart. A notable focus of the galleries is their commitment to building quality relationships with their artists, their support of the craft community and their mentorship of emerging artists. Owner, Judy Gillis describes it as a "toy store for adults" with a kaleidoscope of brilliant colors, exotic materials and imaginative design. Often visitors to the Northwest will remember The Real Mother Goose Gallery as one of their first stops in this beautiful city with the Downtown Gallery located just off of the MAX tracks at 901 SW Yamhill Street. It can be reached at (503) 223-9510. The Washington Square Mall location, in Tigard, can be reached at (503) 620-2243, and the Portland International Airport location can be reached at (503) 284-9929. You can also check out their artists and designs online at www.therealmothergoose.com.

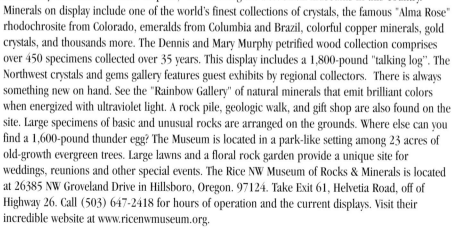

Rice NW Museum of Rocks & Minerals

Meteorites from outer space and one of the world's best petrified wood collections are just two of the exhibits you might find at any given time at the Rice NW Museum of Rocks & Minerals in Hillsboro. Founded by Helen and Richard Rice in 1938 and incorporated as a nonprofit in 1996, the Museum includes mineral specimens from throughout the world. Rock & Gem Magazine recently called the Museum "superb," and "among the best small museums in this country." Minerals on display include one of the world's finest collections of crystals, the famous "Alma Rose" rhodochrosite from Colorado, emeralds from Columbia and Brazil, colorful copper minerals, gold crystals, and thousands more. The Dennis and Mary Murphy petrified wood collection comprises over 450 specimens collected over 35 years. This display includes a 1,800-pound "talking log". The Northwest crystals and gems gallery features guest exhibits by regional collectors. There is always something new on hand. See the "Rainbow Gallery" of natural minerals that emit brilliant colors when energized with ultraviolet light. A rock pile, geologic walk, and gift shop are also found on the site. Large specimens of basic and unusual rocks are arranged on the grounds. Where else can you find a 1,600-pound thunder egg? The Museum is located in a park-like setting among 23 acres of old-growth evergreen trees. Large lawns and a floral rock garden provide a unique site for weddings, reunions and other special events. The Rice NW Museum of Rocks & Minerals is located at 26385 NW Groveland Drive in Hillsboro, Oregon. 97124. Take Exit 61, Helvetia Road, off of Highway 26. Call (503) 647-2418 for hours of operation and the current displays. Visit their incredible website at www.ricenwmuseum.org.

The Bee & Thistle

When searching for the best in designer accessories, visit The Bee and Thistle in Northwest Portland. As the chic and fashionable already know, you will not be disappointed with the large selection and affordable prices. Featuring many local designers and artists, the Boutique is the premier place to find fashionable jewelry, designer handbags, shoes and accessories. With both trendy and classic looks, there is something for everyone who enjoys up-to-the-minute fashions that are always unique at attainable prices. Owner, Kim Lane, and her team of BAT (Bee and Thistle) Girls help turn a simple shopping trip into a fun and exciting experience. A former Nordstrom buyer and jewelry designer, Lane is clearly an expert in the field of fashion. Styles here are amazing and Bee and Thistle customer service is always top-notch. The Bee and Thistle often showcases local designers and offers fabulous seasonal promotions and special events. During the annual holiday open house, Lane offers ten to fifty percent off purchases and the friendly staff is more than willing to charge a purchase over the phone if a customer can't make it in on the day of the big sale. Lane's newest venture is Sole, a boutique located in Portland's Pearl District. The Store carries such lines as Kenneth Cole, BCBG Girls and Pazzo as well as merchandise exclusive to Sole. The Bee and Thistle is located at 2328 NW Westover Road, one block North of West Burnside and Northwest 23rd Place. To speak with a member of the BAT team, call (503) 222-3397 or for more information, visit their website at www.thebeeandthistle.com.

Toy Bear, Ltd.

With more than 20,000 toys to choose from, who could ask for anything more? Dale and Patricia Fiedler have had this wonderful toy store in historic downtown Gresham since 1982. Since that time, they have developed a terrific selection, which includes specialty toys from many smaller toy companies, as well as from the big, well-known manufacturers. They hand-pick only the best of toys that will encourage children to explore their full potential. Just a few of the excellent brands are: Learning Curve, Folkmanis, Small World Toys, Toysmith, Museum Quality Creative Toys, Brio, Playmobile, and Madame Alexander's Dolls. Toy Bear, Ltd., is deeply engaged in the community life of Gresham, taking part in many events like the Teddy Bear Parade that has been entertaining Gresham children of all ages for twenty-two years. In addition, they host numerous in-store events. The Toy Bear, Ltd., is also a Gold Sponsor and an organizer of the annual Children's Festival in Historic Downtown Gresham, which draws more than 2,000 children to participate in its many fun activities. Just a short, ten minute walk from the Max Light Rail, Toy Bear, Ltd. provides a great shopping experience, with gift wrapping and close parking also available. The Store is open daily, and is located at 130 North Main Avenue in Gresham. You can reach them by calling (503) 661-5310, or come in to explore this Oregon treasure. Visit their website at www.toysinportland.com for more information about the Toy Bear, Ltd., store and about the Fiedlers' other store, Child's Play, in Portland.

Scandia Imports

Eero and Tuulikki Harju opened Scandia Imports in 1987 to provide a source of fine gifts for people of Scandinavia descent and people who love Scandinavian culture. Scandia Imports features wonderful items reflecting the Harjus' own Finnish heritage as well as Swedish, Danish, and Norwegian specialties. Catalog sales provide Scandinavian cheer to people all around the world, and since 1998 the Harjus have made their catalog accessible via the Internet. Delicious food is a mainstay at Scandia. Juhla coffee from Finland, lingonberry jam, peparkakor Christmas cookies, are just a few of the selections, and don't miss the imported candy, either! Melkesjokolade is the Norwegian word for milk chocolate, but it spells delicious in any language. Swedish breads and goat cheese are available only at the Store, and they're well worth the trip. At Scandia Imports, it feels like Christmas all year round. Ornaments, wreaths, and traditional decorations such as the Swedish jul bok (Christmas goat) are always available. If you're having trouble coming up with good gift ideas, consider fine Porsgrund porcelain from Norway, lovely Swedish glassware or Iittala glassware from Finland. Children will love the many items featuring the classic Dala horse design – ornaments, mobiles, magnets, cookie cutters, even gummi Dala horses! The Store is open Monday through Saturday throughout the year, and seven days a week during November and December. Every November the Harjus have a Christmas Open House to display their new Christmas merchandise and let people get a head start on their holiday shopping, with tempting discounts offered for enthusiastic shoppers. While you're there, enjoy traditional refreshments such as glögg, the classic Scandinavian mulled drink. Scandia Imports is located at 10020 Southwest Beaverton Hillsdale Highway in Beaverton. For more information, call toll-free, (800) 834-8547, or visit their website at www.scandiaimports.com.

The Monkey & The Rat

For a unique selection of fine gifts and intricate treasures at affordable prices, visit The Monkey & the Rat in historic Oldtown, Portland. This eclectic shop features one-of-a-kind handmade items from around the world. Their customers pick through an amazing array of vintage furniture, teak wood carvings, spiritual statues, beautiful textiles, silver jewelry, bamboo candles, silk scarves and more. This is truly an Oregon Treasure with something for everyone.

Browsing through the Shop is an experience in and of itself, as you enter into the brick-walled setting of the turn of the century. Much of the inventory is hand-picked from Southeast Asia (Thailand, Myanmar, Laos, India), by Owner, Christopher Yarrow. Christopher and his staff are truly passionate about finding the perfect objects to grace his store. The friendly service and attention to detail keep people coming back for more. The Monkey & The Rat can ship merchandise anywhere in the United States, and can even have items custom-made in Thailand. If you have a special item in mind and cannot find it in the Store, the staff will search high and low until they find it. The Monkey & the Rat, open Tuesday through Sunday, is located at 131 NW Second Avenue between the Classical Chinese Garden and the Portland Saturday Market, one block from the Max Light Rail Line. Phone (503) 224-3849 for more information or visit their website at www.themonkeyandtherat.com.

Child's Play

Dale and Patricia Fiedler warmly welcome visitors to their delightful store in Portland. At Child's Play you will find the best assortment of specialty toys, science products, stuffed animals, dolls, games, books, educational items and much more. Child's Play has been located in the trendy NW 23rd Street area, one block from the streetcar to downtown, since the late 1970's. Revisit your childhood with dress-up clothing, Thomas trains, wooden toys, puzzles, hand and finger puppets, and Ginny dolls are all just a taste of what they carry. For the budding musician in your life, browse through their beginner musical instruments or select a trike or wagon for your young traveler. Choose from top brands, including Playmobil, Brio and LaMaze infant toys. On-premise parking is available, as is free gift wrapping. With a friendly and extremely knowledgeable staff, and a great selection of toys for every facet of your child's imagination, visiting Child's Play is a fun and immensely enjoyable experience. Come in to 907 Northwest 23rd Avenue in Portland, Oregon 97210. Contact them by calling (503) 224-5586, or you can find out more information about Child's Play and the Fiedlers' other store in Gresham, Toy Bear, Ltd., by visiting their website, www.toysinportland.com.

Julia's Specialty Gifts

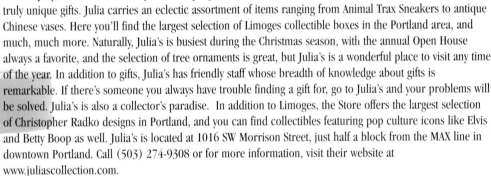

You can't miss Julia's Specialty Gifts because the dazzling front window displays are like no other in Portland. Julia Pollock has been putting her imagination on display here for seventeen years, and people from miles around know that this is the place to come for truly unique gifts. Julia carries an eclectic assortment of items ranging from Animal Trax Sneakers to antique Chinese vases. Here you'll find the largest selection of Limoges collectible boxes in the Portland area, and much, much more. Naturally, Julia's is busiest during the Christmas season, with the annual Open House always a favorite, and the selection of tree ornaments is great, but Julia's is a wonderful place to visit any time of the year. In addition to gifts, Julia's has friendly staff whose breadth of knowledge about gifts is remarkable. If there's someone you always have trouble finding a gift for, go to Julia's and your problems will be solved. Julia's is also a collector's paradise. In addition to Limoges, the Store offers the largest selection of Christopher Radko designs in Portland, and you can find collectibles featuring pop culture icons like Elvis and Betty Boop as well. Julia's is located at 1016 SW Morrison Street, just half a block from the MAX line in downtown Portland. Call (503) 274-9308 or for more information, visit their website at www.juliascollection.com.

The Fossil Cartel

The Fossil Cartel, located at Pioneer Place in downtown Portland, has the largest selection of crystals, minerals, fossils, meteorites and jewelry in Oregon. Owner Susan Landa takes great pride in her stunning museum style shop. Her love of fossils, minerals, unique items and precious stones has led to the outstanding items showcased here. Trilobites are a favorite of hers as are insects captured in amber. She carries Mt. St. Helen's Emerald Obsidianite jewelry, petrified wood, and other Pacific Northwest favorites. Be sure to seek out the Oregon Opal, distinguished from more common Australian opal by it translucent shades of blue, red and yellow and occasionally with an iridescent fire. In this museum of the earth you will find a wide assortment of items ranging from very inexpensive tumbled stones to very expensive meteorites. When you do find that special gift for someone, consider adding a unique hand display to hold the precious item. Made here in Oregon they are crafted to show extraordinary detail. Additional items you can find here include jewelry, crystals, rocks and fossil that can be used in Feng Shui, home/office décor and metaphysical healing. The Fossil Cartel is located at 340 SW Morrison St. in Portland. It can be reached at (503) 228-6998. You can also check out some of their products online at www.fossilcartel.com.

Luv 'N Stuff Flowers & Gifts

Located across the street from Good Samaritan Hospital in Portland, Luv 'n Stuff Flowers & Gifts can deliver your sentiments and smiles locally or worldwide. Says owner Sharon Paulsen, "We take special pride in assuring you that we use only the freshest flowers that have been brought in from select growers. We value your continued use of our flower and gift service and will always deliver your gift with the greatest care." Here is a sample of recent "all occasion" floral arrangements available at Luv 'n Stuff. A Be Happy arrangement: the receiver can't help but feel a little more cheerful when this happy face arrives. Smiles are guaranteed. An orchid plant: the blossoms will last up to six weeks with minimal care. Shades of Purple: perfect for a new friend or a lasting love. Purple irises surrounded by lavender freesia and purple asters and other soft accents. Double azalea: a basket of azaleas great for the Northwest. Will re-bloom for years when planted outside. Dendrobrium orchids: a vase of 10 stems of stunning beauty. The orchids arrive attractively arranged in a glass vase. Arrangements change seasonally, of course. In addition to the flowers and gift baskets, Luv 'n Stuff has teddy bears, chocolates and truffles, balloons, and more. Luv 'n Stuff Flower & Gifts is located across the street from Good Samaritan Hospital, at 2266 NW Lovejoy, Portland, OR 97210. It's on the street car line that connects the trendy Northwest area of Portland with downtown. Call (503) 228-2266 or (800) 451-1764 toll-free. Visit the website at www.luv-n-stuff-flowers.com to place an online order 24 hours a day or phone to order from a trained operator.

Bob's Red Mill

When you go to Bob's Red Mill website, you will recognize Bob Moore's face, which appears on the packages of stone-ground, whole-grain products on every good grocery store's shelves. These products for a healthy, balanced lifestyle have been around for 25 years, since Bob Moore opened his one-of-a-kind business in an old mill near Oregon City in 1978, Stone Ground Whole Grain Products – "The Old Fashioned Way." After living his "first" life in California as a business manager, Bob's wife, Charlee, inspired him with her life-long passion for whole grain foods. Then he read a book that changed his life (the story of the restoration of an old stone-grinding flour mill), and started his first mill. Many of the most popular mixes, like the 10-Grain Pancake Mix and the Date Nut Bran Muffin Mix, were created at that time. When Bob and Charlee moved to Portland, supposedly in retirement, they stumbled upon an old vacant flour mill near historic Oregon City. They purchased the mill and opened up Bob's Red Mill. In 1988, the old mill was completely destroyed by fire and when asked by firefighters what he most wanted to save, Bob replied "Save the stones!" Bob and Charlee were able to rebuild the business at a lake-side location in Milwaukie, Oregon. And it now has two modern facilities totaling 132,000 square feet on six acres, with 115 employees working three shifts. Bob's Red Mill has become a multimillion-dollar business milling and marketing whole grain natural foods throughout the USA and Canada. Their website has a wealth of information and will help you find the closest store that carries Bob's Red Mill products. When you enter their Whole Grain Store at 5000 SE International Way in Milwaukie, you will find a mill outlet store, bakery, breakfast and lunch café. Their cooking/baking school features local and nationally recognized instructors. An eight-minute video gives an intimate look into stonegrinding and packaging. This is the world's premier natural whole grain food supplier. "Try our superb products – We think you will find them to be the finest available anywhere." You can reach them at (503) 607-6455 or visit the website at www.bobsredmill.com.

Beaumont Market

Nestled in the center of a bustling and historic Northeast Portland community, the Beaumont Market is not your typical neighborhood market. The store offers an eclectic blend of food, gifts, drinks, and coffee, while providing you with a unique shopping experience. The Market touts an impressive assortment of specialty beers, fine wines, fresh local produce and meats, plus a large selection of gourmet food. Owners, Richard Johnston and Donna Nelson, and Manager, Scott Klinkhammer have made the Beaumont Market a "destination" stop where you can browse the vast collection of gift and home decor accessories. Locals call it a store small in size but huge in heart and soul. With warm, sincere customer service, you'll leave with a sense that you stepped back in time to the wonder years of old-fashioned service in the "corner market." Come shop and make new friends in this Oregon treasure. The Beaumont Market is located at 4130 NE Fremont Street in Portland, Oregon 97212. From downtown Portland, go east on I-84 to the 33rd Street exit. Travel north on 33rd to Fremont Street. Turn right, and the Market is on the right after approximately three-fourths of a mile. For more information, call (503) 284-3032.

University of Oregon Book Store & Branch Duck Shop of Portland

If you venture downtown near the beautiful Willamette River in Portland you will find a unique retail store full of wonderful collegiate sportswear, gifts and much more. When you enter the Duck Shop it is like going back in time, regardless of where you went to college. Located in a historic building full of old city charm, you will see murals adorning the walls capturing collegiate life from the early days of the University of Oregon until the present. You will find the Duck Shop inviting and elegantly merchandised and it has something for everyone and every pocketbook. You will also find that whether you are a Duck fan or just a visitor, their helpful staff is eager to share their pride in their University and in Portland. The University of Oregon opened the Portland Duck Shop in 1989 to serve the Portland area alumni and friends of the University and give them a way to connect with the campus 110 miles south in Eugene. From the very beginning the Duck Shop has been a success and has helped the University expand its presence in Portland by offering students classes and seminars taught by UO faculty. The Duck Shop is open seven days a week and is located on the corner of Southwest Second Avenue and Yamhill St. To contact them, call (503) 725-3057 or for more information about the Portland store and their other locations, visit their website at www.uobookstore.com.

Portland State University Bookstore

The school that is now Portland State University was born just after World War II, with a different name and in a different place. Returning veterans seeking college education prevailed upon the state legislature to create Vanport College, but when the campus disappeared along with the rest of Vanport during the Memorial Day Flood of 1948, the college was moved to downtown Portland. Portland State College was granted university status in 1969, and the Bookstore has had many locations too since it was formed as a student cooperative at Vanport. You will find the Bookstore now at the PSU Urban Center, where it serves both PSU students and the public. And like other visitors, you may be surprised to find such a wide selection of best sellers, travel books, cookbooks, art supplies, and children's books. The PSU Bookstore's mission is to serve everyone in the Portland area, and it does a great job! The Bookstore offers special benefits to Co-op members, including 10% savings on all books except textbooks. And students from all universities are entitled to a 10% discount on some items, just show your student ID. Fans of the PSU Vikings know that the PSU Bookstore is the first stop for the best selection of official Viking apparel, souvenirs, and gifts. The PSU Bookstore is located at 1715 SW Fifth Avenue. For more information, call (503) 226-2631 or visit their website at www.psubookstore.com.

Rose's Glassworks and Gifts

If you want to get an up-close look at what beautiful custom stained glass is all about, visit Rose's Glassworks and Gifts in Portland, Oregon. Owner Larry Cartales (who named the business in memory of his grandmother Rose) wants you to be virtually overwhelmed when you enter the door with the lead panels, cop per foiled sun catchers, Tiffany reproduction lamps, 3-D floral panels, fused art glass and fused bowls, plates and water fountains. There are mosaic stepping stones for your walkway, benches for your garden, and even glass beads if you want to make your own jewelry. It's the place to revel in stained glass and decide "This is what I want to have custom-made for my home" or "This is what I want to make for myself." If so, sign up for classes and you're on your way. Finished pieces are for sale in the studio, of course, but you might decide you want a similar piece made to fit your home decor. Or you might want to make an appointment with a designer and develop a design that fits your personal lifestyle. Perhaps you are already a stained glass designer and want supplies. They are here too. Whether you're a beginner at or an aficionado of stained glass, Larry wants you to feel welcome in his store. Congenial, with an "I've got all the time in the world" demeanor, Larry spent 20 years in home remodeling before buying the studio in 1997. "I rebuilt the business to make a premier stained glass studio with a really nice classroom area," Larry says. "We make it easy on beginners. For the price of the class, we supply everything they need - all the tools, glass and supplies, plus great teachers - a comment I get constantly." Rose's Glassworks and Gifts is located near the Washington Square Mall at 10105 SW Hall Blvd., Portland, OR 97223. Call (503)246-9897. Visit the web site at www.rosesglassworks.com.

Let It Bead

Let it Bead is your full service bead store right in the heart of downtown Portland. Begun by Susan Landa, Let it Bead has become the "go to" place for all of your beading needs. Her great appreciation of gems, fossils, jewelry and unique items has led her around the world in search of rare and sometimes elusive treasures to share with her customers. The staff shares her passion and it shows in the broad scope of knowledge and friendly, engaging service you will receive. Even if you have yet to take up beading this is the place to come for classes, for restringing and for helpful answers to those trickiest of beading questions. Let it Bead, in conjunction with Susan's other store, The Fossil Cartel, provides very hard to find vintage glass, silver, pearls, semi-precious stones, and hand crafted beads. Take a look at the selection of incredible hand crafted artisan jewelry as well. This is an eye-catching store with a fusion of colors and textures that will inspire the creative jeweler in you. Susan and her crew are happy to help you with special requests, including custom orders and repair. Just let them know what you need and they'll help you make it happen. Let it Bead is located at 733 SW Alder in downtown Portland. You can reach them at (503) 228-1882.

Kitchen Kaboodle

For more than thirty years, the Pacific Northwest has looked to Kitchen Kaboodle for fun and functional products, fine cookware, cutlery, appliances, bakeware, dinnerware, glassware and every kitchen gadget you can think of, and some that might surprise you.

Plus, they have a huge selection of fine furniture for every room in your home; from dining tables and chairs to beds and dressers, to sofas, loveseats and recliners. There's even an extensive assortment of outdoor furniture with which to enjoy that Northwest sunshine!

Because Owners, John Whisler and Lynn Becraft are locals, they know the marketplace and sell products that address the tastes and concerns of people in this area. They delight in their selection of items, about which they say, "So, while we carry our share of just plain useful products, most include a unique twist." In addition to an abundance of merchandise, Kitchen Kaboodle hosts signings by the authors of top cookbooks, and product demonstrations that show the special features of the products they offer. Kitchen Kaboodle's outstanding success has led to their growth from one store to the current six locations in the Portland area. The original Kitchen Kaboodle store, which was recently expanded by fifty percent, is located in the Progress Square shopping center at 8788 SW Hall Boulevard. For locations of other stores, online shopping, and features such as "Gadget of the Month," visit their very informative website at www.kitchenkaboodle.com, where you can sign up for their newsletter and see how they live up to their motto, "Kitchen Kaboodle - we make your house a home!"

Reed&Cross

For a unique shopping experience, don't miss Eugene's elegant Reed&Cross. You'll find something for everyone on your list as well as special treats for yourself! Touted as "One of Oregon's Best Gift Stores" by the Oregonian newspaper, Reed&Cross can best be described as many boutiques all under one roof. For more than 50 years Reed&Cross has offered an eclectic mix of merchandise. You can browse for hours for that perfect gift or treat. Of Grape and Grain, the in-store cafe, is a popular spot to sit back, relax and catch up with friends. Reed&Cross is the largest florist in the area. Their award-winning design team creates every kind of bouquet imaginable including stunning flowers for your wedding or other special event. In addition to an array of fresh flowers, Reed&Cross offers indoor and outdoor plants, plus silks and dried flowers, and garden fountains and decor in The Gardens. A wonderful selection of women's clothing is available for all your informal and special occasions, including Oregon's own Pendleton. Need to accessorize that outfit? Absolutely don't miss their Brighton Shop with so many choices in handbags, jewelry, shoes and even beautiful luggage pieces. The Housewares department is a cook's dream! Gourmet cookware, dinnerware, wine accessories and of course, all the latest in kitchen gadgets. Gourmet foods and gift baskets round out the selection. From October through the end of the year, the Holiday Trim shop is a huge magical place that draws crowds from all over the state! Now if you're tired from all that shopping, unwind at Bello Day Spa and Salon. It's all about pampering yourself. All this and easy freeway access, too! Reed&Cross is located at 160 Oakway Road (where Oakway meets Coburg road). For more information, phone (541) 484-1244. You can also visit their website at www.ReedCross.com.

Hand Crafted for You

Hand Crafted for You, just 1 mile south of the End of the Oregon Trail Interpretive Center in Oregon City, was opened in 2003 by Sheri O'Brien as a means to display her work and the work of many talented and diverse artists from both the local community and around the country. Featuring unusual and high-quality handmade gifts, toys, decorations and crafts, the Store's items range anywhere in price from seventy-five cents to five hundred dollars. Their extensive collection of dollhouses and accessories is quite impressive, and they also carry clothes for the "American Girl" collectible doll series. The displays are always in flux as artists come and go. From stained glass to quilts, hand knit scarves to graphite fly rods, Hand Crafted for You is a sure bet when looking for that perfectly unique gift or treasure. Matilda, the shop cat, will be waiting to escort you in your quest. Hand Crafted for You is located at 1001 Main Street in Oregon City, Oregon 97045. You can reach them at (503) 656 3722 or visit their website at www.craftedforyou.net

Negstad's

One of the most delightful aspects of Western Oregon is the dedication of so many local people to their Scandinavian heritage. In Salem, Paul and Doreen Negstad have opened a store dedicated to providing high-quality Scandinavian gifts, housewares, toys, clothing, candles, stationery, calendars, and foodstuffs. If it's made in Scandinavia, chances are excellent that you'll find it at Negstad's. From well-known brands like iittala, Porsgrund, and Royal Copenhagen to hard-to-find specialty items such as books and videos in the various Scandinavian languages, Paul and Doreen have gone to great lengths to ensure that you won't leave Negstad's empty-handed. But there's more to Negstad's than shopping. There's the charming home setting that Paul and Doreen have created to display their wares. The cheery, peaceful feeling you get when shopping at Negstad's couldn't be more different from the hectic, draining experience of shopping at a mall. Christmas is a special time when all the charming Scandinavian traditions come to life at the store.

Tree ornaments and tomtes (adorable Swedish dolls), colorful mobiles, linens, Christmas plates and cards, and beautiful handcrafted wooden Nativity scenes add to the feeling expressed by many a customer that, "It just isn't Christmas without a visit to Negstad's." If you have a relative of Scandinavian descent, chances are they'd love one of the lovely tapes or CDs of Scandinavian music. Children love the wooden doll houses and trains from Brio, and many other quality toys. Gift wrapping is always provided free of charge. Negstad's is located at 3270 Liberty Road South in Salem, Oregon. You can reach them at (503) 362-9580. Their website is www.negstads.com.

Julia's Tea Parlour

In West Salem, you can dress up and step back in time quite properly, you know, in a Victorian setting located in the historic Harrit House. You can be a part of this activity Tuesdays through Saturdays at Julia's Tea Parlour, run by Ed and Kathleen Sheehan. There you'll have a choice of 50 (fifty!) different types of teas from such makers as Harney and Sons, Taylor, and Numi. In addition there are scones, sandwiches, quiche and a dessert plate. All of this is located in an 1848 house which is listed on the National Historic Register. The House is named after Julia and Jessie Harrit, who traveled from Kentucky west to Oregon along the Oregon Trail. Julia brought along her sweet teas. The House is the oldest home in Salem still on its original log cabin foundation. You can simply enjoy a pot of the tea of your choice, and perhaps add a scone with Devonshire cream and lemon, or quiche, or you can order various combinations. For example, the Cuppa Tea. It has tea, scones, Devonshire cream and lemon curd. Or perhaps you'd prefer the Full Afternoon Tea. This has tea, scones, fresh fruit, four tea sandwiches, the quiche of the day and dessert. If you have young ones with you, they will appreciate the Wee People's Tea. They can choose to have tea or hot cocoa, peanut butter and jelly and cheese tea sandwiches, fruit and dessert. After eating, visit the Gift Shop with its selection of teas, books, lace, linens, hats and home decor items. Julia's Tea Parlor is located at 2280 Wallace Road NW in Salem, Oregon 97304. (503) 378-7060. Reservations are highly recommended, so call for inquiries. For larger groups, remember the Parlour can accommodate groups of up to forty-five people.

Native American youth dances at a western Oregon pow wow

Christmas Treasures

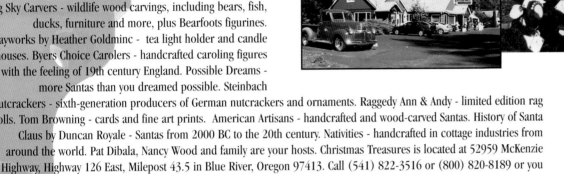

You're driving along McKenzie Highway near Blue River, Oregon in July and you wonder if your eyes deceive you. A Christmas shop, open in the summer? Yes indeed, Christmas Treasures is not only open during the holiday season, but throughout the entire year. This store is known for its great display of Christmas items. Everything from Santas, Nutcrackers, and lights, as well as what is said to be the tallest lighted living Christmas tree in Oregon and third tallest in the world. The tree is 154 feet tall and is festooned with 50,000 lights, which are kept on until midnight daily. Here is a sampling of the recent offerings at Christmas Treasures: Dept. 56 - Heritage Collection-Dickens, North Pole, New England, Alpine, Christmas in the City, Snow Villages and Snow Babies, Big Sky Carvers - wildlife wood carvings, including bears, fish, ducks, furniture and more, plus Bearfoots figurines. Clayworks by Heather Goldminc - tea light holder and candle houses. Byers Choice Carolers - handcrafted caroling figures with the feeling of 19th century England. Possible Dreams - more Santas than you dreamed possible. Steinbach Nutcrackers - sixth-generation producers of German nutcrackers and ornaments. Raggedy Ann & Andy - limited edition rag dolls. Tom Browning - cards and fine art prints. American Artisans - handcrafted and wood-carved Santas. History of Santa Claus by Duncan Royale - Santas from 2000 BC to the 20th century. Nativities - handcrafted in cottage industries from around the world. Pat Dibala, Nancy Wood and family are your hosts. Christmas Treasures is located at 52959 McKenzie Highway, Highway 126 East, Milepost 43.5 in Blue River, Oregon 97413. Call (541) 822-3516 or (800) 820-8189 or you can visit their fascinating website at www.christmas-treasures.com.

Quiltwork Patches

Quiltwork Patches is the store that sets the standard for an innovative shop with a wonderful selection of fabrics. This store in Corvallis is fun to visit, a place where you can revel in an abundance of color in a lovely, well organized space with high ceilings, ample room, and a technically dazzling display of original quilts for inspiration. The fabrics are arranged by color, and you walk through the full spectrum of the color wheel as you walk along their 3,200 bolts of fabric. Quiltwork Patches carries a lot of fabric types and styles: batiks, Japanese prints, florals, flannels, plaids, paisleys, stripes, 1930s reproductions, and much more. All are available in fat quarters. Quiltwork Patches provides quiltmakers from the local area and throughout the Pacific Northwest with extensive, knowledgeable help. From a busy schedule of basic and advanced classes to answering questions all day long, the staff continually teaches the principles of quilting on a one-to-one basis as the customers come in to find what they need for their individual projects. Their website at www.quiltworkpatches.com has a full list of the classes (22 of them when we checked), including topics like Easy Baby Quilts, Curved Piecing by Machine, a Quilting Mystery, Hand Quilting and Hand Appliqué, or making a "Raggy Jacket."

You can even design your own class if you and a group of friends all want to learn the same thing. The classes are kept small and are held during the day, evening, or weekend so that everyone who wants to can attend. Quiltwork Patches has the absolute highest quality of fabric and quilting supplies. Tools are an important part of their inventory and they scout for them all the time, then test the ones they stock. Finally, the staff can demonstrate and answer questions about all of them. Come in to this friendly, creative store at 212 SW 3rd Street in Corvallis. Call (541) 752-4820 and soon you can enjoy the quilts the staff makes up "in unexpected ways" to inspire their customers to try pattern variations of their own. At Quiltwork Patches you will be welcomed and inspired, and very glad you came.

Ralph's Pharmacy & Gifts

Ralph's began as a family-owned drugstore with a few gift items. Over the course of more than forty years in business, more and more gift items were added as the store became increasingly popular with the large group of Scandinavian-Americans living in the Junction City area. Now Ralph's, with the largest selection of Scandinavian-themed gifts and specialty foods in Lane County, is a popular stop for tourists and antique searchers, as well. Owners Orine and David Brunscheon have recently branched out, along an International theme, to include traditional German and Russian gifts, Delft china, and English bone china. As you might imagine, the Christmas season is an especially popular time to shop at Ralph's. Refreshments are served Friday and Saturday in November and December, and people love the traditional Swedish Dala horses, imported nutcrackers, candle arrangements, Santa Claus figurines, and ornaments. Beautiful scarves and sweaters from Russia, Norway, and Sweden help ward off the winter chill in style and Danish cookies are a perfect treat on Christmas Eve. If you're feeling ambitious, you can buy a kransekake form and make a traditional Norwegian almond wreath cake. And that's just a small sample of the wonderful gifts available! Another fun time to visit is August, when the Scandinavian Festival is held, a tradition dating back to 1961. Ralph's is a major presence – be sure to visit their Festival booth in front of the Junction City Post Office. People come to Ralph's all-year round to enjoy the hospitality and pick up their favorite foods. Swedish coffee and lingonberry preserves, chocolates from Norway and Sweden, Finnish cookies and mints, lefse (traditional Norwegian bread), Danish aebleskivers – if you're from a Scandinavian family, you already know how wonderful these are, and if you're not, now is the time to find out! If there's a favorite dish you can't find, just ask – special orders are no problem. Ralph's is located at 665 Ivy Street, just off Highway 99. You can call (541) 998-6780 or visit the website, www.ralphsrxgifts.com for more information.

Amish Workbench Furniture

Aurora, Oregon, might not seem like the most likely place to find beautiful, durable, handcrafted Amish furniture, but in Oregon, you have to expect the unexpected. The founders of Amish Workbench Furniture, Jay and Carol Titsworth, came to Oregon from Pennsylvania, where they developed a deep love and respect for the Amish and their ways. When they decided to set up their own business, it was only natural that their thoughts turned to Amish crafts and furniture, not widely available in the Pacific Northwest. Jay and Carol's motto is "Simply the best … Not the most expensive." If you were surprised to come across their store, you'll be even more pleasantly surprised to discover that their commitment to quality is matched by their commitment to providing fair prices to their customers. The inviting nature of the store will impress you the minute you walk inside. It's more than just a showroom for furniture. Jay and Carol also sell juried handcrafts, including handmade quilts, many made with traditional and stunningly beautiful 19th-century designs. Any of these quilts would make a perfect complement to the elegant beds available, such as the Spindle Shaker, all of them made in four different sizes. Dining room tables come in different sizes as well, ensuring that you can find one to meet the needs of your home space. All of the furniture at Amish Workbench is handcrafted by Amish artisans in Indiana, using only real woods. No particle board, Masonite, or laminate is ever used. Kiln-drying methods, superior to chemical treatments, ensure a more stable grain in the red oak and cherrywoods, and all furniture is coated with a specially formulated varnish that is amazingly damage-resistant. The Amish Workbench Furniture store in Aurora has proven so successful that Jay and Carol have opened a branch store in Salem. The Aurora store is located at 14936 Third Street N.E.; the Salem store is located in the historic Reed Opera House. For more information, call toll-free (866) 678-7799, or visit the Web site, www.amishwbf.com.

Parson's Canby Pharmacy

It wasn't too long ago that a family owned pharmacy was the standard and a chain pharmacy was the exception. These days it is hard to come by a quality family pharmacy, so while in Canby be sure to take a moment to visit Parson's Canby Pharmacy in its expansive 15,000 square foot store. Since 1954, the friendly, professional and knowledgeable staff have been serving area residents. Parson's is a full service general store and carries an abundance of gift choices and card selections including Hallmark Gold Crown cards and collectibles. As a Dept. 56 Gold Key Showcase dealer you will find special Dept. 56 items you aren't likely to find in any other store near you. It is more than just a full service pharmacy, it is also the place to get your photo finishing completed and to ship out gifts from their UPS Shipping site. Check out their Fenton Glassware showcase and Peggy Karr Glassware displays. A nice selection of Vera Bradley Handbags and Zoppini Charm bracelets, decorator lamps and accessories round out their broad selection. You will find Parsons on the corner of 2nd and Grant in downtown Canby. You can reach them at (503) 266-2233.

Greenbaum's Quilted Forest

When you visit Greenbaum's Quilted Forest, a fourth generation business, you will be inspired to take up quilting. This shop is filled with a gallery of beautiful hand-made quilts and all the supplies you'll ever need to make your own. Founder, Isador Greenbaum, started the store in downtown Salem selling dry goods in 1900. Now granddaughter, Sylvia Dorney carries on the tradition by selling high quality fabric and supplies for quilting. "Quilting is part of our heritage, enrichment, and fulfillment. We quilt, we love what we do, and we want to share it with you," said Sylvia. With an action-packed class schedule and a colorful shop it's no wonder why Greenbaum's Quilted Forest was recently featured as a U.S. Top 10 Quilt Shop by Quilt Sampler Magazine, a special publication by Better Homes and Gardens. Classes are targeted for beginners to advanced quilters with an emphasis on a "you can do no wrong" attitude. The relaxed and playful approach to each class caused a recent student to comment, "Everyone was very helpful to me as a beginning quilter. Informative without being pushy and willing to cut fabrics in any amount to fit my needs." Teachers strive to keep the classes innovative and one step ahead of the competition. From the basics of log cabin, to free form and artistic, Greenbaum's Quilted Forest will have you cutting and stitching in no time. You can make a quilt of any size, a frilly Victorian lampshade or a beaded bag. There are even classes to get the next generation of quilters started like the Quilt Camp for Kids. It's the highlight of every summer. Greenbaum's Quilted Forest is the oldest family owned business in Salem still in its original location. Stop by at 240 Commercial St., in NE, Salem, Oregon 97301. Call (503) 363-7973, or (877) 700-2233. Visit their website at www.quiltedforest.com for the latest fabrics, kits, locally designed patterns and the shop newsletter.

Holly & Ivy, Ltd

When in search of the perfect Christmas tree ornament or gift, look no further than Holly and Ivy Gifts, in Oregon City, Oregon. Operating out of the historic 1867 Fellows house, built by Ship Builder and Engineer, E.B. Fellows, since 1999, Owners, Shirley Smith and Diane Petrasso have decorated every available nook and cranny with ornaments from top brands including Old World Christmas, Fitz and Floyd, and Dept., 56. Heartwood Creek by Jim Shore. Perhaps even more famous than their ornament collection is their upside-down Christmas tree. Raised to the ceiling but supported from the floor these trees are made to look as if they were hanging from the ceiling. The combination of uniqueness, elegance, and space saving practicality make these trees a wildly popular item. During the summer months, relax on the patio with a cup of tea, as you tour the yard display, and then in the winter months, enjoy cookies and spiced cider. In addition to the 35 to 40 decorated trees, they carry wind chimes, wall sconces, candleholders, lanterns and numerous garden and patio items. So, whether you are gearing up to deck your halls with fantastic new ornaments or just want a dose of the holiday spirit during the off-season, visit Holly and Ivy Gifts where it's Christmas all year long. Open seasonally July 1st thru January 5th. During off season they will open by appointment only for small or large groups. Holly and Ivy Gifts, 416 S McLoughlin Blvd. in Oregon City, Oregon 97405. Call (503) 723-5511 or visit their website at www.hollyandivygifts.com.

OSU Bookstore Beaver Fan Shop

For a large variety of Beaver memorabilia for men, women, children and infants, come to the Oregon State University Bookstore's Beaver Fan Shop in the heart of downtown Portland. Located in the Bank of America Building, this store brings the presence of the OSU campus to Oregon's largest city and makes it easy to keep up the ties to the Corvallis campus for alumni and fans of the OSU Beavers. Open since 1994, the Portland Store is a branch of the OSU bookstore that has been serving Oregon State University students and friends since 1914. Over the years the campus bookstore, now one of the largest bookstores in the area, has changed from a cooperative to a diversified non-profit with more than 140 employees, OSU Bookstore, Inc. Now offering computer equipment and best sellers, and hosting book signings, the Store serves both OSU students and Corvallis residents. The Beaver Fan Shop has given OSU a presence in the Portland metropolitan area. For students, alumni, friends of the University and Beaver sports fans, the OSU Bookstore in Portland or Corvallis is a wonderful source. For over ninety years the Bookstore has been serving the needs of OSU students, faculty and friends in Corvallis, and now in Portland as well. The Corvallis Bookstore is located in the Memorial Union Building on the OSU Campus. The Portland Store is located at 121 SW Morrison Street, Suite 120 on the corner of SW 2nd and Alder. For more information, visit the website, www.osubookstore.com or call (503) 525-2678.

Lafayette Schoolhouse Antique Mall

With owls in the belfry and ghosts among the antiques, the antique dealers who call the Lafayette Schoolhouse their address greatly enjoy their vintage setting. What started as a schoolhouse in the early 1900s is now the largest antique mall in Oregon, and it hasn't lost an iota of its attraction or historical interest. Nestled in Oregon's wine country, the town of Lafayette is full of history. The three-story, 1912 schoolhouse is now filled with the wares of more than 100 antique dealers. The adjacent gymnasium (built in 1933 as a WPA project) houses displays of antique oak, pine and mahogany furniture. This treasure trove of the rare and collectable is the destination of serious antique hunters, as well as a source of great enjoyment for the casual tourist visiting the wine country. And the tales of ghosts just add a layer of intrigue to the mix. Stories seem to have started with a gypsy curse, and even recently, on a calm day with few visitors, the staff was taken aback when the glass doors on a display case were suddenly opened and slammed shut by an invisible hand. And occasionally the dealers also see an owl, one of the denizens of the belfry, silently flying through on mysterious business of its own. Manager, Cricket Propp, is assisted by Vicki Johnson. The Lafayette Schoolhouse Antique Mall is open seven days a week from 10am to 5pm (except on Christmas, Thanksgiving, and Easter). Also open on weekends in the upstairs is the Winter Hills Winery, which offers wine tasting right in the Schoolhouse. You can go to www.myantiquemall.com/lafayette for more information, or call (503) 864-2720, or e-mail them at lafsh@onlinemac.com.

Hazelnuts, an Oregon Favorite

Umpqua Indian Foods

It's not often that the words "moist" and "tender" come to mind when biting into a piece of jerky. Indian Beef Jerky created by Umpqua Indian Foods, has found global appeal as far away as the United Kingdom. Made in the Native American tradition, UIF's Indian Beef Jerky is made in Oregon from only the finest USDA Choice beef. Unlike most jerkies which are made from less expensive steak that is smoked, UIF uses pectoral cuts which are hand trimmed and air dried. Spices, water and cure are used for the marinade which, of course, is mixed by hand. Finally, the jerky is vacuum sealed to lock in the freshness and deliciously unique flavors for which their jerky is famous. But it doesn't stop there. Beef sticks and salamis are additional specialties of Umpqua Indian Foods. "Umpqua Indian Foods' products are wonderful because of the excellent quality of meat and spices used and the time taken in production. It's the best because it tastes the best. It's that simple," says Sue Shaffer, Chairwoman of the Cow Creek Band of Umpqua Tribe of Indians. Also packaged under the Umpqua Indian Foods label is a delectable selection of jams, sauces and other gourmet delights. With the commitment, vision and community involvement of people like Shaffer, Umpqua Indian Foods became part of the Umpqua Indian Development Corporation in 1999. Located in historic Canyonville, the company's recent expansion required a relocation of their storefront to 315 Main Street, right across the road from their production plant. The quaint shop fitted out with traditional artwork made by local artisans, also sells a wide variety of Native American, Oregon made and Pacific Northwest food products. Unique gift baskets are also custom made for any occasion and, along with their gourmet meats, are available online at www.indian-beef-jerky.com.

Just Bears and Stuff

There's something about a Teddy Bear that just makes you feel good inside and this full-service gift and collectible store has one of the largest selections in the nation. After enjoying the beautiful drive to rural Myrtle Creek you'll find all of your favorite designers in this truly unique shop. There are Steiffs, Deb Canhams, Boyds, Ganz Cottage by Lorraine Chien, World of Miniatures and much, much more. Owner Patricia Twitchell's lifelong passion has been to pass on the comfort and joy she gets from Teddy Bears. Her dedication has been featured in the books, Workplace Miracles, Inspiring Stories and Thoughts of Possibility. You're sure to find that perfect gift at Just Bears & Stuff. Who knows? You may even leave with a gift for yourself. Just Bears & Stuff is located at 113 S. Main Street in Myrtle Creek, Oregon, or you can call Patricia at (541) 863-6037 or check the website at www.justbearsandstuff.com.

Savannah Faire

If you are looking for fine examples of quality handmade crafts, chances are you'll find them at Savannah Faire Crafters' Outlet & Gift Shoppe in Grants Pass, Oregon. Since 1994, the Chapman family has owned and operated this bazaar, turning it over to daughter-in-law Mandy and their son Cole in 2001. Savannah Faire hosts over 100 local crafters and artisans, many of whom have been there for 11 years, each with unique handmade or embellished items. Savannah Faire also offers fine gifts, gourmet foods and sweets. With a huge selection of reasonably priced quality craft items, Savannah Faire has been voted "Favorite Store Downtown" and "Favorite Gift Shop" for the last five years. Savannah Faire is open seven days a week. Be sure to check them out when you're in Grants Pass. Savannah Faire Crafters' Outlet and Gift Shoppe is located at 311 SE 6th Street in Grants Pass, Oregon. You can reach them by calling (541) 479-4808.

Northwest Nature Shop

The Northwest Nature Shop in Ashland, Oregon is one of those rare places where you can find unique gifts for others, but inevitably will want to keep them for yourself. Items from and about nature abound in this one-of-a-kind store. Northwest Nature Shop is filled with a wide variety of books, cards, games, clothing, rock hounding items, and a huge collection of educational toys. Northwest Nature Shop also has one of the largest map selections of this area from the U.S.G.S. and the U.S. Forest Service. The staff is always ready to suggest special gift ideas, help you find the perfect item to complement your collection, or help you to improve the ability of your yard to attract birds. If you're at all interested in the natural world around you, this shop has enough to keep you intrigued for hours. Stop by 154 Oak Street, just off of Hwy 99, in Ashland, Oregon to see how exciting the natural world can be. You can visit their fascinating website at www.northwestnatureshop.com. or phone them at (541) 482-3241.

Allyson's Of Ashland

Gourmet Welcome. If you believe the kitchen is the heart of your home, you'll feel right at home at Allyson's, in the heart of downtown Ashland. First, stroll through a myriad of high-quality utensils from a precision grater to a state-of-the-art toaster -- items you won't see in any other retail store in America. If you're looking for the perfect gift or if every meal you prepare is the gift to yourself and your family, you'll find everything you need in this amazing shop. Once you enter Allyson's it won't be long before mouth-watering aromas inevitably draw you downstairs where the deli offers a frequently updated lunch menu and hard-to-find foods from around the world. At frequently scheduled wine tastings, you can sample from over 2500 wine labels and an assortment of delicious cheeses. For a satisfying lunch, try the scrumptious King Lear sandwiches, made with Prosciutto, fresh arugula, mayonnaise and a drizzle of truffle oil on a ciabatta roll. One of several freshly-made salads melds meaty seared Portobello mushrooms with a garlic-soy vinagrette on succulent mixed greens with garden vegetables. While you're settling in, get your name on a list for one of many cooking classes offered to expand your skills in your favorite cuisine. They're the talk of Southern Oregon , so be sure to sign up early. Allyson and her husband were newly engaged when they first visited Ashland. They fell in love with the area, quit their "city" jobs, and brought their expertise along with the finest of gourmet specialties to Oregon. Come and see how they've created their own little slice of heaven right here in Southern Oregon. 115 East Main Street, Ashland, OR 97520 (541) 482-2884, www.allysonofashland.com.

Pico's Worldwide

Walk through the doors of Pico's Worldwide in downtown historic Jacksonville, Oregon and you will be greeted by Pico the bearded collie, Store Proprietor and Mascot. He is just one of the many fantastic finds you will be pleased to discover at this unique shop, established in 2004 by Bethany Mulholland and Michael Richardson. Pico's is your Southern Oregon source for hemp, organic cotton, recycled cotton and other eco-friendly clothing, as well as a large selection of other environmentally and socially responsible products-both imported and domestic. Shop Pico's for a full complement of home accents and personal accessories such as jewelry, handbags, scarves, genuine Panama hats, soap, soy candles, weavings, lamps, wall decorations, world music and a wide variety of other fun and functional products. When you're in Jacksonville, remember to leave plenty of time to visit Pico's Worldwide. You will need it to peruse all of the interesting items that'll tickle your fancy! Pico's Worldwide has two locations. The first is at 160 E. California Street and the other is located at 165 E. California Street in Jacksonville. For inquiries, dial (541) 899-4400.

The Web•Sters Inc

If you're looking for high quality, one-of-a-kind articles of clothing, look no further than The Web•Sters in historic Ashland. Since 1984, Owner, Dona Zimmerman has been producing and selling her own top-quality wool. The progression from raising her own flock of Romney sheep, a breed from the Romney Marshes of England, to opening up Web•Sters was natural for Zimmerman. As a result, her store has become a destination for even the most serious knitters, weavers and hand-spinners. In addition to specializing in natural fiber, hand-made clothing, she also offers knitting, weaving and spinning workshops. Web•Sters also carries hats, handbags, and a wide assortment of knitting, spinning and weaving tools, books and materials. When in Ashland, visiting Web•Sters is a must. Web•Sters is located at 11 North Main Street in Ashland, Oregon 97520. Call Dona and her knowledgeable staff at (541) 482-9801 or visit their website at www.yarnatwebsters.com.

Rising Suns

Rising Suns in Cave Junction, sells local and west coast Oregon art, candles, jewelry and paintings. Realizing the lack of available jobs, Owner and Founder, Todd Johan, moved to Oregon from Southern California, originally opening Rising Suns in Selma, Oregon and then moving to Cave Junction. Since 1999, Todd and his mother, Audrey Moore, have featured works-of-art including hand-made silk scarves in a gorgeous array of colors, quality water color paintings, hand-crafted glass earrings and necklaces, Raku rattles, and spirit horses. Rotating their merchandise monthly ensures that their customers are

exposed to the latest in local art. Rising Suns is sure to carry that unique gift you've been searching for. Rising Suns is located at 146 S. Redwood Highway in Cave Junction, Oregon 97523. To speak with Todd or Audrey, call (541) 592-2430 or visit their website at www.gifts4you.com.

Rare Earth

Rare Earth is filled with rare treasures! This store on the Plaza in Ashland, is an Aladdin's Cave of the unusual, fun and marvelous. Rare Earth is where you will find thousands of small treasures, including great imports you won't find anywhere else. Store Manager, Jim Carney, describes it as "gifts galore," but you're bound to find plenty you won't want to part with. As Ashland's premier gift shop, Rare Earth offers an eclectic mixture of merchandise, something for everyone – jewelry, incense, candles and holders, home décor, tapestries and rugs, toys, kitchen equipment, quality bath products, including brands like Terranova Toiletries and Burt's Bees. Rare Earth's selection of clothing for young people is especially notable. This is where you find clothing and shoes when you want something positively unique. But what Rare Earth is most known for is its large selection of goods that are made in other corners of the world. New items arrive continually. They can ship non-breakable items for you, and the helpful staff is friendly and welcoming. Come in to see for yourself why this Store is a very popular, favorite with the locals. Rare Earth is located at 33 North Main, right on the Plaza, in the heart of Ashland. To learn more, you can phone them at (541) 482-9501.

Scheffel's Toys

Scheffel's Toys Inc., is a small specialty toy store, oriented toward one-on-one customer service. As befits a store that welcomes families, Scheffel's is family-owned and operated by Bill & Linda Graham, who have dedicated themselves to furnishing customers with the highest quality toys and collectibles available, at very affordable prices, for the young and young at heart. In its picturesque setting in the historic village of Jacksonville, the Store, with its whimsical window displays, almost seems like a vision of the small-town toy stores of yesteryear. Linda's parents, Jim and Judie Scheffel, opened the store in 1983. Originally the focus was on antiques, but Jim and Judie began to focus on toys out of frustration at being unable to find high-quality toys for their grandchildren. After visiting the original FAO Schwartz store in Manhattan, they were spurred to recreate that experience in their own store. In 1986, they decided to dedicate the store entirely to toys, and in 1992 Bill and Linda took over the store and have been running it happily ever since. Scheffel's doesn't do trendy – it does good! The toys here are unique items from respected manufacturers such as Playmobil. They sell well because of their quality rather than television hype. Bill and Linda's vast product knowledge ensures that customers can find what they're looking for, whether it be a beautifully hand-crafted historical figurine, an authentic die cast plane, or an LGB Garden Railway Set (Scheffel's is the only LGB dealer in Southern Oregon). There are toys for toddlers, books, games, dolls, and science and craft kits. Scheffel's offers international shipping and free gift wrapping. Customer satisfaction is the number one priority here. Small wonder that some of Bill and Linda's customers have told them that the store represents "what a toy store SHOULD be." Scheffel's Toys is located at 180 West California Street in downtown Jacksonville. For more information, call (541) 899-7421, or visit their website at, www.scheffels.com.

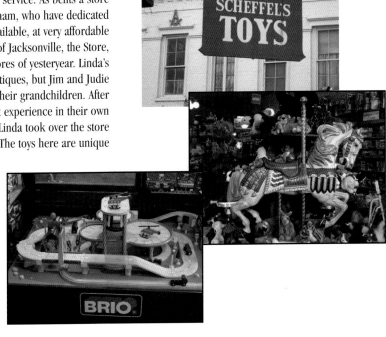

Ashland Mountain Supply

You can rely on Ashland Mountain Supply to take the mystery out of outdoor gear. Their motto is "Keeping the Fun in the Outdoor Experience," and they mean it. They provide quality gear at affordable prices, "value-oriented, not price-oriented." The shop inventory at Ashland Mountain Supply changes as the seasons change, and the staff's knowledgeable service is one of the Store's biggest assets. From rafting gear to everything you need for fly fishing, hiking, or any other open-air activity, they have it. Owner, Bill Gilliam, and his wife, Bea, have extensive familiarity with the outdoors and the local area in Southern Oregon. Sharing their knowledge with customers is their pleasure as well as their life's work. Bill came to his love of the outdoors as a young child through growing up in a family that appreciated the wonders of nature. The continuing love of nature is evident when you meet the Gillams and their friendly staff. Since 1983, Ashland Mountain Supply has been located at 31 North Main Street on the Plaza in Ashland. Whether you're looking for skis, custom-fitted boots, backpacks, tents, or top-notch hiking boots, come in to Ashland Mountain Supply to find the perfect item to suit your needs. You can also reach the Gillams at (541) 488-5402.

The Furniture Depot

The Furniture Depot, located in Ashland's historic railroad district, is an ideal place to find a wide selection of furniture, lighting, and home décor items. Owners Loren and Sheryl Clear carefully select their merchandise from small North American manufacturers, with styles that combine harmoniously to create a contemporary feel. Loren, a cabinetmaker and furniture builder before being drawn to retail sales, and Sheryl, with her background in art and business, have developed a store unique in the retail furniture business. Assisting customers with furniture selection and interior designs since 1994, the pair's passion for creating individualized home interiors has earned them a reputation for consistently providing high quality, personalized customer service with stylish, top quality products. Whatever your style, the Furniture Depot's unique selection and spacious showroom will delight your senses and please your taste for beautiful yet functional furniture. The Furniture Depot is located at 498 Oak St., Ashland, OR 97520. Call: (541) 482-9663 or visit them on the web at www.furnituredepot.com.

Yanase Jewelers

Opened in 1989 by Michael and Karen Yanase, Yanase Jewelers in Kerby, Oregon is a terrific place to find reasonably priced custom-made jewelry. With over thirty years of jewelry-making experience, Michael and Karen, experienced gemologists, cast and create unique pendants, earrings and rings using a variety of stones including Mexican fire opal, differently colored sapphires, amber and garnets. Many people assume that a piece of custom jewelry will be out of their league, but by eliminating the middle man and dealing directly with the Goldsmith rather than a jewelry store you save money and have something truly unique. Their work in recreating a piece of jewelry from an existing piece is always artistically done, and their express service is greatly appreciated by customers. In addition, they carry a selection of jewelry by several local artists. Their greatest pleasure is a satisfied customer so next time you're in Kerby, stop by Yanase Jewelers, a true gem of a place. Yanase Jewelers, 23772 Redwood Hwy., Kerby, OR 97531. Phone: (541) 592-4838 or visit them on the web at: www.yanasejewelers.com.

Cripple Creek Music Co.

Ashland, Oregon is home to Cripple Creek Music Company. Visit Southern Oregon's unique and unusual music store, featuring hundreds of musical instruments from all over the world. Since 1976, Cripple Creek Music Company has provided beginner to professional musicians with all their musical needs. They have a diverse stock of instruments and instrumental accessories. There's a dazzling variety of guitars, Celtic harps, mountain and hammered dulcimers, mandolins, violins, saxophones, and exotic instruments like the sitar. All the staff members from the owner to the repair technicians are musicians. If you are looking to buy a vintage banjo, a new hand-made guitar, or get your tuba repaired, this is the place you'll find professional service. Repairs are done in the store and our technicians are available to set up or repair woodwinds, brass, and stringed instruments. It's easy to get started musically with Cripple Creek Music's Band and Orchestra "Easy Play Rent to Own Program." If you want to play music, the musicians here want to help you. Cripple Creek Music Company also offers a huge variety of print music and musical gifts. From traditional to New Age, whatever your taste in acoustic music; Bluegrass, Folk, Jazz, Latin, World, or Ethnic; Cripple Creek Music will start you on the right note! Cripple Creek Music Company is a family business built on the traditions of quality service, knowledge, and integrity. Cripple Creek Music Company is located at 353 E. Main Street in downtown Ashland. Call (541) 482-9141 or go to their website www.cripplecreekmusic.com Visit Cripple Creek and experience the sights and sounds of music.

Inti Imports

Inti Imports Marketplace carries distinctive clothing, jewelry and gifts. Inti specializes in comfortable, fluid clothing for young and old. They are the exclusive venue for the "Manta" line of great clothing. It moves the way you move, it flows, it stretches. It dances in a joyful celebration of color, texture and form. Experience this clothing which is eco-conscious, natural and made of pre-shrunk cotton. It's wonderfully suited for retreats, travel, yoga, massage, T'ai Chi and just plain everyday relaxing. Inti also carries jewelry featuring rings, necklaces and semi-precious stones that are designed to complement the "Manta" clothing line. Also available; are Giclee prints by award winning multi-cultural Artist, Betty LaDuke, African masks and artifacts, and Batik jackets and sarongs from Bali. Percussion instruments from around the world are featured in the "Rhythm Section." You'll find everything from maracas, shakers, claves, didgeridoos and so much more. Owned by Catherine and Sean Van Ausdall, Inti Imports Marketplace has been located at 45 N. Main Street in Ashland since 1995. Visit their website at www.yogaclothes.com or call (541) 488-2714 for further information.

Maizy's Bath, Body & Home

Owner, Sharon Fleck, prides herself on carrying the best fine linen selection in Southern Oregon at Maizey's Bath, Body & Home. Linen name brands to choose from include; Bella Notte, Peacock Alley, Pine Cone Hill, Dea Dans Nos Maison fine linens and more. There is a large display of Couleur Nature table linens. Bath and body products include special treats from Fresh. Also featured are Vera Bradley handbags, Palm Press greeting cards and Connie Brooks jewelry. Casafina stoneware is in abundance. There is a selection of unique furniture, lamps and rugs from a variety of manufacturers. Men's luggage from Baekgaard is among the merchandise to browse. Bamboo vases and decorative items round out the eclectic merchandise from which you may choose. You are sure to find a unique treasure among the many possibilities that have been personally chosen by Sharon. Established in 1996, Maizey's is located at 90 N. Pioneer in Ashland. For further information check their website at www.maizey's.com or call (541) 482-6771.

Quiltz

The focus of Quiltz is getting their customers hooked on the enjoyment of quilting. Besides having fun, clients can create a custom product to treasure or give as a hand crafted gift. Owner, Debra Barth, and Manager, Sharon Cervantes, provide Quiltz devotees with a large selection of quilting fabrics, notions, patterns, books and Husqvarna-Viking sewing machines. Debra and Sharon are more than business partners, they are sisters who share the love of quilting. Quilting classes for all levels are conducted throughout the year. Examples of the art of quilting are on display throughout the store and serve as inspiration for what is possible. Quiltz is located at 1666 Ashland St. in Ashland, Oregon. For further information about the store or to inquire about one of their enlightening classes, call (541) 488-1650.

Soundpeace

A special place in Ashland since 1986, Soundpeace offers books, music and gifts for self-discovery, celebration and exploration. Soundpeace is often described as a New Age store, but Owners, Steve Cole and Stephanie Cook, like to think of it as a place focused on spirituality and personal growth. The hand-picked inventory reflects their personal taste and knowledge of their customer's preferences. Unique greeting cards are available and many are handmade. The jewelry selection is another customer favorite. There is a large variety of compact discs ranging from calming and relaxing to upbeat and danceable. At Soundpeace all CDs can be previewed before purchase. Most of the staff members have worked at Soundpeace for many years and are often asked, "Are you the owner?" Regular customers come from around the world and say they just can't come to Ashland without visiting Soundpeace's calming, peaceful, relaxing atmosphere. Soundpeace is located at 199 E. Main Street in Ashland. You may find out more about them by accessing www.soundpeace.com or by calling (541) 482-3633.

Studio K of Jacksonville

Since 2004, Studio K of Jacksonville has been a haven for those seeking the latest and greatest in home and garden products. Owner, Kirsten Neale, a native of Copenhagen, Denmark, draws on a lifetime of experience apprenticing in the home and garden shops of Copenhagen to bring together a delightful collection of furniture, gifts, art, and other home décor products. With a constantly changing product line influenced by seasonal changes, Studio K features gifts from Tea Forte, Department 56, Global Views, Austin and many more. Furniture items include armoires, chests, trunks, tables, benches and chairs, some hand-painted by Neale. Visit the outdoor garden to find a special assortment of fountains, urns and garden furniture, a majority done in the European style. Situated in the Milo Caton Building, built in 1902, Studio K provides a feast for even the most ravenous home and garden collector. Studio K of Jacksonville is located at 135 S. Third Street in Jacksonville, Oregon 97530. You can also contact them at (541) 899-5712.

Bloomsbury Books

For twenty-five years, Karen Chapman and Sheila Burns have shared their love for reading with visitors to Bloomsbury Books in Ashland, Oregon. This independent, locally-owned store takes pride in its breadth of selection (including an excellent children's section and periodicals selection) and its friendly customer service. The staff of former (and practicing) writers, artists, actors and teachers are always eager to share their recommendations, from the latest page-turner to a forgotten classic or a just-published provocative political analysis. The large, comfortable store, open until 10pm, hosts weekly author signings and poetry readings in its lively upstairs coffeehouse. It is a Southern Oregon institution and a community gathering place for readers of all ages. Bloomsbury Books is located at 290 E. Main Street in Ashland, Oregon 97520. To learn more about this true Oregon Treasure, call (541) 488-0029.

Looking Glass Beads & Jewelry

Owner, Mary Moore, began her bead business in 1990 and has established a fine reputation for having an especially large selection of beads from around the world. Mary personally chooses her unique and diverse merchandise. The variety is pleasantly mind boggling! You will find custom fine jewelry, high quality gemstones, antique, and collector beads. Among the gemstones you may select from pearls, rubies, sapphires, emeralds and more. Also available are beautiful embellishments for clothing. The Store provides excellent customer service and will try to provide you with information on any questions you may have about beads and jewelry making.

Looking Glass Beads holds regularly scheduled beading classes. They will teach you how to make your own unique gifts. You can learn the origin and history of the many beads on display. Their staff will also repair your beaded jewelry. If you are looking for a special hand-crafted item that you can't find on display, they will custom make it for you. Looking Glass Beads and Jewelry is located at 283 E. Main Street in Ashland, Oregon 97520. They may be reached at (541) 482-7000. You can also visit their interesting website at www.LookingGlassBeads.com.

Wild Seahorse Swimwear

If it's a cold day in Medford, Oregon, hey -- it's a warm day in Bermuda, right? And you can get there from here in just a few minutes! Well, figuratively speaking anyway. What you really can do is stop in at Wild Seahorse Swimwear on Biddle Road and step into one of the "mood" dressing rooms. With names like Bermuda, Aruba, Jamaica, Bahama, or Key Largo, they'll all inspire you to find the perfect outfit. No matter what your figure, Wild Seahorse has a suit for you. The selection comprises over 10,000 suits. That's right, ten thousand! This amounts to an infinite variety of styles and sizes for people of all ages. If you want a two-piece suit, you can buy the top and bottom separately, for a custom fit. The Store opened in 2001, after Owners, Vicki and John Hardey wanted suits for a winter trip to warmer climates but found that most stores stock swimwear only during the summer. They opened their store with 1,000 suits but customer demand has caused expansion to the present capacity of over 10,000. There is an extensive variety of Hawaiian shirts for men, too. And the Wild Seahorse is open year-round, not just during the summer. It is offered in a venue where Vicki provides the kind of customer service and assistance not seen since the days of June Cleaver. Says Vicki, "Owning the Store is like having a third child to nurture and enjoy." So, "See ya in Bermuda!" on a journey starting in Medford. Wild Seahorse Swimwear is located at 1390 Biddle Road in Medford, Oregon 97504. For more information, call (541) 772-7946.

Tobiano

Tobiano is an inviting clothing boutique which features European contemporary fashions. The clothes range from casual to elegant and all are personally selected by Owner, Donis Rothstein. You will find fashions not found anywhere else at Tobiano's. Donis travels widely to seek out special fashions for her store and customers. She often visits Paris to guide her in her next fashion selections and direction. If you wish, Donis will provide personal assistance. Tobiano originated in 1992 and is located in beautiful and historic Jacksonville at 120 S. Third Street. For further information, call this remarkable clothing boutique at (541) 899-7205.

Taylor's Sausage

Since 1924, sausage making has been a Taylor family tradition. After emigrating from Europe, Great Grandpa Taylor settled in Santa Monica, California selling sausages made from his secret recipes. Starting in 1932, his son and apprentice, Grandpa Taylor, went on to sell the sausages at the world famous Farmer's Market in Hollywood. Following WWII, he moved to San Francisco and opened a store, with the addition of two other sausage kitchens in Oakland and Hayward across the Bay. For ten years third generation sausage maker Charles Taylor worked at the Oakland store, finally leaving the big city in 1970 for the Illinois River Valley in Josephine County, Oregon where he opened up Taylor's Sausage. The store is still a family operation and a labor of love. A landmark in Cave Junction, Taylor's sells their handmade sausages, as well as an assortment of meats, fine wines, cheeses, pickled items and gifts. Using the finest meats, natural spices, natural casings, natural smoking hardwoods and a minimum of preservatives for their sausages, Taylor's has a devoted following. Not only are people attracted by their delicious food but also by Taylor's live music, catering, ten different micro beers, community events and open microphone nights. Taylor's is a must-go the next time you're in Cave Junction. You'll find Taylor's Sausage at 202 S. Redwood Highway in Cave Junction, Oregon 97523. You can call them at (541) 592-5358 or visit their website at www.taylorsausage.com.

Nimbus

Ken Silverman, Owner of Nimbus, has collaborated with Carol Brookins to create a fascinating hybrid that's both a craft gallery and an upscale contemporary clothing store. In business since 1971, Nimbus features the best work of contemporary American craftspeople in blown glass, ceramics, handmade jewelry, and woodworking, plus a complete line of men and women's clothing, with an emphasis on the unusual and hard to find. Ken personally selects the items in the men's department and Gallery. Carol oversees the women's department and the shoe selection. Gallery selections are continually changing and the clothing selections are updated frequently. This reflects not only Ken and Carol's personal tastes but the requests of the many longtime customers who've come to depend on Nimbus for items they can't find anywhere else. Nimbus is located at 25 East Main Street right on the Plaza in Ashland, Oregon. For more information, call (541) 482-3621.

Legends Furniture

Have you ever dreamed of owning the kind of furniture you see in art museums or historic houses? Legends Furniture is the place where your dreams will come true. Dale and Chris Porter, and their son Ryan, have created a furniture store that will take your breath away. Handcrafted reproductions of the most elegant antiques, from Chippendale chairs to Queen Anne-style beds to Empire sofas abound. Rich mahogany and teakwood, farmed from renewable plantations, are used to create armoires, highboys, dressers, and much more. You might think craftsmanship like this would cost a fortune, but the prices at Legends are just as amazing as the furniture. Dale and Chris moved to the Rogue Valley from Kona, Hawaii, after visiting their son Paul at Southern Oregon University in Ashland and falling in love with the area. Though retired, Dale and Chris wanted to find something to do that would enable them to combine their love of fine furniture with their love of helping people fulfill their dreams. When Dale discovered the factory that now supplies them with their amazing reproductions, he knew he'd found the answer, and the Store opened shortly thereafter. For more information, call (541) 245-5555 or visit their inspiring website at www.legendsmedford.com. You'll want to make a special visit to the area just to visit Legends, located at 4024 Crater Lake Highway (Route 62), just north of Costco. You'll be glad you did!

Terra Firma Home

Krissy and Mark Millner have created a homeowner's dream store in the middle of Medford. Their motto is "art + you = home." Terra Firma Home is dedicated to providing sophisticated interiors, handcrafted furniture, and accessories from around the world, but there's more. The Millners offer in-home design consultation and service for whole room makeovers, and the largest selection of fabrics and textiles in Southern Oregon, with an emphasis on natural fabrics such as silks, wools, Irish linen and fine cottons. Enhance your decoration options with custom lighting, one-of-a-kind tribal rugs and sculptures, Asian antiques, and wall art and carvings unique to Terra Firma Home. There's a complete line of leather sofas and chairs, sectionals and ottomans, dining room tables and chairs. Krissy and Mark also have another Terra Firma store located in historic Jacksonville, a gift shop that offers up an array of items not found elsewhere, including; toys, music, books, and a wide assortment of beautiful gift ideas. Terra Firma Home is located at 309 E Main Street in Medford, Oregon and the Jacksonville gift store is located at 135 West California Street in Jacksonville, Oregon. Call (541) 770-2728 or visit their newly updated website, www.terrafirmahome.com.

Health & Beauty

DuBois Salon & Rainforest Spa

Whether you are looking for a new hairstyle, a soothing massage, or a relaxing overnight stay at a luxury bed and breakfast, go no further than DuBois Salon & Spa.

Owner, Cheryl DuBois has created a unique partnership that is sure to please and delight clients to her historic downtown Gresham business. Her salon offers the finest in care and service. Precise razor and scissor cuts, luminous color applications, and treatments such as perms, straightening, and deep conditioning are available. The stylists use only Redken and Bumble & Bumble of New York products. The Rainforest Spa is the perfect place to be pampered. Spa facials, massages, manicures and pedicures, rainforest showers, and seaweed wraps will rejuvenate the mind and spirit. For those wanting to share their relaxing time with friends or family, spa parties are available.

DuBois Salon & Spa has opened a four-star bed and breakfast, TLC, on the upper floor of this elegant Tudor building. TLC features four elegant bedroom and bath suites. Guests to the Bed and Breakfast receive priority booking in the salon and day spa. This is the perfect place for bridal parties, slumber parties, or romantic weekends. Guests will love to have a luxurious place to lay their newly coiffed heads or beautiful bodies for a restful sleep. The DuBois Salon & Spa also offers Bridge the Gap Academy, an instructional program for licensed technicians. The Academy provides additional training for recent beauty school graduates and dedicated professionals who desire to better their skills and income potential. Visit DuBois Salon & Spa at 700 North Main Street in Gresham. For more information, call (503) 618-1020.

Desirant Day Spa & Salon

With its wonderful custom-made furniture, mirrors, sinks and cabinetry, and its superb spa services at affordable prices, Desirant Day Spa & Salon in Sherwood is truly "the day spa you've been wishing for." Opened in 2004 by Zena Doherty, Desirant offers customized services including: haircuts, styling and treatments, nail therapies, facials, microdermabrasion, waxing, and numerous body massages and steam canopies. Placing its clients on a pedestal and catering to your every whim, they will arrange whatever special service you desire, be it hot air balloon rides, picnics or wine tastings. Desirant Day Spa & Salon will also provide a limo to take you to your shopping or other combined spa destination. With its goal of personalized customer service by highly trained technicians, Desirant is the perfect place to treat yourself or a loved one to a full day of pampering. Desirant Day Spa & Salon is located at 20510 Roy Rogers Road, Suite 140, Sherwood, OR 97140. Call (503) 625-8822 or visit them on their website at: www.desirant.com.

Olena's European Spa & Salon

Olena's European Spa & Salon in Portland, Oregon is a unique spa that provides excellent service as well as great results. Here you can escape from reality to a world of complete European serenity for a truly relaxing experience. Since 2003, Owner, Olena Trone's salon has earned a reputation as a highly desirable, full-service day spa. Olena comes with 15 years of training in Russia, the Ukraine, Paris and the U.S. Olena is able to utilize the latest technology and finest available products to relax and rejuvenate her customers. The salon offers European technique facials, detoxifying deep hydrative wraps, Swedish massage and a variety of other luscious body treatments. Olena's also offers hair salon services and wonderful pedicures and manicures for men and women alike. Why not try some of Olena's signature services such as the ultimate unique caviar facial, vitamin response facial, alpha-clear anti-pigmentation treatment, air-brush spray tanning, French silky smooth body treatment and many other varieties of stimulating body treatments. Hydrotherapy, Finland sauna and many spa packages are offered, especially for couples. Gift certificates make wonderful presents. A visit to Olena's ensures that you will leave feeling rested, pampered and ready to visit again while you're in Portland. Olena's European Spa & Salon is located at 8101 SE Cornwell Street, Portland, OR 97206. Phone (503) 775-0900 or visit them on the web at: www.olenasdayspa.com.

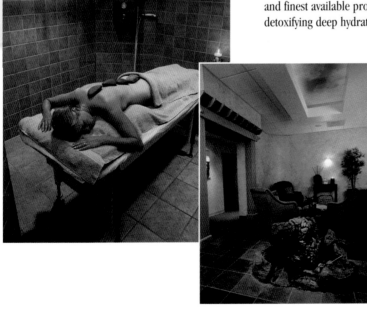

The Pointe Spa

Once you enter the Pointe Day Spa and Hawthorn Farm Athletic Club, you realize you've entered a rare and special place. This award winning private club, complete with three pools, basketball court, group exercise classes, Pilates plus workout facilities, is the home of the Pointe Day Spa. Open to the public, the Spa offers a full menu of services and individualized, friendly attention from their highly skilled staff. Getting to experience their treatments is an encounter in relaxation and bliss. You are greeted by a warm and friendly Client Coordinator, who answers any questions you might have, while gently easing you across the threshold to your appointed services. Sauna, steam and Victor Zuzin, one of the licensed massage therapists, effortlessly start your day. Victor, one of the many massage therapists, is in high demand. His background includes being former physician with the Russian Olympic Ice Skating Team. Victor's easy demeanor and his understanding, skill and knowledge of the body make his massages perfect. A favorite of its regulars, the Chocolate Papaya Mud Wrap is a must. This signature treatment includes rinsing off in a shower with a cascading waterfall and finishing with a nourishing shea butter. Services to choose from include massage, facials, wraps, nails, waxing, and make-up applications. Let the client coordinator help you select the services to make your day special. Plan some extra time and visit the Hawthorn Farm Athletic Club. The spa offers full use of the club on the day of your services. You may enjoy the Bistro where the executive chef prepares a sumptuous meal. Or schedule a personal Pilates session, among many other things to do. This high-end club offers it all. The Pointe Day Spa and Hawthorn Farm Athletic Club are located along the MAX Light Rail line at 4800 NE Belknap Court in Hillsboro and are easy to get to from almost anywhere. You may make reservations by calling (503) 640-6404 or visiting www.thepointespa.com .

Salon Nyla "The Day Spa"

You will find Salon Nyla the Day Spa, an Aveda Concept salon, right in the lobby of the Embassy Suites hotel in downtown Portland. It's hard to resist its invitation to a day spa where body wraps massage therapy, and Aveda facials refresh and energize; while hair services, nail treatments, and complimentary make-up applications will help you look as great as you feel. Owner Nyla Thomas has been providing services in downtown Portland for the past 18 years. She and manager Ann Bailey are devoted to the principle that "the body is our most precious possession." Signature treatments such as the Elemental Nature Facial for Self-Renewal provide an experience of total skin rejuvenation and relaxation. Aveda flower and plant essences are used to enhance all their fantastic treatments. Their friendly, experienced staff help ensure that every customer leaves feeling pampered and satisfied. In addition to "a la carte" services such as, the Elemental Nature Massage, Hot Stone Massage, Rosemary mint pedicure, and so many more, Salon Nyla the Day Spa offers special packages ranging from three hour Spa Sampler to a full day of bliss Salon Nyla the Day Spa is well known for their fabulous Bride and Groom packages and Special Occasion parties. Salon Nyla the Day Spa is located at 327 SE Pine St. Walk in appointments are welcome, but an advance appointment will help ensure availability. Call (503) 228-0389 or (503) 279-9000 ext. 6191. See their website at www.salonnyla.com for a list of all their fabulous services.

TAVIN

TAVIN in Portland is a top skin care studio, specializing in facials, waxing, make-up and nail care for both women and men since 2002. With its extensive selection of services, including Deep Cleansing, Vitamin C, Microdermabrasion, Full Body Waxing and Airbrush Tanning, the salon attracts clients who want only the best when it comes to their skin. Appealing not only to women, TAVIN also offers numerous treatments specially designed for men, including facials. Owner, Tavin Moore, skilled aesthetician for 11 years, also produces her own line of spa products available at the studio. You'll also notice locally designed jewelry and glass available for sale there as well. A top finisher in the NW Stylist & Salon Cover Contest, TAVIN will leave you glowing both inside and out. TAVIN is located at 811 NW 19th, in Portland, Oregon 97209. For questions, call (503) 222-5001 or for more information, visit their website at http://portland.tavin.com.

Rejuvenation Day Spa

The Rejuvenation Day Spa in Portland, Oregon is one of the premier spas in the area. Since 1999, Owners, Diana Governalé and Shari Jacobson have sought to provide a sanctuary of harmony and healing. A place where both men and women can escape to rejuvenate physically, mentally, emotionally and spiritually. At Rejuvenation, the air and water is vigorously purified, and all the plants, herbs and minerals used in the treatments are as natural and curative as possible. With treatments ranging from the spa's signature Aromatherapy Facial to the Tangerine Dream exfoliating skin treatment, as well as holistic body wraps and hot stone therapy, Rejuvenation provides the latest in self-renewal. Their studio offers numerous yoga and Pilates classes, and frequent workshops are held that emphasize a holistic approach to well being. Whether you visit the spa, or buy a gift certificate for a deserving someone in your life, rest assured that the Rejuvenation Day Spa will leave you with a newfound feeling of serenity. Rejuvenation Day Spa is located at 6333 SW Macadam Avenue, Suite 105, in Portland, Oregon 97239. For inquiries, call (503) 293-5699 or visit their website at: www.rejuvenationdayspa.com.

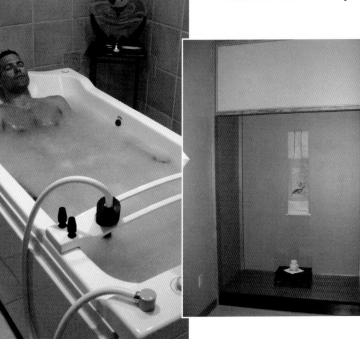

Yoga in the Pearl

Yoga in the Pearl in Portland, Oregon is just that, a pearl. Owners and instructors, Alice Boyd and Jennifer Preisler, opened their yoga studio in 2002 with the goal of creating a clean, beautiful space with good energy and excellent, high-quality instructors. With a well-designed, state-of-the-art facility complete with locker rooms, they have succeeded. Alice and Jennifer offer several different yoga classes, from Power Vinyasa to Prenatal Yoga to Ashtanga. Their visiting instructors and lecturers provide introductions into exercises beyond what they traditionally offer. However, if you prefer something other than yoga to relax, you may choose from Pilates, massage therapy, acupuncture, naturopathic medicine, and energy healing. Their Boutique carries yoga clothing and accessories, books, candles, jewelry, cards and more. When you're finished with your classes for the day head to Blossoming Lotus, their vegan café for a smoothie or fresh squeezed juice and a sandwich or other healthy light fare. Yoga in the Pearl is a jewel of a find. You can visit them at 925 NW Davis in Portland, Oregon 97209. Call (503) 525-YOGA or visit their website at www.yogapearl.com.

Loprinzi's Gym

Visiting Loprinzi's Gym is a pleasure. Loprinzi's is a low-key, non-trendy place that's genuinely dedicated to fitness. Sam Loprinzi helped to pioneer the fitness craze when he started the Gym in 1948 with help from other family members. The equipment is all still there, and Loprinzi's has one of the few local freestanding weight rooms. The original equipment was handmade, even some of the dumbbells. After Sam met the legendary fitness guru Jack LaLanne while they were serving in the Navy during World War II, the two men taught strength and fitness to sailors on San Francisco's Treasure Island. They shared ideas and discovered that they both had many of the same ideas about training and fitness. "This is an iron gym. This is a real gym. Not a lot of pretenses here." a long-time member states. Bob Hill bought the gym in 1994, and notes that it is probably the most comfortable gym in town. With photos of Sam and Jack and other past greats like Steve Reeves and Frank Zane along the walls, you can experience history as you take your workout with the same type of equipment once used by these great bodybuilders. Keep your body fit at the second oldest continuous workout gym in the state while experiencing a true Oregon Treasure at the same time. Loprinzi's Gym is located at 2414 Southeast 41st Avenue. For more information, call (503) 232-8311.

Spa Sassé

Located in the heart of Portland, Spa Sassé is an oasis of calm dedicated to the art of beauty and well being. Inside, experienced technicians provide a professional atmosphere encompassing a variety of spa packages including sea algae body treatments, full body massages and a delicious spa cuisine meal. Since 1983, Owner, Sara Sassé, has emphasized a holistic approach, utilizing the earth's natural ingredients such as sea extracts, organic clays and flower essences for the Spa's treatments. The signature Crescendo Treatment is an hour and a half experience that includes full body massage, a Salt-Glo Body Scrub with Dead Sea mineral salts, a Vichy shower and a soothing scalp massage. Other offerings include the Thalasso Hydromassage Bath, the St. Tropez Polish and Bronzing Treatment, and wonderful Couple's treatments for a relaxing interlude together. A variety of facial treatments, peels and waxing are also available. Complete salon services are provided including hair, manicures and pedicures, as well as laser hair removal. Spa Sassé is open seven days a week and offers gift cards. Beginning in the summer of 2005, the Spa will also offer Heli-Spa retreats in the Canadian Rockies of British Columbia. They are a combination of helicopter touring, deluxe lodging, spa treatments, hiking and other exciting adventures. Next time you're in the city, visit Spa Sassé, located at 630 SW Alder in Portland, Oregon 97205, where specialists will pamper, refresh and rejuvenate you. Call (503) 228-8266 for additional information and reservations or visit their website at www.spasasse.com.

Rafting in the High Country

Kathy's Oasis Salon and Day Spa

Kathy's Oasis Salon and Day Spa in Salem, Oregon, invites you to "Come on in and relax; leave your troubles and pressures outside." Says owner Kathy Bell, "This is a place to relax, renew, and refresh, a refuge of serenity where you can forget your stresses and leave feeling more beautiful and calm than when you arrived." Kathy's, in operation for 44 years, offers hair design and coloring, skin and spa services, and nail services -- each of which with an extensive list of choices and options. "Our mission," Kathy says, "is to provide an experience of relaxation and renewing of the soul." Among the skin and spa services are body treatments, and primary among them is Kathy's exclusive Dead Sea Body Masque. As you luxuriate with a rich mud masque applied to your entire body, you receive a relaxing facial, scalp, and foot massage. Then a rich moisturizing cream is applied to your body. Among facial skin care procedures, the chemical or double peel is popular with many guests. Nail services include the classic pedicure. At Kathy's you enjoy a therapeutic soak in a whirlpool foot tub, followed by exfoliating scrub, foot and leg massage, hydrating moisturizer and flawless polish application. And by the way, not all of this is reserved for women -- men

are welcome, and popular among men is the deluxe hair cut, in which you indulge in Tea Tree, The Experience, featuring a neck massage and essential oil aromatherapy. Kathy's Oasis Salon and Day Spa is located in the Liberty Plaza at 285 Liberty St NE, #130, Salem, OR 97301. Parking is free and easy. Call (503) 362-7488. Reservations are highly recommended. Visit the web site at www.kathysoasis.com.

Museums

Portland Children's Museum

This lively, entertaining, and totally captivating enterprise is now called the Portland Children's Museum 2nd Generation, or CM2 for short. The new name came with a move from cramped quarters to a spacious new location close to the Oregon Zoo. But it's just the newest face of this children's museum that has been serving Oregon since 1949 – the sixth oldest children's museum in the United States. The mission of the Children's Museum is to foster creative behavior in people, especially children. They do a fantastic job, and CM2 serves approximately 250,000 children and parents per year. Go to their very colorful Web site at www.portlandcm2.org to see a full schedule of children's favorite activities here. They have areas for dress-up, water play, and music-making, as well as regularly scheduled story times. They have an interactive "Animal and Animal Homes" exhibit, a puppet theater where

puppeteer Penny Walter has built a loyal following for her productions, a studio where children get their hands into clay and make wonderful things out of it, and "Wonder Corner" where they can draw plants and rocks, using microscopes to get a closer look at the usually unseen natural world. The newsletter, CM2 and You!, tells members all about their activities – and with a wealth of benefits for membership at a wide variety of levels, joining CM2 is an investment that every family will profit from. CM2 has pointers in their newsletters that help parents with many facets of their children's growth and well-being, like how to support imagination and literacy in the home. As well as describing all the great things you can do with your kids at the museum. Volunteers play a critical part – playing with the kids, building exhibits, sewing costumes and props, doing art with children, reading stories, and much more. Individuals, service organizations, and corporate groups are all invited get involved. (503) 471-9909.

Oregon Historical Society

The Oregon Historical Society opened its first office and museum in Portland City Hall and began development of a regional research library and collection of historical artifacts. In 1917 OHS moved into Portland's Public Auditorium, and in 1966 moved to its current location at the corner of SW Jefferson and Park in downtown Portland. OHS has published the Oregon Historical Quarterly continuously since 1900. Over 150 books on Oregon history, politics and culture, as well as biographies, field guides and exhibit catalogs, have also been published by OHS since 1929. The OHS artifacts collection comprises over 85,000 items and the Research Library contains one of the country's most extensive collections of state history materials. The Library's photographic archives include over 2.5 million images from pre-statehood to the present day. OHS also sponsors Education Programs. The Oregon Historical Society Museum at 1200 SW Park Avenue in Portland, Oregon, is open seven days a week. Visit them to enjoy world-class exhibits offering a refreshing glimpse into the history of the Pacific Northwest. For information, call (503) 222-1741 or visit their incredible website at www.ohs.org.

Oregon Museum of Science & Industry

If you're visiting Oregon, one of the most important places you can go is the Oregon Museum of Science and Industry, better known as OMSI. Located in the heart of Portland, this 219,000 square foot building has the largest science outreach education program in the United States. It also has more popular exhibits that have been featured throughout North America and Europe than any other institution. OMSI first evolved from a donated house in 1955 to a hand-built brick building constructed solely by volunteers in 1957. It finally found its home on a donated eighteen-acre site, with its new facility completed in 1994, where it now entertains one million visitors. OMSI has dedicated a significant portion of its space to teaching children science and math in new, stimulating and fun ways, from its Science Playground where young children can learn activities through playing games and inspecting the resident reptiles and critters, to the Physics, Chemistry, Laser and Holography Labs equipped for teens and young adults. But OMSI isn't just a great place to bring young ones, with its exclusive state-of-the-art 330-seat dome screen OMNIMAX Theatre and 200-seat planetarium, there's a place for everyone interested in creative experiences. All without making a dent in their pocketbook! If exploring becomes too demanding, there's always the Science Café that faces the river for a little time to relax before jumping back into the learning process. With hundreds of different activities for the young and old, as well as residents and travelers, OMSI is a priority "must see" for anyone who loves to discover. OMSI is located at 1945 South East Water Avenue in Portland, Oregon. To contact them for museum hours, rates, and events, call (800) 955-OMSI.

World Forestry Center

Newly renovated, the World Forestry Center Discovery Museum (opening summer2005) gives you a hands-on, interactive experience that teaches about the forests and trees of the Pacific Northwest and the world. Exhibits are designed to show visitors how we interact with the forests and their importance in our lives. The "Dynamic Forest" provides both an underground "root crawl" experience and a canopy walk through the upper branches. While the simulated smoke jumping and whitewater rafting exhibits demonstrate how people work and play in the forest. Upstairs, you can take a journey through some exotic places in the world and learn of boreal, sub-tropical, temperate, and tropical forests as well as explore temporary exhibits about art, culture, and history. The World Forestry Center in Portland's Washington Park is a five-acre campus that includes the Center's Discovery Museum. Since 1971, the Center has been providing an exciting and educational experience for adults and children alike. The Museum's history traces back to the Lewis and Clark Centennial American Pacific Exposition and Oriental Fair held in Portland, Oregon in 1905. One of the most popular buildings at the fair was the Forestry Building; a giant log cabin built out of huge logs with the bark still attached. The building was so popular that when the fair ended, it was turned over to the state of Oregon and became a Portland landmark until August 17, 1964 when it burned to the ground. Out of the ashes of the fire, civic leaders conceived the Western Forestry Center, a non-profit educational institution that would later be renamed the World Forestry Center to reflect its international mission. The World Forestry Center's Discovery Museum is housed in a massive wooden building commanding magnificent hilltop views across the park and the city beyond. The building is considered a masterpiece of Cascadian style architecture. The World Forestry Center campus also has two other beautiful wooden buildings which can be rented out for social functions and business meetings. For more information, call (503) 228-1367 or visit their interesting website at www.worldforestry.org.

Pittock Mansion

Open to the public since 1965, Portland, Oregon's Pittock Mansion is a community landmark. Completed in 1914, Pittock Mansion was home to Portland pioneers, Henry and Georgiana Pittock from 1914 to 1919. The Mansion was designed by Architect, Edward Foulkes and incorporated Turkish, English and French designs, but Oregon craftsmen and artisans and Northwest materials were used to build it. The grand staircase alone is a magnificent structure. Home to the Pittock family until 1958, the Pittock Mansion Estate was purchased by the City of Portland in 1964 and restored over a fifteen month period. A nexus that unites all of Portland's community in a volunteering effort to preserve history, Pittock Mansion invites you to share a unique experience of Portland's past. Situated a thousand feet above Portland, the Mansion is nestled on forty-six acres. It's the perfect place to spread your picnic blanket and enjoy an exclusive view of the city while savoring the scents of one of the most famous gardens in Oregon's history. Bring your picnic basket to 3229 Northwest Pittock Drive in Portland, Oregon. Call (503) 823-3624 for more information or visit the Mansion's website at www.pittockmansion.com.

Historic Cemetery, Jacksonville

Evergreen Aviation Museum

It only flew once, in 1947, but it remains one of the greatest legends in aviation history: Howard Hughes' H-4, famously nicknamed the Spruce Goose – is the largest wooden airplane ever built, and now the star attraction at the Evergreen Aviation Museum in McMinnville. The Museum was the dream of Captain Michael King Smith, a McMinnville native who served in the U.S. Air Force and the Oregon Air National Guard. He loved flying and envisioned a living museum that would educate the public about aviation and exhibit historic air craft. In 1992, Evergreen acquired the Spruce Goose from the Aero Club of Southern California, and after an epic journey from Long Beach to McMinnville by land and by sea, the legendary flying boat arrived safely at its new home. Sadly, Captain Smith died in an accident shortly afterwards, but his father, Delford Smith, Founder of Evergreen International Aviation and Co-Founder of the Museum, persevered and made sure that the Museum would open, a tribute to his son's vision. Since its opening, the Museum has become one of the most popular attractions in Oregon, fulfilling its mission to inspire and educate, to promote aviation history, and to honor the service and sacrifice of America's veterans. In addition to the Spruce Goose, there are more than fifty aircraft on display, ranging from a replica of the Wright Brothers' first successful airplane to the ultra-modern SR-71 Blackbird. The Museum also offers educational programs and special events. Call (503) 434-4180 or go to the museum's website, www.sprucegoose.org, for more information. To get to the Museum, located at 500 NE Captain Michael King Smith Way, drive south from Portland on Highway 99W through Newberg and Dundee, go left onto Highway 18 and head west for about four miles. The Museum is on the right. Be sure to visit the Museum's Spruce Goose Café, and Rotors Wings and Things store   The Museum's admission is free for children under the age of five and Evergreen Aviation Museum members.

Hallie Ford Museum of Art

Willamette University, the first university in the West, has a wonderful collection of art. Originally intended for the enrichment of the students and to preserve the priceless works, the collection continued to grow for more than a century. Six years ago it also became an Oregon treasure, a museum where you are welcome to share the significant works of art. Founded by Methodist missionaries in Salem in 1842, the University has collected of European, Asian, and Native American, historic and contemporary regional art. One example of the rich resources of Willamette's collection is its Native American baskets, many given to the early Methodist missionaries by Clatsop Indians on the Oregon Coast and Kalapuyan Indians in the Willamette Valley, and more coming from a 1930s Native American collection of two prominent Salem collectors. Native American art is one of the most interesting and exceptional parts of the collection to this day. In 1996, fortune helped in the creation of the Hallie Ford Museum of Art when a great building, one block from the campus, became available. It featured an enclosed garden on the ground floor, marble panels on the second, and 27,000 square feet of floor space. Long-time University benefactor, Hallie Ford helped to acquire it for a new museum, and the former telephone company building was transformed into a museum of art with space for permanent and temporary galleries, offices, a lecture hall, and work and storage areas. They used warm colors, natural materials, and curves throughout the building to create a warm, dynamic space, "a jewel-box." Prints, sculpture, and paintings, all of the best are here for you to see. Don't miss this wonderful, ever-changing part of Salem's cultural setting as the collection grows and more special shows are mounted. Each one is designed to instruct and delight. And the Carl Hall Gallery and the Northwest collections reflect the Museum's special commitment to preserving, presenting, and interpreting the art of this region. The Hallie Ford Museum of Art is open Tuesday through Saturday at 900 State Street in Salem. For more information, call (503) 370-6855 or visit their website at www.willamette.edu/museum_of_art/.

Springfield Museum

When visiting Springfield, Oregon, be sure to stop in at the Springfield Museum for a fun and educational journey into the town's past. Located in historic downtown Springfield, the Museum is housed in the former 1911 Oregon Power Company transformer station. This unique brick building is listed on the National Register of Historic Places. Founded in 1980 and opened to the public in 1981, the Museum is separated into three distinct areas. The first floor exhibits, the second floor Interpretive Center and the Museum Store. The first floor features special exhibits that change throughout the year. Contemporary and fine arts and crafts, antiques, and historic memorabilia have all been displayed. The second floor is home to the Interpretive Center. Opened in 1996, the Interpretive Center focuses on the men and women who built the community of Springfield. Visitors to this engaging center will learn what life was like for pioneers of a small mill town in the 1880s and early 1900s. They will learn about the arrival of the railroad, farm life, the Kalapuya Indians. The daily life of pioneer men, women, and children is also featured. The Museum Store features work by local artists, a large selection of books, heritage toys, Springfield Museum logo merchandise, and collectibles. The Springfield Museum is located at 590 Main Street. Their hours are 10am. until 5pm. Tuesday through Friday and 12pm. to 4pm. on Saturday. Admission is $2 for adults. Children under 18 are admitted free. For more information on this fascinating Oregon Treasure, phone (541) 726-3677.

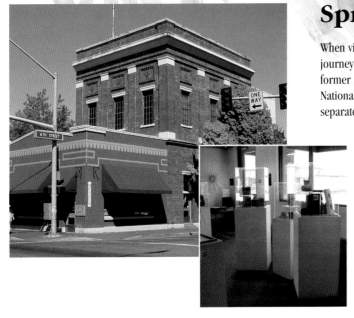

Mission Mill Museum

When visiting Oregon's capitol city, be sure to tour beautiful Mission Mill Museum. With its manicured grounds and hands-on exhibits, this is truly an Oregon Treasure. Located on a historic five-acre site, Mission Mill Museum tells the history of the early settlers to Salem, including Methodist Missionary, Jason Lee. Visitors can tour three historic houses and a church that have been restored and furnished to look the way they did when built during the 1840s and 1850s. The Jason Lee house is said to be the oldest remaining frame house in the Pacific Northwest. The church was built in 1858 and is the oldest Presbyterian Church in the Pacific Northwest. The

Thomas Kay Woolen Mill is also located on the Museum grounds. This red building produced wool products from 1889 to 1962. Visitors can view working equipment that was used in the mill and the original water-power turbine. Children and adults alike will enjoy the hands-on exhibits that range from learning to spin, card and weave wool. Costumed speakers bring history alive for visitors. The museum offers daily and group tours, children's programs, living history exhibits, and many special events throughout the year, such as the Sheep to Shawl Festival that demonstrates how wool fabric is made from beginning to end. The Museum Store offers fine textiles and woolens, a large selection of books, art created by local artists, home decor, jewelry, cookware and kitchen items, and reproduction toys. The beautiful grounds are the perfect place for your next special event. Many weddings and meetings take place on this historic site. With many activities, interesting exhibits, and a beautiful backdrop, Mission Mill Museum is sure to please. The Museum is located at 1313 Mill St. SE in Salem. Phone (503) 585-7012 for more information. Or visit their website at www.missionmill.org.

Jordan Schnitzer Museum of Art

The University of Oregon's Jordan Schnitzer Museum of Art, reopened in January 2005, after a five-year, $12.72 million dollar renovation and expansion that transformed this 70-year-old building into a modern, state-of-the-art facility. Says Susie Pape, President of the Museum Board of Directors, "We look forward to providing visitors with new and outstanding gallery installations and public programming." The Museum, listed on the National Register of Historic Places, was awarded $6.36 million in state-serviced bonds. The funds were matched through a combination of grants, estate gifts and contributions from more than 750 individual donors. The largest private gift came from Portland philanthropist and cultural leader, Jordan D. Schnitzer. The Museum bears his name in recognition of his generous donation. The Museum opened its doors to the public in 1932. It was designed by Ellis F. Lawrence, University of Oregon's Dean of Architecture at the time. It was built to house the Murray Warner Collection of Oriental Art. With its elegant exterior brickwork, decorative moldings and iron grillwork, plus the restful Campbell Memorial Courtyard, the museum building remains one of the most distinctive architectural structures in Oregon. It houses collections of American, European, Korean, Chinese, and Japanese art. A Changing Exhibitions Gallery covers nearly 4,000 square feet of floor space. An educational suite contains an interactive discovery gallery, art-making studio and lecture hall. There is a new cafe and enlarged museum store, plus a special events hall available for public rental. The Museum is fully accessible to disabled persons. The Museum staff makes a special effort to reach out to school children via tours. For example, "Learning to Look: An Introduction to the Gallery," is an interactive tour recommended for pre-kindergarten through 12th grade. "Art Moves You: Dance Through the Museum of Art," also intended for students from pre-kindergarten through high school, is an interactive tour that engages learners by using movement, dance, and theater techniques to explore the Museum. All tours are led by specially trained Exhibition Interpreters. The Jordan Schnitzer Museum of Art is located at 1223 University of Oregon Street in Eugene, Oregon 97403. To contact them, call (541) 346-3027 or visit their fascinating website at http://uoma.uoregon.edu.

ScienceWorks

ScienceWorks Hands-on-Museum in Ashland, Oregon is an exciting and educational museum dedicated to the exploration of science through fun and interactive exhibits. Founded in 2001, ScienceWorks provides people of all ages with over one hundred themed hands-on exhibits. The exhibits include; Art and Science, the Dark Science Tunnel, the Hall of Illusions, the Bubble-ology Room and the Science Playroom. In addition, they are currently in the planning stages for an outdoor interactive Water Exhibit. Serving school children and educators throughout the region with innovative programs, the Museum works to promote science literacy and inspire a love of learning through informal learning environments. Its Discovery Lab, Kirlin Community Lecture Series, Sciencelive! Performances, summer festivals and numerous special events, provide visitors to ScienceWorks a variety of activities to choose from. A visit to ScienceWorks will leave you inspired, intellectually stimulated and eager to go back the next time you're in Ashland. ScienceWorks is located at 1500 E. Main in Ashland, Oregon 97520. To learn more, call (541) 482-6767 or visit their website at www.scienceworksmuseum.org.

Restaurants

The Brown Derby Restaurant

Since 1935, The Brown Derby restaurant (named after the famous Brown Derby in Hollywood) has been a landmark in Banks, Oregon. And since 1975, Ed Clark has been involved in this archetype Oregon restaurant. Open for dinner, the Restaurant serves traditional Northwest cuisine, including seafood, steaks, and salads. They feature many of Oregon's excellent wines (including all of the Shafer Vineyard Cellar wines), high quality food and service. You will find a great top shelf of liquors. In addition, the Coffee Shop is open Monday through Saturday Early morning for Espresso, Pastries, Quiche, and it also serves a light lunch menu. Everything they serve is cooked to order and made from scratch, including all of their excellent desserts. The Brown Derby Restaurant is particularly known for their chocolate brownies. The Brown Derby is used as a landmark when local residents give directions, and it is the traditional starting point for some of the famous local parades. It can also be a very special place for birthdays, anniversaries, reunions, retirement dinners and any other special event. Or you can always just take advantage of their expertise, and use the Brown Derby as the caterer for your home event. Banks is a small town where the residents enjoy a relaxed country lifestyle in rural Washington County, but it is located close to the bustling metropolitan area of Portland. Banks has retained its friendly small town atmosphere. You will find Banks in the scenic foothills of Oregon's coast mountain range, just 30 minutes from the city and less than an hour from the coast. Award-winning wineries are located nearby, and are just some of the attractions you will find close to The Brown Derby Restaurant located at 181 North Main Street, Banks, Oregon. You can call for reservations at (503) 324-7866.

Fireworks over Portland

Corbett Fish House

For some fun and great food check out the Corbett Fish House for what is widely regarded as the best fish and chips in Portland. The menu at Corbett Fish House is a fabulous composition of favorite seafoods selected based on the guidelines of the Monterey Bay Aquarium in order to utilize fish that are abundant, well managed, and caught or farmed in environmentally friendly ways. You can rest assured that whatever choice you make from the menu will also be delicious and perfectly prepared. At the Corbett Fish House they use rice flour and clean, hot, high quality oil to produce fried fish with very little oil absorbed. In addition to being gluten free, rice flour also provides for a light and crispy exterior to all of their perfectly fried options. Because Celiac Disease is the most common genetic disorder in America, and limits dining choices for over 2 million Americans, all meals are gluten free except for the bread used on sandwiches. Walleye and Lake Perch are the secret to their meaty and succulent fried fish. Enjoy the Oyster Shooters, calamari, scallops, mussels, clams, salmon, chile fried catfish, halibut, ono and yellowfin tuna too. If you are a Packers fan and want to see the game, head over to the Corbett Fish House where all Packers' games are aired. The Corbett Fish House is located at 5901 SW Corbett Avenue in Portland. You can reach them at (503) 246-8080. Check out their website at www.corbettfishhouse.com for more information on their menu, Celiac Disease or the Monterey Bay Aquarium guidelines.

Helvitia Tavern

Sometimes simplicity wins out over all others. For over 25 years the Lampros family have operated this low-key tavern and have been offering their patrons a classic tavern meal done right. Very little has changed in all of these years because there isn't any need to. The menu is simple at Helvetia Tavern where you can choose from four classic burgers or a garden burger, three sandwiches or grilled chicken or halibut. There are fries or onion rings on the side and plenty of drinks to choose from. This is the home of the Jumbo Burger and a pile of fries. When you go to Helvetia Tavern you know what they have and you know you'll get free refills of soda while your little ones under ten get free sodas with their meals. The atmosphere is consistent with its casual farmland setting and friendly folks. Adults can enjoy the back patio with its gorgeous sunset views while imbibing imported, domestic, microbrewed beers, hard lemonades or wine. When you visit Helvetia be sure to bring cash as they don't take credit cards, but they do have an ATM if needed. You will find Helvetia Tavern off Highway 26, take the NW Helvetia Road Street exit about two miles past the train trestle to the big red barn at 10275 NW Helvetia Road in Hillsboro. You can reach them at (503) 647-5286.

El Gaucho

Owners, Paul Mackay and Franco D' Amico, have brought the premier Steakhouse of El Gaucho to Portland. Listed as one of the top twelve steakhouses in the nation, the exquisite décor, world class dining, exhibition kitchen and superb table side service are just the beginning of your fine dining experience here. Top quality 28 day dry aged certified Angus Beef charcoal grilled to perfection lends to the impressively prepared selection of steaks. Try their Chateaubriand of Tenderloin, Rippe's Signature Steak with Rippe's double shot espresso rubbed into a 12 oz filet with a cinnamon chocolate chipotle demi-glace, or the Gaucho Steak, an 8 oz Top Sirloin topped with Lobster Medallion and Bèarnaise Sauce. While El Gaucho is widely known as the place to get the best steaks in town it also offers an array of lamb, ribs, ostrich, fish and lobster prepared with the same care and quality patrons have come to expect. Peruse their extensive fine wines list and complete your dining experience with a tableside flambe of Coffee Diablo for dessert while relaxing to the live music presented nightly. If you are seeking a refined lounge experience try out their cocktail lounge accentuated with a wood burning fireplace, overstuffed couch, chairs and full service waitstaff. Separately, you will find an intimate cigar lounge staffed by attendants with a broad knowledge of the finer points of their extensive cigar menu. For those very special occasions there are three private rooms available for up to 35 guests as well. Located at 319 SW Broadway in Downtown Portland. You can reach them at (503) 227-8794 or by visiting their website at www.elgaucho.com.

Café Allegro

For an authentic Italian meal that is sure to satisfy, try Café Allegro in Tigard, Oregon. The owner has created an inviting atmosphere with delicious food. Located in a turn-of-the-century building in historic Old Town Tigard, Café Allegro has provided guests with mouth-watering dishes for over ten years. The setting is quaint and cozy with an outside patio to be enjoyed during warm weather. This is a favorite spot for both romantics and families with young children. The Chef prepares appetizing meals from scratch and uses only the freshest ingredients. The menu is extensive and includes such things as traditional Italian specials like lasagne, fettucine, and calzones, wonderful seafood sautes, gourmet pizzas, and delicious soups and salads. For a special treat, try an indulgent Chocolate Fudge Brownie or one of the other freshly made desserts. Beer and wine are available. For those unsure of the best wine to choose, just ask the friendly waitstaff. The Café Allegro's courteous staff is more than willing to offer advice or a taste to ensure the wine is to your liking. Café Allegro now offers catering services as well. The same care and fresh ingredients are used to make any event memorable. Rehearsal dinners, wedding receptions, company parties, or other events will be enhanced by the experienced staff at Café Allegro. Off-site catering is available, or groups can meet in the banquet room or rent the entire restaurant. The Restaurant can comfortably accommodate 120 guests if the outside patio is available, or 100 guests during the cooler months. Open for lunch and dinner seven days a week, Café Allegro is located at 12386 SW Main Street in Tigard. For reservations, phone (503)684-0130.

Maggie's Buns

Maggie Pike loves baking and has for a long time. Her passion for food is what led her to start Maggie's Buns several years ago in Forest Grove. Today her little college coffee shop has legions of loyal fans and is known far and wide. Making over 200 crowd pleasing gooey, decadent and massive cinnamon buns each day isn't all that keeps them talking. And it's not just the home-style food served in belly-filling portions at prices college students can handle. The real draw here is the outspoken, eccentric, and motherly Maggie and the eclectic bakery that reflects her independent nature. As soon as you visit Maggie's you'll recognize that this isn't your run-of-the-mill small town hang out. They make it a point to learn customers' names for a more personal experience. Upon the walls are sculptures of disembodied arms, legs and golden buns amidst colorful artist displays that keep your eyes occupied and your mind entertained. The menu is simple and made from scratch. For breakfast you can enjoy Maggie's trademark Cinnamon Buns in their traditional form, or split in half and fried up French Toast style. Lunch provides quiches, vegetarian options, wraps and soups. For dinner you can count on four course meals that can include: Chicken Picatta, Beef Stroganoff, Prime Rib and even Salmon options. With undeniably decadent desserts to top it all off you can see why Maggie's has the loyal following it does. Come find out what keeps them coming back for more. Maggie's Buns is located at 2007 21st Avenue in Forest Grove. You can reach them at (503) 992-2231.

Castagna and Café Castagna

Castagna and Café Castagna bring a unique blending of Mediterranean style and Pacific Northwest flavors to Portland. Acclaimed as the Restaurant of the Year by The Oregonian only months after it opened in 1999, Castagna has continued to build a reputation for fine dining in a setting of understated elegance. Co-Founders, Kevin Gibson and Monique Siu, first met at Portland's legendary Zefiro, which Siu also co-founded. Zefiro was one of the first restaurants to bring truly modern dining to Portland. With Castagna, Gibson and Siu continue to innovate. Married since 1995, they have brought the best features of Zefiro with them to Castagna, along with the experience Gibson acquired working as a chef in Costa Rica and for two other renowned Portland restaurants, La Catalana and Genoa. Café Castagna, next door to the main restaurant, offers lighter fare in a bistro setting. Castagna's minimalist yet lovely décor provides a unique setting, reflecting Siu's experience as an artist and printmaker. Artwork by Ming Fay and cork floors help create a peaceful, hushed atmosphere. Café Castagna has a more casual ambience in keeping with its emphasis on lighter fare, but whichever you choose, you will be pleased by the emphasis on service and dining comfort. The extraordinary food keeps people coming back to Castagna. Copper River salmon and Red Haven peaches are among the fine Northwestern ingredients that complement exotic European specialties like Cabecou cheese and Gianduja chocolate. Be sure to try Gibson's signature dish, pan-seared scallops with oyster mushrooms. An extensive selection of fine wines ensures you can find something to accompany anything you choose to order. Whether you have a full, formal dinner in the main Restaurant or a casual repast in Café Castagna, you will be dazzled and delighted by the experience. Located at 1752 SE Hawthorne Boulevard, Castagna is easy to find, but not necessarily easy to get into. Reservations are not required, but they are recommended! For inquiries, call (503) 231-7373. The Restaurant is open Wednesday through Saturday. Café Castagna is open for walk-ins seven nights per week.

Jake's Grill Catering

The most elegant place to hold your next function or catered event in downtown Portland is Jake's Grill, located in The Governor Hotel. For a unique and unforgettable dining experience, "as elegant as the White House," Jake's Grill is the premier place to have an event. The restaurant in this beautiful hotel, built in 1909 and renovated to its former glory, has been transformed into breathtaking ballrooms and private dining areas. The abundant rich, dark wood takes diners back to another era, while the white table linens evoke an impressive contrast. Jake's Grill serves classic American cuisine. The traditional full bar serves hand-mixed cocktails and a large selection of single malt whiskeys. Located at 611 SW 10th Avenue, Jake's Grill is open daily for breakfast, lunch, and dinner. Sample Jakes' cuisine for a taste of available possibilities for your next catered event. For reservations or catering arrangements, call (503) 220-1850.

Tucci

If you're looking for an elegant Italian dining experience in Lake Oswego, Tucci is THE place to go. Family-owned and operated, Tucci is more than a restaurant. It's a celebration of modern Italian cooking with a Pacific Northwest spin. Owners, David and Suzanne Regan, were raised in an atmosphere of traditional Italian dining where every meal was an event for the whole family. They've recreated that atmosphere at Tucci, even down to the name, which honors their Grandma "Tucci," an employee at Portland's famous Lido restaurant for more than fifty years. (That's not the only tangible reminder of Grandma's influence. You can see an original sign from Portland's Lido at Tucci's Lido Bar.) At lunch or dinner, you'll find a wealth of choices, with antipasti like Beef Carpaccio with Arugula or Dungeness Crab and Avocado Bruschetta, delectable soups and salads, and entrees including Tucci's signature dishes, Pan Seared Sea Scallops with Pesto Potatoes and Roast Filet Mignon with Morel Mushrooms. At lunch you can also enjoy Tucci's Paninis (grilled Italian sandwiches) and their traditional-style pizzas, baked in their wood-fired oven, with toppings like Calabrese sausage and spicy shrimp. A selection of limited-production artisanal Italian wines is available to complement your choice. Try to leave some room for dessert so you can enjoy classic Italian favorites like tiramisu and gelati that are made from scratch. Or perhaps you'd like to try another house specialty – Orange Crème Caramel served with roasted figs. Whatever you choose, you'll finish the evening offering a hearty "Bravo!" to Chef and Co-Owner, Pascal Chureau and Pastry Chef, Andrea Bowers. Tucci is located at 220 A Avenue in downtown Lake Oswego. Calling ahead for reservations is strongly recommended at (503) 697-3383 or fax (503) 697-3387. Lunch is served starting at 11a.m. Monday through Saturday, and dinner is served Tuesday through Sunday. If you're planning a party, Tucci is available for rental on Monday nights, and they also cater. For more information, call www.tucci.biz.

Café Beignet

New Orleans style Chef, Adam Anaforian, and his family have been serving up scrumptious Bayou flavors to those lucky Oregonians who have found this Louisiana transplant. Now, you too can find this little bit of Louisiana heaven hidden in Aloha. Their signature offerings are beignets with powdered sugar or fruit topping. Beignets are light pillows of doughnut–like pastry either sprinkled with powdered sugar or topped with fruit toppings. Crisp and lightly browned on the outside and warm and soft on the inside, they please just about any palate. Traditionally served alongside cups of rich coffee, they make a great start to any day. At Café Beignet you will also find options for lunch and afternoon snacks ranging from Po' Boy sandwiches, Cajun Chicken Wraps, Cajunmac Salad and skillfully prepared fresh green salads, to Auntie Sher's special recipe chicken salad and sandwiches. Don't miss the one-of-a-kind Dark Chocolate Voodoo Cake with rich cherry filling or the Praline Cinnamon Rolls. Coffee drinks, espressos, frappes, teas and excellent milk shakes await your palate as well. All food is freshly prepared onsite with care and attention to flavor. You will find Café Beignet at 18385 SW Alexander in Aloha. Look for a Bourbon Street style building and you're there. Open Early Morning to late afternoon Monday through Saturday. You can reach them at (503) 642-0807 or check out their website at www.café-beignet.com.

Mint Restaurant

Mint Restaurant and Bar in North Portland offers delicious Latin American dishes and inventive cocktails. This is the perfect spot to relax with friends and try something new. Lucy Brennan has created a hip hangout that is sure to please. Head Chef, Lyle, is a culinary master, well-known for his mouth-watering fresh ceviches and other seafood creations. He uses only the highest quality local ingredients and changes the menu every three months. The Bar serves inventive cocktails that are sure to please. This is no ordinary lounge, but an innovative laboratory where customers are lucky enough to try the original drinks created by Lucy. Her specialties include the very popular blended Avocado Daiquiri and the "Bella," which is made with blackberry puree, vodka, a squeeze of lemon and lime and served up in a sugared martini glass. The drinks are unique and absolutely delicious. Although the Restaurant is relatively new, having opened in 2001, it has already made its mark as a hot spot in the minds of Portland's diners. With its delicious dishes and one-of-a-kind cocktails, this is truly an Oregon Treasure. Mint Restaurant and Bar is located at 816 N. Russell Street. For inquiries, call (503) 284-5518, or for more information visit their website at www.mintrestaurant.com.

Cool Runnings Cafe

Opened in 2002, Cool Runnings Café and Brewery in Portland serves up a delicious fusion of Cajun, Creole and Island cuisine. The name Cool Runnings means "have a good day" and "Peace be the Journey." Appropriately named by Owners, Cal and Heidi Ferris, the intention was to create a restaurant with positive vibes, good food and a fun, tropical atmosphere. Moving from Malibu, California to Portland, Oregon to realize his dream of opening his own restaurant, Cal uses his own recipes, as well as some learned from his grandmother. Cal works diligently to prepare the spicy dishes, stews and soups that the Café is best known for. Brewmaster, Craig Nicholls, lends his skills to the operation by producing fine brews including the Island Red, a nice complement to their spicy menu. Special events include their Fat Tuesday and Valentine's Day parties. With its warm Caribbean décor, comfortable setting and tasty food, Cool Runnings Café is worth stopping for while you're in Portland. Cool Runnings Café, 4110 NE Fremont, Portland. You can reach them by calling (503) 282-2118.

Taqueria Nueve

Since its opening in 2000, Taqueria Nueve in Portland, has received wide-spread acclaim as a top Mexican restaurant. Named Best Mexican Restaurant by City Search Editors for the past three years, it also ranks as one of the top ten Mexican Restaurants in the Nation (City Search) and was honored by the Oregonian with its "Rising Star" Award in 2001. Since meeting in college, Owner/Head Chef, Billy Schumaker, and Owner, Stephen Speiser, have worked in the restaurant business. After taking several months to travel to Mexico and learn about its culture and cooking styles, the pair opened the Restaurant with the intention of providing a true taste of Mexico as reflected in Billy's authentic, unique and extremely tasty recipes. While their menu changes seasonally, their use of the freshest and highest-quality ingredients does not, and they rely on local farmers to provide their produce and meat. Billy and Stephen share an intense passion for both Mexican culture and its food, which is evident in Taqueria Nueve, a must-go restaurant for anyone in the Portland area. Taqueria Nueve is located at 28 NE 28th Avenue in Portland, Oregon 97232. For menu information, call (503) 236-6195.

John Street Cafe

John Street Cafe is the current incarnation of Jamie and Marie Noehern's long time affair with great food and service. With loyal customers following them from their Hawthorne District restaurant to the John Street Cafe several years ago, they had the basis for what would become a neighborhood favorite. With their wonderful breakfasts being a hallmark of their style you can count on ample portions that are affordable and skillfully prepared. Probably best known for their 'from-scratch' cooking philosophy, Jamie and Marie are devoted to fresh ingredients made to a higher standard. At John Street Cafe, you can try one of their signature omelets, such as the Bacavo: bacon, avocado, and Monterey Jack topped with blue cheese, or create one of your own from a list of ingredients. Aside from fabulous omelets, their huge from-scratch pancakes are available in buttermilk or black currant and filbert. Lunch is not to be overlooked though. Check out their high-piled Reubens, the Blackened Snapper Sandwich or their Chicken in the Garden Salad. Jamie and Marie will provide you with great service and great food at a great price. John Street Cafe is located at 8338 N. Lombard in Portland on the north side of St. Johns Bridge. You can reach them at (503) 247-1066.

Salty's On The Columbia

Salty's on the Columbia has been in existence since 1987 and likes to be known as "fun dining." The Restaurant is situated along a particularly scenic area of Marine Drive just west of the Portland Airport. It is next to the Portland Marina and features two levels of floor-to-ceiling windows with a 180-degree panoramic view of the Columbia River. Personalized service and individual attention is apparent. While you enjoy your meal, Salty's will even lend you a pair of binoculars so you can get a closer view of the ever-changing river scenes. You can dock your boat at the marina and come in for a casual lunch or dinner. Salty's is also considered one of the most romantic restaurants in Portland. Salty's features Northwest seafood, local and organic foods. Executive Chef, Jeremy McLachlan's "market sheet" changes frequently depending on what foods are the freshest available. Pastry Chef, Darla Swanson's specialties include Key Lime Pie, Blackberry Silk Tart and Chocolate Raspberry Tart. For a real treat try Salty's Sunday Brunch. Salty's is the perfect spot for the most romantic wedding, social event or important business meeting you've ever held. Their Private Wine Room seats 30 to 40 reception-style. Their North Shore View Room seats 250 (including outdoor decks) or 200 reception-style. Call them for availability. Salty's also offers the best of Portland's Happy Hour menus. Featured are generous portions and friendly service. Salty's food has earned numerous awards for Best Seafood, and Best Brunch. The wine list is one of the best in the Northwest and features many regional wines. Live entertainment is featured regularly. Salty's in Portland is located at 3839 NE Marine Drive. You may phone them at (503) 288-4444. You can also make reservations online at www.saltys.com.

McMenamins

In Portland you can stop just about anyone and ask about a McMenamins. Watch their eyes light up as they point you in the direction of the closest one. McMenamins is the name behind over fifty destination pubs, microbreweries and hotel spots in Oregon and Washington. With fun and entertaining atmospheres that are kid and adult friendly you will find that many folks have been to at least one and most have a bona fide favorite. Started in 1974 by the McMenamin brothers as a philosophical pursuit of fun, funky and friendly gathering spots for good food and good beer, the concept has found a captivated audience and a region of devoted fans. Now providing neighborhood pubs, movie houses, microbreweries, hotels, bus tours, music venues and ballrooms, there seems to be no end to the magic created by these two truly inspired entrepreneurs. Each location is entirely unique unto itself but retains historical preservation, artistic diversity, musical style and a neighborhood allegiance that is unsurpassed. Consider visiting one each week and you'll be busy all year! Some of the fabulous sights you'll see on your journey through their "Kingdom of Fun" are the 360-degree view from Hotel Oregon's Rooftop Bar, the floating floor at the Crystal Ballroom, the Kennedy School's Detention Bar, the Mission Theater Pub, and the new Old St. Francis School in Bend, offering lodging, restaurants and even a mosaic tiled Turkish style pool. There is so much more to these locations, but you will just have to see them to understand. Give McMenamins a call at (503) 223-0109 for more information on their locations, or just for fun visit their website at www.mcmenamins.com.

Bluehour

Bluehour is the premier modern restaurant in the Pearl District of Portland. Owner Bruce Carey opened the doors four years ago and has earned the accolade from Gourmet Magazine as "the most exciting restaurant in Portland" with "the most sophisticated menu in town." Kenny Giambalvo, Executive Chef, specializes in classic French and Italian food. Your fine dining may be accompanied by an array of specialty cocktails. In French, "bluehour" describes any time of day "of heightened emotion." In Portland, it has come to mean "a great place to dine." For special occasions, business parties and family celebrations, reserve their private dining room, "L'heure Bleue" that can accommodate up to 60 people. Bluehour is located in Portland's Pearl District at 250 NW 13th Avenue (between 13th and Everett). View Bluehour's unique website at www.Bluehouronline.com. Inquiries and reservations may be made by calling (503) 226-3394.

Typhoon Restaurant

Opened in 1995 by Thai native, Bo Kline, the Typhoon Restaurant quickly became known as a gourmet restaurant featuring the best in Thai cuisine. Praised by magazines like Bon Appetit, Bo is recognized as one of the top chefs in America. The unique flavors of Typhoon are inspired by such diverse sources as the Thai peasants' pushcarts and the dining halls of Asian palaces. Bo demands the best quality ingredients and will not compromise. For example, several years ago, severe storms in Southeast Asia caused Thai chili peppers to become scarce. Bo found and imported the peppers from different countries around the world for three solid months to ensure that every dish maintained the standards she had built her reputation on. Whether you try a familiar favorite or take a taste adventure, Typhoon will serve you a delicious meal that will be unlike anything you have ever had before. Typhoon has several locations in the Portland area, and all restaurants are open from 11:30am until 2:00pm for lunch Monday through Friday, 5:00pm until 9:00pm for dinner Monday through Thursday, 5:00pm until 10:00pm Friday and Saturday and 4:30pm until 9:00pm Sunday. Portland's Typhoons are located at 410 SW Broadway in Portland (503) 224-8285 and 2310 NW Everett Street (503) 243-7557. The Beaverton location is 12600 SW Crescent Street in Beaverton (503) 644-8010. Gresham's Typhoon is located at 543 NW 12th Street in Gresham, Oregon. They can be reached at (503) 669-9995, or for more information, visit the website at www.typhoonrestaurants.com.

Kelly's Olympian

New owners Jeff Mincheff and Ben Stutz have breathed new life into one of Portland's oldest bars, Kelly's Olympian, which opened in 1902. The town was a little rougher then – Kelly's used to have showers in the basement for the benefit of lumberjacks who stopped by on their way to and from the local logging camps. Ironically, Kelly's new look is an old look – historical photographs line the walls, vintage motorcycles hang from the ceiling, and museum-quality neon signs and gas station memorabilia create an atmosphere that makes the past come alive, and dance, especially when there are live bands performing and live DJs providing late-night entertainment. Jeff and Ben maintain the traditions that have made Kelly's a popular meeting place for over a century. The bar features 26 beers on tap, and is one of the few remaining bars in Portland that still serves Olympia Beer (indeed, Olympia Beer put the "Olympian" in Kelly's name). Breakfast, lunch, and dinner are also served here in classic diner style, right down to the "Blue Plate Special." And the prices may make you think you're in a time warp. Along with the pancakes, hamburgers, French fries and other traditional fare, Kelly's features specialties you won't find elsewhere, such as the beer-battered deep-fried macaroni and cheese bites and the grilled spam sandwich on Wonder Bread. Kelly's Olympian is in the heart of downtown Portland at 426 SW Washington Street. Call (503) 228-3669 for more information.

Veritable Quandary

At Veritable Quandary you can find a truly authentic Portland experience. Founded by Dennis King in 1970 in a historic building near the Hawthorne Bridge, Veritable Quandary offers a look back at Portland's rich past while providing diners with the best of the present – superb food and superb ambience in the glass-walled dining room. Chef Annie Cuggino creates daily menus that are always fresh and different, combining expertise acquired at some of New York and New Orleans' finest restaurants, the best of the Northwest's farm-fresh ingredients, and her own superb style. Though the menu is constantly changing, one item stays time after time – the fantastic Veal Osso Buco. And the Chocolate Nucello Soufflé is another treat that diners come back for time and again. The "VQ" features a wine cellar with over 900 bottles of the finest Northwestern and European vintages, including over 40 selections that diners can try by the glass. Whether you're enjoying the gorgeous blooms of warm spring weather on the patio, or watching the beautiful lights of the winter dusk in Portland from the comfort of the dining room, you'll see why the VQ calls itself "a Dining Oasis in the Heart of the City." Veritable Quandary is located at 1220 SW First Avenue. Call (503) 227-7342 for reservations. More information is available at www.veritablequandary.com.

Irvington Corner Table

Tired of "corporate" restaurants? Try a favorite local gathering place, the Irvington Corner Table in Portland, where everything is made fresh to order and customers are treated with neighborly service. The menu offers both traditional and exotic fare, with appetizers ranging from calamari to Antijitos (grilled tortillas filled with jalapeños and black-olive cream cheese), and entrees from prime rib to the vegetarian Portobello Wellington (chopped shiitake and seasonal mushrooms with herbs, cream cheese and almonds, on top of a whole Portobello mushroom baked in puff pastry). The shepherd's pie is a hearty treat, a meal in itself, and desserts like rum cake and key lime pie provide the perfect finish. Owners Tony and Pamela Karais bring fourteen years of restaurant experience to the management of the Irvington Corner Table. Their commitment to the community has made the restaurant a destination for people who come not just to eat but to meet friends, relax, and perhaps play a game of darts or billiards. A special children's menu helps families feel welcome. The Corner Table calls itself "A neighborhood place for the whole city," and the whole city agrees. The Corner Table at 1700 NE Broadway in Portland is open seven days a week for lunch and dinner, and for brunch on weekends. Reservations are recommended; call (503) 331-1200. Visit the website, www.thecornertable.com, for more information, including the full menu, which has much more than we can include here. But here's a hint – smoked salmon pizza!

Stepping Stone Café

No, you won't get designer food or fancy décor at Stepping Stone Café. For over 55 years they've managed to remain the vintage hideaway everyone is looking for, serving huge portions at small prices to longtime Northwest residents and the lucky few who happen to find them. Old friends and new converts enjoy the breakfast menu containing a dozen massive omelets, griddle cakes, waffles, biscuits and gravy to die for, and homemade cinnamon roll French toast. The full lunch menu includes sandwiches, soups and salad selections, and dinners are the good-old-fashioned kind you would expect from a vintage café. With late night dining until 3am Thursday through Saturday, they serve breakfast and other selected items, while providing full bar selections until 10pm. Stepping Stone has affordable prices, a bright atmosphere, great music, motto-bearing underwear and an edgy staff. Is this the perfect environment or what? They were listed in the Oregonian's 2004 "Oregon's Best Breakfasts" and were the Examiner's "Best Breakfast in the Northwest" pick. Sure, they might give you some friendly attitude (after all their motto is, "You Eat Here Because We Let You." sm) but they are just far enough off the beaten path of NW 23rd Avenue and will serve such good old-fashioned food that it's worth getting there and putting up with them. Located at 2390 NW Quimby Street in Portland, Oregon 97210. You can reach them by calling (503) 222-1132 or visit their website at www.steppingstonecafe.com.

The Old Spaghetti Factory

Tiffany lamps. European antiques. And isn't that an old trolley car over there? Welcome to the world's spaghetti leader, the place that's served enough noodles to go to the moon and back – twice. It was drizzling in Portland, Oregon on January 10, 1969, the day The Old Spaghetti Factory opened its doors for the first time. Standing there to greet the few customers who wandered in was the owner, Guss Dussin. Total gross sales for the night were a paltry $171.80 and many in the business who knew Dussin were convinced his harebrained idea was a complete bust. They couldn't have been more wrong. One week later, the evening's receipts rose to $900 and by the end of the year, the restaurant had sales of almost $400,000. In 1970, two more restaurants were started and company sales rose to $1.3 million. Today The Old Spaghetti Factory is an international restaurant company serving more than 10 million customers annually. Families and friends come to enjoy the delicious food, charming atmosphere and friendly service, at unbeatable prices. Dine amidst fine antiques, collected from around the world, while savoring perfectly cooked pasta and spaghetti sauces, freshly made, and using only the finest ingredients. The staff continually strives to provide guests with a relaxing and enjoyable dining experience. Whether a first-time diner or a frequent guest, you are sure to find the food, service and surroundings to your complete satisfaction. Visit one of the following locations, or see a complete list at www.osf.com. Clackamas: 12725 SE 93rd Ave., (503) 653-7949; Hillsboro: 18925 NW Tanasbourne Dr., (503) 617-7614; Portland: 0715 SW Bancroft St., (503) 222-5375; Vancouver: 730 SE 160th Ave., (360) 253-9030.

Stanich's LLC

If you're looking for the "World's Greatest Hamburger" and you're in Portland, Oregon, you're in luck. Head for Stanich's, it's that simple. Stanich's opened in 1949 by George Stanich, who became known as the Philosopher of Fremont Street. His motto was "Success is luck, ask any failure." The business has remained in the family and is currently run by George and his wife, Gladys and their three children, Steve, Patty and Diana. In 1949 George and Gladys set out to create a restaurant with a friendly and comfortable atmosphere that made a delicious burger. The "W.G.H." consists of a quarter pound of fresh ground chuck topped with bacon, ham, a fried egg, cheese, onion, tomato, lettuce, and sauce sandwiched in a five-inch sesame seed bun. The two-pound burger has won numerous state and national awards, including being mentioned as one of Oregon's "Most Memorable Hamburgers" during Summer 2004's 100th Anniversary of the American Hamburger celebration. The walls of the establishment are full of sports memorabilia, with pennants, high school and college banners, cartoons, and candid photos of George and Gladys and their many friends and customers. Steve tells many stories about his parents. In 1949, places like Stanich's were mostly men's territory. The main draw was beer, discussing sports and philosophy, and Mom's cooking. It was not until the 1960's that women felt comfortable entering the hallowed halls and downing a beer or wine cooler. Stanich's has two locations: 4915 NE Fremont St., Portland, OR 97212, and 5627 SW Kelly St., Portland, OR 97239. Call (503) 281-2322 or (503) 246-5040. At either location, you'll feel welcome, you'll receive outstanding service in a clean family atmosphere, and you can enjoy a fantastic hamburger.

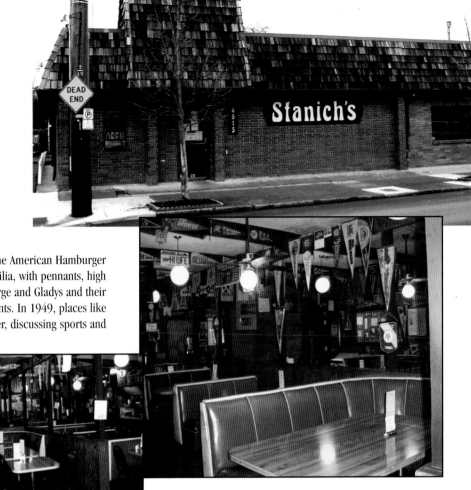

Capitol Coffee House & Bistro

Capitol Coffee House & Bistro in Portland, Oregon is a virtual melting pot for food. They offer a mélange of international cuisine. While the Capitol Bistro's menu draws largely from French cuisine, Owner/Chef, Kevin Peck (along with his wife and Co-Owner Colleen), also infuses flavors and techniques from Italy, Spain and Cuba. Opened in 2002, the Capitol Bistro is located in the former home of the Transit Station for the Red Electric Commuter Rail Line, a charming, two-story building saturated with dark wood and windows, giving it the feel of a European inn. The downstairs coffee house uses only the finest Caffe Umbria coffee, imported from a fourth generation Italian coffee-growing family. Upstairs, the Bistro serves lavishly delectable and savory dishes, including an incredible cheese menu. Some of their outstanding dishes include Coquilles Saint Jacques Au Gratin, a classic French bistro dish, and Lemon Mousse, their signature dessert. The full bar is stocked with a nice selection of Northwest Oregon, Washington and European fine wines and beers. The restaurant also offers live music on many weekends. The Capitol Bistro is a great dining destination, where international cuisines are perfectly fused to provide diners with the ultimate in innovative gastronomic delicacies. Capitol Coffee House & Bistro is located at 6446 SW Capitol Hwy., Portland, Oregon 97239. Call (503) 297-1455 or visit their website at, www.capitolbistro.com.

Gubanc's Pub & Restaurant

When you're running a pub and restaurant with patrons who dine with you as often as five days a week, and their parents and grandparents before them, did the same, you know you are doing it right! Tony and Anne Gubanc, founders of Gubanc's Pub and Restaurant in Lake Oswego, discovered their niche when they opened this neighborhood establishment in 1976 serving an array of soups, salads and sandwiches. The public keeps coming back for the consistent quality food and unassuming service. Plus, Gubanc's is a very comfortable atmosphere that regulars find charming. Michael Buck, General Manager, along with Randy Richards, Executive Chef, instill the high standards and participate in the daily ritual of luncheon and dinner specials – as they have for over twenty years. Visit them yourself and try the featured soup of the day which could be Santa Fe Chicken and White Bean or Chicken and Pear. The Chef selects from over eighty soups personally created with the Northwest palate in mind. Favored choices include Halibut Provençal, Grilled Rueben, Southwestern Pork Wrap, and Chicken and Dumplings. For dessert, the incredible Fresh Fruit Cobbler may tempt your appetite and keep you coming back for more. Gubanc's Pub is located at 16008 Boones Ferry Road, Lake Oswego, Oregon 97035. For more information, call (503) 635-2102.

Nob Hill Bar & Grill

Don't judge a book by its cover – that's the lesson of Nob Hill Bar & Grill. This unassuming exterior in the midst of the trendy boutiques of Portland's NW 23rd Avenue hides a restaurant whose award-winning hamburgers are a magnet to burger connoisseurs from all over the nation. Nob Hill Bar & Grill (sometimes referred to by those in the know as "Nobby's") is the only place you can find such specialties as the Gastronomical Burger – two patties topped with pepper jack cheese, jalapenos, and a special sauce that really is special. Other perennial favorites include the "Ambulance Chaser" (a quarter-pound patty topped with pepper jack) and the Nobby Burger, two patties topped with cheese and either ham or bacon. Nob Hill caters to all tastes – vegetarians can enjoy the Garden Burger, a meatless patty adorned with Swiss cheese. Burgers are the main event at Nob Hill, but there are plenty of other attractions. Breakfast features luscious dishes like the Prime Time Omelet, made with mushrooms, onions, Swiss cheese, tomatoes, and guacamole. If you're temporarily burgered out, try the Turkey Club sandwich, a bowl of homemade chili, or perhaps the Crispy Chicken Salad. And as you'd expect from a bar, there's a wide variety of wines and beers available to complement your meal. Nob Hill Bar & Grill is located at 937 NW 23rd Ave. Call (503) 274-9616 for more information or visit the website at nobhillbg.citysearch.com.

Shari's Restaurant

Back in 1978, Ron Burquist opened a strange-looking six-sided structure along Highway 395 in Hermiston, Oregon. No one knew at the time that this was only the first of what would become a chain of over 100 restaurants. Today, Shari's is the largest full-service restaurant chain based in the Pacific Northwest, taking pride in serving guests from rural communities to major cities, preparing meals and building friendships. Over the course of a single year, Shari's pours over half a million cups of coffee, cracks a quarter million eggs, and fries over five miles of sausage links! In just one week, the chain can go through a ton of potatoes, 360 heads of lettuce, 300 pounds of beef and 150 pounds of chicken and turkey, and no wonder, on a typical day they serve more than 1000 customers. Breakfast, lunch, dinner, and dessert, Shari's has it all. The unique six-sided design that initially puzzled passersby is one of the secrets of Shari's success: maximizing the indoor space, it provides quick customer seating, low noise levels, and efficient server traffic patterns, so customers know they won't have to wait and they can eat in comfort. And they eat well. Shari's motto is "Good People Serving Good Food®", and they live up to their motto each and every day. Visit their website at, www.sharis.com, for restaurant locations and other information.

Il Piatto

Is your stomach crying "Italian!" tonight? Then head for Il Piatto on SE Ankeny in Portland. The house cure Prosciutto Risotto ought to satisfy, don't you think? Or perhaps their Gnocchi or Tiramisu is what you're seeking. Wash it down with one of over 150 Italian regional wines and save room for the Homemade Gelatto. Included with all of the delightful food is Il Piatto's warm, romantic ambiance. Since its opening in 1994, Il Piatto has developed an almost cult-like following. Says Bon Appetit, "It's quite a special place." Adds the Vancouver Columbian, "Il Piatto gets a big bravissimo!" Let's take a look at a few recent entrees. Pollo Ripieno: Breast of chicken stuffed with leeks, mozzarella, coated with crushed hazelnuts and bread crumbs, served with an apricot and marsala demi glaze. Zuppa di Pesce: Italian fish stew with clams, fennel, tomatoes, saffron, and potatoes. Saltimbocca: Thinly sliced pork loin with sage leaf and prosciutto; served with polenta and vegetable. You'd rather have pasta? Try the Spaghetti Al Carbonara. It's served with house-cured pancetta and parmesan in a cream sauce. Or delicious Pomodoro Al Forno, an oven-roasted dish including roma tomatoes sautéed with garlic, leeks, artichokes and olive oil, all served over spaghetti. Try an appetizer like Panzanella. It's toasted bread, tomatoes, cucumbers, red onions and fresh basil in a red wine and olive oil vinaigrette. Don't forget to save some room for dessert. The Gelatto is wonderful! Il Piatto is located at 2348 SE Ankeny St., Portland, OR 97214. Call (503) 236-4997. Visit their website at www.ilpiatto.citysearch.com. For food delivered directly to your home or office, log in at www.delivereddish.com. Il Piatto can also customize a party to your needs and they will cater groups of up to 80 people.

McCormick & Schmick's Seafood

This is the restaurant that was so acclaimed that it led to a collection of great eateries all across the country. You will find the original McCormick & Schmick's Seafood Restaurant in Portland's Henry Failing Building, built in 1886. The setting is full of history and the ambiance is just one of the reasons why this is such a popular gathering spot for locals and a terrific find for tourists. From the striped awning outside to the gleaming rows of glasses and bottles behind the bar, a trip to McCormick & Schmick's is a gratifying experience for all the senses. The Oregonian described it in 2000, "A crisply attired, highly professional waiting staff and an abundance of oak and brass contribute to the timeless aura, while the top of the menu proclaims what's up-to-the-minute here … the freshest fish and seafood from around the world." The keystone of McCormick & Schmick's success is wonderful seafood and wonderful service. Menus are printed every day, reflecting the best food available at that particular time and including up to 100 freshly prepared items. The Restaurant is located at 1st and Oak Streets, and is also renowned for its very popular and lively bar. For reservations, call (503) 224-7522.

McCormick's Fish House & Bar

They describe themselves at McCormick's Fish House as a place for "Great seafood and other regional favorites", but in the Pacific Northwest, those favorites can include such items as Button Mushroom Sauté with fresh herbs and demi glaze, Tomato Basil Bruschetta, with grilled baguette and Bay Shrimp, Roasted Red Pepper and Pesto Torta with crackers and cucumbers, Jarlsberg Cheese Fondue, or Yakatori Chicken with peanut curry sauce, and those are just some of the items from the Happy Hour menu! On the dinner menu you will find appetizers like Black and Blue Ahi with Wasabi and Pickled Ginger, and main courses like Oregon Sturgeon grilled with basil, black pepper, and dijon beurre blanc, or Hawaiian Tombo braised with Port wine, cranberries, oranges, and bok choy. Add to that an immense list of soups, salads, pasta, meat and poultry dishes, fish house classics and more, and you have a delicious world of possibilities. You can read the full McCormick's Fish House menu online at www.McCormicksFishHouse.com, but keep in mind that it is a sample menu only, since they add fresh items every day according to what is in season.

McCormick's Fish House & Bar is in Beaverton, in the southwest suburbs of Portland, at 9945 SW Beaverton-Hillsdale Highway. McCormick's features a full, popular bar (where you can get the wonderful Happy Hour fare at the incredible price of $1.95). They can be reached at (503) 643-1322.

McCormick & Schmick's Harborside Restaurant

Part of a collection of great seafood eateries, McCormick & Schmick's Harborside at the Marina combines the best of McCormick and Schmick's great eating traditions with its own distinctive flair. Located in the scenic River Place Marina, it gives you an incomparable view of the Willamette River to enjoy with your excellent meal. This is Portland's Premier Riverfront dining, bringing together fine food, top-notch service, and a wonderful natural setting. Also right next to the Harborside Restaurant is the very popular Pilsner Room, home of the Full Sail Ale microbrewery. The combination makes for an evening of great food and fun. The Oregonian's Restaurant Guide says it has, "an impressive fresh list of seafood from around the Pacific, some intriguing preparations, and a rousing bar scene." You can check out the menus at www.McCormickandSchmicks.com (they are sample menus only, since they change their offerings daily, according to what is fresh and best that day), including their "large party menu" and the menu for one of the features that is unique to McCormick and Schmick's restaurants, the $1.95 Happy Hour fare. At the Harborside this includes such delicious items as Japanese Tempura Onion Rings, Escargot, Inferno Fries, Four Cheese Pizza, and much more. You will find McCormick & Schmick's Harborside at the Marina Restaurant at 0309 SW Montgomery, and you can call (503) 220-1865 for a reservation.

Saucebox

It's swanky, it's sexy, it's delicious. That is what is said about Saucebox! Saucebox was Oregon's Restaurant of the Year in 1998. Its reputation as a popular late night hang out has continued ever since then. Saucebox has been featured in the New York Times, where Chef, Adam Kekahuna's salmon was lauded, "As good as salmon gets." Bon Appetit and Travel and Leisure have also sung praises for Saucebox. After starting Portland's specialty cocktail movement, Saucebox evolved to include a professional staff serving unique food that incorporates Hawaii regional and Pan-Asian cuisines. They also pioneered the DJ Café movement in Portland. Every night after 10:00pm, the lights go down and a live DJ comes on. Special events at the Saucebox include, Happy Hour from 4:30pm to 6:30pm Tuesday through Friday and Dance Parties with a live DJ are featured on Saturday nights. Sunday and Monday the restaurant is closed, but is available for private parties. Located at 214 S.W. Broadway in Portland, co-Owners, Joe Rogers and Bruce Carey can be reached at (503) 241-3393 or by e-mail at info@saucebox.com. Check out their lively website at www.saucebox.com.

Cadillac Café

If you're in Portland on a Saturday or Sunday morning and you see a long line of people, chances are they're waiting to eat at the Cadillac Café. Since 1989, Owners, Rod Brackenbury and Terry Hughes have enticed customers with their innovative breakfast and lunch fare served in a family-friendly environment. As soon as you enter the Cafe, you'll see the authentic signature pink Cadillac. Yes, the Cadillac is inside the Café! With a menu featuring fabulously delectable dishes, a full bar serving their signature Pink Cadillac martini and their ever-popular milkshakes, the Café has earned its ranking among the Oregonian's 100 Best Restaurants in Portland for four consecutive years. Next time you're in Portland, visit the Cadillac Café and taste what all of Portland is raving about. The Cadillac Café is located at 1801 NE Broadway in Portland, Oregon 97232. For more information, call (503) 287-4750.

Original Pancake House

Les Highet and Erma Hueneke founded the Original Pancake House in 1953. Since then it has become a second- and third-generation family business with over one hundred franchises from coast to coast, and the very first restaurant in Portland is still going strong. Drawing upon years of experience in the culinary field and their matchless working knowledge of national and ethnic pancake recipes, the Original Pancake Houses have been able to offer a unique and original menu that has gained national acclaim. Their pancake recipes demand only the finest ingredients, the purest butter and 36% whipping cream, fresh grade AA eggs, hard-wheat unbleached flour, and the restaurant's own sourdough starter recipe. The batters and sauces are made fresh in each restaurant's kitchen. But there's more than pancakes to the Original Pancake House. Their unique omelets are rolled in a skillet and then oven baked for a light, moist delicacy. Their gourmet crepes include the Cherry Kijafa, a blend of tart cherries and sweet Danish cherry wine. Their signature coffee is blended, roasted and ground just for the Original Pancake House restaurant. It is their pleasure is to serve you the finest food with pleasant and courteous service. In Portland, go to 8601 Southwest 24th Avenue, just off of Exit 296A on Interstate 5. Other Oregon locations are in Salem, Bend, and Eugene. For more information, call (503) 246-9007 or visit their excellent website at www.originalpancakehouse.com.

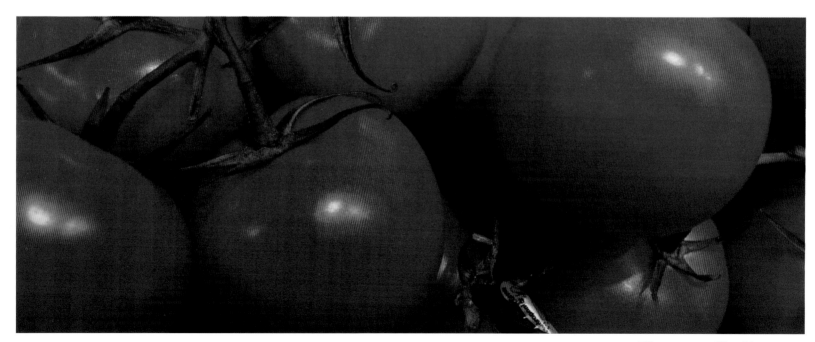

Willamette Valley Tomatoes

Fife

Fife Restaurant is the realization of a dream – the dream of one of Portland's most gifted chefs, Marco Shaw. Located in the heart of the Beaumont Wilshire area, Fife has been catering to Portland natives since December 2002 and has been earning raves since their opening day, which was Friday the 13th (so much for bad omens). Fife is a cozy, intimate, casual, yet elegant restaurant. With stunning architectural treatments and superb interior décor, Fife's atmosphere is achieved through a flowing, home-away-from-home design. Chef/Owner, Marco hosts guests nightly in this elegant environment. Stringent standards of excellence in service, food presentation, and quality ingredients, married with delicious and innovative concepts in cuisine, all combine to complete this wonderful dining experience. The menu changes daily to reflect the bounty of the Northwest; Marco and his team, Sous Chef, Mickey Minko and Pastry Chef, Steve Smith, work with local farmers and ranchers and use organic ingredients whenever possible. A three-course dinner at Fife opens with a light dish, perhaps a Dungeness crab and smoked bacon chowder, then moves on to a savory entrée such as roasted duck breast with chanterelles. For the final course, try a coconut cream tart with golden plum sauce or any of the other memorable desserts. A wine list with a wide array of local and imported vintages and a superb selection of after-dinner drinks round out the menu. Fife is located at 4440 NE Fremont Street. For reservations, call (971) 222-FIFE (3433) For detailed menus and additional information, visit their website at www.fiferestaurant.com.

Kells Irish Pub

"If you can't go to Ireland, go to Kells!" Portland's Premier Irish Establishment has one of the Northwest's most extensive selections of single malt Scotch and Irish Whiskeys, plus a large selection of microbrew and imported beers on tap. Kells offers live satellite feed for selected International sporting events. Kells is annually acclaimed as one of the Top Ten Irish Establishments in America. Kells has an excellent lunch and dinner menu that can be previewed on their website www.kellsirish.com. In addition to great food and drink, Kells also offers some of the area's most elegant private event facilities with accommodations for up to 250 people. Kells is host to one of the West Coast's largest annual St. Patrick's Day Irish Festivals. The festival features over a dozen live bands, Irish Dancers and Kells' own Irish Pipers. Kells is located at 112 SW 2nd Avenue. For reservations, please call (503) 227-4057.

Delta Cafe

Within Portland's bohemian-affected Woodstock district you will find a true herald of traditional home cooked southern comfort food awaiting you. Delta Café is well-known amongst the easy-going set, as well as by gourmands, as the place to go on a chilly night when you need a bit of southern fare. At the Delta Café, Anastasia Corya and Anton Pace serve up supreme portions in a 1960's style expressive atmosphere from 5 to10pm nightly. Until 2am, the Lounge serves up drinks, a small menu and a DJ as well. But the inviting ambiance and friendly service are not just what keeps them coming back for more, it is the food, and what food they have! Southern fried goodness warms the soul, from their chicken and okra to their hushpuppies and sweet potato fries. Enjoy their BBQ ribs and chicken or ample sides of black-eyed peas or collard greens with your blackened catfish, mac-n-cheese or great big po' boy sandwich. But don't miss the savory chicken and pillowy soft dumpling soup, or their jumbalaya and gumbo, all of which are great. One of the hallmark bargains here is the 40 oz. champagne style bottle of Pabst in a bucket of ice. So, for a relaxing and comfortable evening, stop by the Delta Café at 4607 SE Woodstock in Portland. Sometimes it gets really busy, so give them a call at (503) 771-3101 to put your name on the waiting list before you arrive.

Jake's Grill

For "classic American grill" cuisine you can't do better than Jake's Grill in Portland. This old-fashioned restaurant serves up excellent "comfort food" entrees such as Pot Roast, Sirloin Steak, Prime Rib, Pork Chops, Meat loaf and gravy, as well as terrific seafood classics like Crab and Shrimp Louie, Jake's Seafood Sampler, or Oysters On the Half-Shell. And there are items like Rock Shrimp Spring Roll with Thai Dipping Sauce, or Ahi and Hamachi Sashimi with Asian salads as well. Jake's Grill is situated in a historic building just next to the Governor Hotel at Southwest 10th and Alder Streets. Their hours of operation and their wonderful and very extensive menus for breakfast, lunch, dinner, and Happy Hour can be viewed online at www.JakesGrill.com, and like the other McCormick and Schmick's restaurants, their delicious Happy Hour fare is only $1.95. All this is complemented with a full, traditional bar. Jake's Grill is "The classic Portland combination of elegance, informality and history" according to The Oregonian-A&E Diner, Restaurant Guide. Call (503) 220-1850 for reservations, and come in to enjoy Jake's for yourself at 611 SW Tenth Avenue.

Jake's Famous Crawfish

A downtown Portland landmark for more than 110 years, Jake's Famous Crawfish has its name in lights on its historical marquee. And when you follow this sign, you will find yourself enjoying one of the top ten seafood restaurants in the nation, a place that must not be missed on a trip to the city and is also a favorite for Portland residents. Established in 1892, and run now by renowned restaurant Owners, McCormick and Schmick, a full menu from Jake's can be found on their website at www.JakesFamousCrawfish.com. This is a sample menu because the Restaurant features more than 30 varieties of fresh fish and seafood flown in daily, "making a true Pacific Northwest statement using fresh Northwest products and served in a traditional and timeless presentation." In Willamette Week's Portland's Best Restaurants listing, they complimented not only the food, but also the "friendly, knowledgeable staff," always an essential part of a great restaurant experience. At Jake's, you will have a wealth of fine food to choose from: Salmon Roasted on a Cedar Plank, Oregon Dungeness Crab, Chinook Salmon Stuffed with Crab, great pasta, poultry dishes and an outstanding selection of prime steaks. Jake's has been voted the Best Seafood Restaurant by CitySearch.com. You can find all this at 401 SW 12th Avenue at Stark Street. They are also justly proud of their very popular bar, "a tradition for generations." You can call Jake's Famous Crawfish at (503) 226-1419.

Heathman Restaurant

"Where cuisine takes center stage!" That's the Heathman Restaurant & Bar. Found at the stylish Heathman Hotel, this first-class restaurant serves breakfast, lunch, dinner, and desserts, and is best known for transforming fresh Northwest ingredients into the best of French cuisine – their own style of "French Northwest." The man responsible for this delightful transformation is Executive Chef, Philippe Boulot, whose achievements include winning the 2001 James Beard Award for Excellence, and working in some of the world's greatest hotels – The Nikko in Paris, London's Four Seasons Inn on The Park, San Francisco's Four Seasons Cliff Hotel, and The Mark Hotel in New York. For an account of his culinary gifts and experience, go to Chef Boulot's profile on the Hotel's website at www.heathmanhotel.com/heathmanrestaurant. He has been at the Heathman for ten years now, relishing working with the finest products from the region's growers and producers, selecting those that resemble the bounty of his native Normandy, and crafting his award-winning cuisine. The Heathman also has a private dining program to meet all your needs for business and personal get-togethers. They can accommodate groups from 10 to 150, and the eight banquet/meeting rooms range from 325 to 1600 sq. ft. While a separate kitchen serves business meetings and private parties, these services are still supervised by the Executive Chef. Call to make a reservation or to find out more about catering or private dining at, (503) 790-7752. The Heathman Restaurant and Bar is at 1001 SW Broadway.

Laurelwood Public House & Brewery

The Laurelwood Public House and Brewery in Portland is the only certified organic brewery in Oregon. With two locations established in 2001, new Owners, Michael DeKalb and Cathy Woo-DeKalb are working hard to ensure that Laurelwood remains well respected as a family-friendly pub with great service and even better beer. Brewmaster, Christian Ettinger has led Laurelwood to numerous honors, including being named World Champion Small Brewery and World Champion Small Brew Pub Brewmaster at the 2004 World Beer Cup. Their Ettinger Amber Ale won a silver medal at the 2003 Great American Beer Festival, and their Organic Free Range Red took home a silver medal at the 2003 North American Brewers Awards. Head Chef, Bonnie Downey, prepares pub fare with an upscale twist, including vegetarian dishes, as well as creating new and tantalizing specials daily. If the weather is nice, opt to drink and dine on the Laurelwood's patio, available only at their northwest location. Laurelwood Public House and Brewery is unique to Portland. The friendly atmosphere will welcome you as you sip one or more of their delicious brews. Laurelwood Public House and Brewery is located at 1728 NE 40th Avenue in Portland, Oregon 97212. For questions, phone (503) 282-0622. Their other location is at 2327 NW Kearney in Portland 97210. The telephone number is (503) 228-5553. You can also visit their interesting website at www.laurelwoodbrewpub.com.

Rose's Deli

Nearly 50 years ago, in 1956, a little widow from Toledo, Ohio named Rose Naftalin opened a small restaurant on 23rd Avenue in Northwest Portland. It was the same year Eisenhower was president, neither Alaska nor Hawaii were states, the Hoola-Hoop was all the rage, and Elvis Presley made his national television debut. Little did Rose know that by the time she retired in 1967, the restaurant bearing her name would be a well-established Portland landmark.

Rose's is well known by locals and visitors alike as the place for authentic, New York-style full service deli fare, famous pastries, cakes and desserts. During the 1980's, Rose's star began to fade, and the original restaurant closed in the early 1990's. Richard Werth, a transplanted restaurateur originally from New York, purchased Rose's in 1992 and set about the task of restoring Rose's name to its former prominence. Local entrepreneur, Jeff Jetton became a partner in the venture in 1998, and together, their efforts have Rose's legacy flourishing once again throughout the Portland metro area. In 2001, Rose's re-opened a store on NW 23rd Avenue, only a few blocks from the original location. Other Rose's locations have recently been opened in Portland, downtown Vancouver and in the Sherwood Cinema Center. In mid-2005, additional stores will be open in Beaverton and Camas, Washington. Serving breakfast, lunch and dinner seven days a week, the current menu features many favorite dishes inspired by Rose's original recipes, including the "world famous" Reuben Sandwich, Pot Roast and Gravy, Giant Cinnamon Rolls, colossal cakes and rich, European-style desserts. Werth notes, "I feel as if we are the caretakers of a legacy that belongs to Portland. It is our duty to see that Rose's continues to 'blossom,' serving our loyal patrons and their families for another 50 years." You can reach the original downtown Rose's Deli at (503) 590-4400. For menus and information about their other locations, see the website at www.rosesdeli.com.

Miller's Homestead Restaurant

The most pleasant and enjoyable dining experience possible. That's the goal of Miller's Homestead Restaurant in Tigard. In 1985, Don and Evelyn Miller opened the Restaurant with walls adorned with family photos, and custom-sculpted wooden benches depicting the Oregon Trail. When you step into the entranceway, you know you've entered a true Oregon Treasure. Inside the dining area country pictures, paintings, and "homestead" memorabilia overlook the tables and booths. And the food has a true down-home feeling, too. Miller's Homestead is especially famous for breakfasts, featuring chicken-fried steak, Belgian waffles, omelets, pancakes, and outstanding Eggs Benedict. Don and Evelyn opened their first restaurant in 1969, the Chalet Pancake & Pie House. Don was a truck driver before he became a restaurateur, so he knows first hand what makes a restaurant great from the customer's point of view, and he's not afraid of hard work. He worked at both the Chalet and his truck driving job for four years before the Millers could afford to hire a manager! Great word of mouth has made the Homestead increasingly popular among locals and visitors, who enjoy the hearty food, the fine service, and the whimsical touches like the authentic covered wagon in the front yard. It's there because Don likes covered wagons. The windmill and water wheel make the Homestead an unmistakable local landmark as well as a great place to eat. Miller's Homestead Restaurant is located at 17933 SW McEwan Road in Tigard, Oregon. For inquiries, call (503) 684-2831.

Bryant Station

Located on the north side of historic downtown Gresham, Bryant Station serves up a delicious, gourmet feast. Opened in 2004 by Owners, Phillip and Lori Bryant, the Restaurant sits in an old home built in 1901, its beautiful décor accented with dark wood touches. In an atmosphere geared toward casual fine dining, guests can enjoy the International-Northwest cuisine that Chef, Phillip prepares using prime cuts of meat and top quality ingredients. In addition to its great wine list, top shelf liquor and espresso, Bryant Station provides outstanding service. While the Restaurant intimately seats 46, the staff often caters to small parties. With its appetizing delicacies and relaxed, easy-going environment, Bryant Station is a great place to eat while in Gresham, Oregon. Bryant Station is located at 835 N. Main St., in Gresham, Oregon 97080. Reservations are highly recommended, so call (503) 674-8961.

Photos by Lyla Emery Reno

Stanford's

Pacific Coast Restaurants invites you to experience the art of wood-fire grilling at Stanford's in Lake Oswego. The warm interior and club-like ambience provide a wonderful setting to discover what a real wood-fire grill can do for steaks, seafood, chicken, and burgers, by cooking them to perfection over an open flame. Stanford's has become one of Portland's favorite places to dine out. You can start with a Grilled "Half Rack" of Spare Ribs, or try the Grilled Flatiron Steak Salad, then select an entree such as Pork Tenderloin with Bourbon Apricot Glaze, Herb-crusted Top Sirloin, or Rock Salt Roasted Prime Rib, and find out what you've been missing! As with other Pacific Coast Restaurants locations, Stanford's features a Happy Hour specialties menu. From 3pm to 6pm daily, 9pm to closing Sunday through Thursday, and 10pm to closing Friday and Saturday, enjoy a Cheddar Cheeseburger, Penne Pasta & Roma Tomatoes, or one of the other delicious selections for just $1.95! The Lake Oswego Stanford's is located at 14801 Kruse Oaks Drive, just off of I-5 at the Lake Oswego exit, their telephone is (503) 620-3541. You can also find Stanford's at RiverPlace, Lloyd Center, and Jantzen Beach in Portland (in 2005, a new branch will be opening at Portland International Airport). Stanford's also has locations at Clackamas Promenade in Clackamas, Tanasbourne in Hillsboro, Southcenter in Tukwila, Washington, and Broadway Plaza in Walnut Creek, California. Happy Hour times vary by location. For hours, menus and more, visit their website at www.stanfords.com.

clarklewis

Imagine putting up a "humble little eatery" in an obscure neighborhood on the East side of Portland, Oregon. A place with high ceilings, visible air ducts and concrete floors. Imagine being so modest that you insist on no capitalization in the spelling of your name, and likewise no capitalization on your website. Then imagine within a year of opening the door, the Portland Oregonian names you winner of its 2004 Restaurant of the Year award! That is followed by the Zagat Guide naming you to its list of Top Ten New Restaurants of 2004. Then Food and Wine Magazine names you winner of its Tastemaker Award. It all happened just that way to Michael Hebberoy and Morgan Brownlow, owners of the clarklewis restaurant. How did they do it? With a "highly seasonal rustic Italian" bill of fare. clarklewis features a menu of top quality organic food, from six homemade pastas daily to the fresh eggs and produce. Morgan, the chef, does all the butchering by purchasing entire animals to assure top organic quality. The result is seasonal dishes made from local ingredients borrowing from rustic Italian food tradition. One of the most popular menu items is a chef's menu in which Morgan cooks three or more courses for you of his choosing. clarklewis serves lunch and dinners to a growing group of fans. From the pastas to the seafood to the lamb, beef, and pig, you know from the first bite why this unique restaurant continues to grow in popularity and earns the recognition it deserves. Said one happy reviewer recently, "clarklewis will set the bar to the next level and redefine the way we eat." clarklewis is located at the corner of SE Taylor Street and 10th Avenue in the East Bank area of Portland. For inquiries, call (503) 235-2294. Visit the web site at www.ripepdx.com.

Monteaux's Public House

The idea of an American "public house" is not a new one. The first public house in America was opened by the Governor of New York, who was too busy to entertain strangers and travelers in his own home. The building became City Hall and was used for that purpose until the 1880's. During the American Revolution, the tavern was the customary venue of political planning sessions. In 2000, four fellow innkeepers founded Monteaux's, an American gathering place dedicated to bringing great food, drink and service to Washington County in a modern version of the public house. Owners, Larry & Lisette Crepeaux, and Sal & Lisa Montcalegre, (Monteaux's combines their surnames) have a long history of hospitality. They managed large hotels together, first in California before settling in the Westside of the Portland metro area. Desiring to own and operate their own place, they found a location in a new building and set out to make it look like it had been around awhile. Long and narrow with high ceilings, Monteaux's dark woodwork and cavernous aspect is at odds with its more modern menu and clientele. Their mural tells the really BIG story of this area's transition from farm and forest to sneakers and hi-tech. Monteaux's Public House is truly an American gathering place. A classic menu, with worldwide favorites sprinkled in, welcomes all ages for lunch, dinner and Sunday breakfast. Try the Black & Bleu Burger, Chicken Saltimbocca or the Olallies Salad and leave room for one of the house-made cheesecakes made by Lisa herself. To drink, enjoy one of the many and constantly rotating draft beers, wine and an inventive cocktail menu. To find Monteaux's Public House simply get to 16165 SW Regatta Drive (Walker Road at 158th) in Beaverton, Oregon or check the information on their website at www.monteauxs.com. To speak with them directly, call (503) 439-9942 with delivery through www.bizeats.com. Stop in, eat, drink and tell some BIG stories…the Owners are never too busy for a good story!

Southpark Seafood Grill and Wine Bar

What do you want when you open a bottle of wine with dinner? If you want it to complement your food, head for Southpark Seafood Grill and Wine Bar in Portland, Oregon. There General Manager, Karin Devencenzi and her staff offer dishes influenced by the traditions of Spain, Portugal, Greece, Italy, France and North Africa. Southpark Seafood Grill and Wine Bar also has a Wine Program that emphasizes those same Mediterranean flavors. Southpark's wine list is comprised of 130 selections from a dozen countries and nearly 50 varietals. They are proud of the fact that they stock many "obscure" wines, with names like Gros Manseng, Coullioure and Arbois Rouge, all offering terrific value for the money. Says the staff, "We encourage you to order wine by taste rather than by familiar label, name brand, or score. We want you to experience some of the wonderful flavors that occur in wines from more obscure regions and try wines you might normally overlook." Southpark's Wine Program is serious enough for the wine cognoscenti, yet friendly and fun if you just want a good glass of wine. Their wine list has won numerous awards from publications including Sante Magazine, The Wine Spectator, Bon Appetit, Wine and Spirits Magazine, Restaurant Hospitality, and The Oregonian. As to the food, Southpark serves authentic Mediterranean-inspired cuisine. Windows of the wine bar open on to the sidewalk, allowing tables to spill outdoors in the European cafe tradition. Southpark Seafood Grill and Wine Bar is located at 901 SW Salmon Street in Portland, Oregon 97205. To make inquiries, call (503) 326-1300. You can also visit their website at www.southpark.citysearch.com.

Main Street Ale House

Main Street Ale House is a product of the dreams of Owner, Adam Roberts and Manager, Adam Klimek. The relaxing atmosphere, great tasting ale and incredible food all combine to create the perfect place to enjoy yourself with family or friends. Located in Historic Downtown Gresham, Main Street Ale House brews 12 delicious ales with names like Black Roots Blonde, Demented Duck Amber, Roberts Red Ale and Powell Porter. Main Street Ale House features a main bar where you can sip a brew while you watch them make their ales, the Black Roots smoking lounge, and a main family dining area. And if you have a special event coming up, they offer a private dining area for families or groups. The menu, prepared by Executive Chef, Will Adams, includes a full selection of mouth-watering appetizers, entrees, sandwiches, salads and pizzas. Visit their website at www.mainstreetale.com and learn about their Passport Program. Main Street Ale House is located at 333 N. Main Street in Gresham, Oregon. Reservations are recommended, so call (503) 669-0569.

Pizza Schmizza

Founded in 1993 by André Jehan and his wife, Carla, Pizza Schmizza has been serving New York-style pizza in a fun and friendly environment. When André moved out west to realize his destiny and open a New York-style pizza joint, his father's response was "pizza, schmizza…get a real job." Well, the name stuck, and Pizza Schmizza has grown to include over 40 locations, each offering a unique atmosphere and a curiously adventurous menu. Initially encouraging their employees to create their own pizza, they now serve over 72 different pizza varieties. With toppings such as spaghetti and meatballs, baked potatoes, alligator and marinated steak, it's not surprising that people flock from all over to enjoy the delicious, New York-style pizza that Pizza Schmizza has to offer. Pizza Schmizza specializes in pizza by the slice and has recently added a line of pasta and salad products. Pizza Schmizza Headquarters is located at 1055 NE 25th, Suite C in Hillsboro, Oregon. Call (503) 640-2328 or take a look at their website at www.schmizza.com.

Alameda Brew House

Alameda Brewhouse Owners, Matt Schumacher and Peter Vernier, show passion in everything they do. From their friendly, intimate atmosphere to their signature recipes and award winning ales you are in for an enjoyable and unique dining experience. Matt, a formally trained chef, and John Eaton, a formally trained master brewer, joined together eight years ago to create a memorable menu that includes seven signature brews and great food at great prices. Ranked as one of the best neighborhood restaurants in Portland you will find a fusion of traditional pub foods with a twist that only Alameda Brewhouse can provide. For starters why not try the Hand Dipped Beer Battered Onion Rings with an avocado-cilantro dipping sauce? Next how about their Black Bear Stout Turkey Pot Pie or the Famous Whiskey Crab Bisque? Want something you can really sink your teeth into? Check out their Whiskey BBQ Babyback Ribs. For dessert try the Brewhouse Brownie topped with vanilla ice cream and their chocolate stout sauce. These are just a small sample of the menu items to choose from. Alameda Brewhouse offers a wide variety of libations including hand crafted ales, mixed cocktails and a large assortment of wines. Take a moment to savor the pleasure of their hand-brewed Grandma Mary's Rootbeer, brewed in-house using birch, sarsparilla and honey. Their Klickitat Pale Ale is an award winning smooth ale and a definite favorite. Alameda Brewhouse is located at 4765 NE Fremont Street in Portland, Oregon. You can reach them at (503) 460-9025.

Portland City Grill

The Portland City Grill is another gem in the Pacific Coast Restaurants collection. Hailed as "one of the Nation's Top 50 Restaurants" by Restaurant & Institutions Magazine, the City Grill is high up on the 30th floor of the Unico/US Bancorp Tower. It is one of the hot spots in Portland and a place to see and be seen in, especially as the lounge has become a popular place to meet up. A very attentive and professional staff serves you from the moment you come off the elevator and meet the hostess. The Grill offers superb food, spectacular views of the cityscape and Mt. Hood, and live piano music nightly in the lounge. In addition to a full menu of wonderful dishes such as Seafood Pappardelle Pasta with Riesling Cream Sauce and Macadamia Nut Crusted Chicken Breast, the City Grill also features a complete Sushi Bar. Order à la carte or enjoy a makimono (roll) combination such as the California Roll, with crab, avocado, cucumber and sesame seeds, or the Lobster Tempura. An extensive wine list includes delightful rarities from Oregon's finest vineyards. As with other Pacific Coast Restaurants locations, the Portland City Grill features a Happy Hour specialties menu from 4:30pm to 6:30pm, Monday through Saturday, 10pm to closing Monday through Thursday, and 4:30pm to closing on Sundays. Dine in the Lounge and enjoy a selection of delicious offerings at prices ranging from $1.95 to $3.95. Three private dining rooms make the Portland City Grill a spectacular location for corporate dining events, anniversary celebrations, business lunches and other special occasions. Private groups of up to 112 can be accommodated for sit-down meals. For dinner reservations, call (503) 450-0030. For private dining and banquets, call (503) 525-5260. For more information, visit their website at www.portlandcitygrill.com.

Newport Bay Restaurant

What better location for a seafood restaurant than a marina on the Willamette River? Newport Bay Restaurant at RiverPlace Marina, Oregon's only floating restaurant, has been drawing enthusiastic patrons since October 1985, and no wonder, with a scenic location offering both a breathtaking view of Portland's beautiful bridges, and delectable dishes such as the Hot Dungeness Crab and Bay Shrimp Sandwich, Pan Fried Alaskan Razor Clams, and Northwest Salmon with Raspberry Beurre Blanc. Whether you come to Newport Bay for lunch, Sunday Brunch, dinner, or to enjoy the $1.95 special menu during Happy Hour, you'll leave satisfied. Also, whether you're a vegetarian or in the mood for red meat, there's something great for you at the Newport Bay Restaurant. An excellent selection of wines, including favorite Oregon and Washington vintages, provide a perfect complement for any entree. And don't forget to ask about the daily fresh specialties. Newport Bay is the place "Where Fresh Seafood Comes Ashore"! In addition to RiverPlace Marina, Newport Bay has restaurants at Jantzen Beach and Mall 205 in Portland, Highway 99 and Washington Square in Tigard, Tanasbourne in Beaverton, Burnside Road in Gresham, Market Street in Salem, and three locations in Washington State. They are Vancouver Plaza in Vancouver, Southcenter in Tukwila, and Northup Way in Kirkland. Reservations are recommended for the RiverPlace Marina. For inquiries, call (503) 227-3474. For directions, sample menus, hours of operation and other information, visit their website at www.newportbay.com.

Manzana Rotisserie Grill

"Manzana" is Spanish for apple, and at Manzana Rotisserie Grill, apple-themed art adorns the walls and food is cooked on a real apple wood grill. The minute you walk in the door you know you are at the right place. You'll find a casual environment with dark wood booths and tables, the lighting is just right. It is a busy place during the week, but don't forget to come back on Saturday and Sunday for the Prime Rib. Besides all the other regular items, they offer a lighter fare, such as Smoky Grilled Artichoke and Tortilla Soup with Avocado. It is close by to the Portland City Street Car which can make for a fun outing combined with the Manzana Rotisserie Grill. Northwest specialties with a Southwest flair are featured here. At the core of Manzana's menu is Fire Roasted Rotisserie Oregon-raised Chicken, seasoned with a special blend of 30 spices. Delightful appetizers like Tuscan White Bean Hummus and a full assortment of soups, salads, sandwiches and desserts round out the menu. Apples are a recurring theme on the menu as well. For example, fresh Fuji apples are chopped into salads, and Granny Smith apples baked into the Grill's luscious old-fashioned Apple Crisp. On weekends Manzana also offers a full breakfast menu. Like other Pacific Coast Restaurants locations, Manzana features a Happy Hour Menu with specialty items such as Chipotle Barbecue Pork Quesadilla, Citrus Honey Chicken Wings, Barbecue Beef Sandwich, and Caesar Salad. At the Manzana Grill, as at all Pacific Coast locations, you'll find a commitment to food quality and a devotion to Guests unequalled in Oregon. Manzana's has two locations. The first is in the Pearl District of Portland at 1203 NW Glisan Street. Their telephone number is (503) 248-1690), and in Lake Oswego at 305 First Street. To reach them call (503) 675-3322. For hours and more information, visit their website at www.manzanagrill.com.

Henry's 12th Street Tavern

The former Blitz-Weinhard Brewery in northwest Portland's Brewery Blocks is now home to Henry's 12th Street Tavern. Henry's is a unique 14,500 Square foot restaurant and bar named in honor of Henry Weinhard. Henry's also pays tribute to the original brewery by offering a hundred varieties of beer and hard cider on tap! The cavernous brick interior with 24-foot ceilings is home to such state-of-the-art innovations as a built-in frozen drink rail in the bar that keeps poured drinks from getting warm. Flat screen and plasma TVs are set up throughout the bar, but Henry's is about more than the bar. The extensive menu offers much more than standard "pub grub," beginning with appetizers like Crispy Salt and Pepper Calamari and Gorgonzola Fries. Fresh seafood from the Pacific Northwest highlights the entrees, with specialties such as the Cumin-dusted Pacific Swordfish. Seems this place comes in two parts: half flashy bar, half upscale restaurant. Henry's has now become one of Portland's hot spots to gather. As with other Pacific Coast Restaurants locations, Henry's also features a Happy Hour specialties menu from 3pm to 6pm daily, with items ranging from $1.95 to $3.95. On the upper level of Henry's, there's another special treat. Seven custom, regulation-sized billiards tables and yet another full-service bar. Whether you're shooting a round or relaxing in one of the overstuffed leather club chairs, it's the perfect place to relax after a meal. Henry's 12th Street Tavern is located at 10 NW 12th Avenue in Portland, Oregon. Call (503) 227-5320 or visit Henry's website at www.henrystavern.com.

Portland Steak & Chophouse

The historic Old Multnomah Hotel in downtown Portland, now home to Embassy Suites, is also home to the Portland Steak & Chophouse. Here you will find one of the best examples of elegance and tradition in a dinner house that has all the modern looks, including things like custom natural gas-fueled light fixtures, plus the coziness and intimate feeling of the Lounge. Mahogany woodwork and booths upholstered in Italian leather create a sumptuous 19th-century ambience, a luxurious setting perfect for enjoying a Rib Eye Chop with Roasted Garlic Herb Butter or a New York Strip Steak with Angel Hair Onion Rings. And there's much more to enjoy: Wood Oven Pizza, pasta dishes (perhaps the Dungeness crab and Rock Shrimp Ravioli?). Of course you'll want to start with an appetizer. Perhaps you'll choose something like Almond-crusted Brie, or Oysters Rockefeller? Choose the perfect accompaniment from an extensive wine list featuring fine wines from the Willamette Valley, Napa Valley and other Pacific Coast vineyards. And wait until you see the dessert list! The Portland Steak & Chophouse is located at 121 SW Third Avenue. For reservations, call (503) 223-6200. From 3:30pm to 6:30pm and 9:30pm till closing, Monday through Saturday, and Noon till closing on Sundays, enjoy the Happy Hour specials at the bar, with delightful treats such as the Sourdough Bruschetta, Tillamook Cheddar Cheeseburger, and Chipotle BBQ Chicken Wings. All are available at prices ranging from $1.95 to $3.95 (minimum drink order required). For more information see their website at www.portlandchophouse.com..

Philadelphia Steaks and Hoagies Restaurant & Micro Brewery

Where are you from? Ever eaten a Philadelphia Cheese Steak? A Hoagie? How about a submarine, hero, grinder, poor boy, or wedge? Did you know that those names all describe very similar sandwiches? In Portland, the place to get one of these sumptuous sandwiches with only the freshest ingredients of beef, onions and cheese is the Philadelphia Steaks and Hoagies Restaurant and Micro Brewery. Owner, Steve Moore, offers a filling and healthy sandwich, and complements the food with a choice of 11 microbrews. The location is Oregon's smallest licensed microbrewery. So how are your taste buds doing right now? How about an Italian Special Hoagie with ham, Genoa salami, Capocola ham, Provolone cheese, lettuce, pickles, tomato, sweet or hot pickled peppers, oil and spices? Or perhaps a Mushroom Cheese Steak with grilled steak, fresh sliced mushrooms, grilled onions and melted American cheese appeals to you? In addition to the steaks and hoagies, there are chicken sandwiches, various Italian favorites, low-carb specials, low-calorie choices, breakfast hoagies, a kids' menu and "Party Time" favorites. By the way, Italian immigrants working at the Hog Island shipyard in Philadelphia invented hoagies at the turn of the last century. In Maine they are known as submarines, heroes in Los Angeles, grinders in Ohio, poor boys in Louisiana, and wedges in New England. Now you're ready to eat, and you've had a history lesson for free. Philadelphia Steaks and Hoagies Restaurant and Micro Brewery are located at 6410 SE Milwaukie Avenue in Portland, Oregon 97202. You can phone them at (503) 239-8544. A second location is open at 18625 Highway 43 in West Linn. To reach their West Linn location, call (503) 699-4130. If you'd like to guarantee a large order, it's best to phone ahead.

Apizza Scholls

Acclaimed by the Oregonian as "the Portland area's best pizza," the pies at Apizza Scholls are something to write home about. Owners, Brian Spangler and Kim Nyland, have heard nothing but raves since setting up their own pizza parlor. The dough is made entirely by hand and takes a full twenty-four hours to prepare. Their "less is more" philosophy results in a perfect balance of ingredients on pies like the Margherita, which features mozzarella, fior di latte, grana padano, parmigiano-reggiano, extra virgin olive oil, basil and garlic (all herbs and vegetables are picked fresh, and the cheese is flown in from Wisconsin). Meat lovers can get classic toppings like sausage and pepperoni as well as Italian hot capicollo. Apizza Scholls is open Wednesday through Sunday. You'll want to get there early, because the demand is so great that sometimes they run out of dough! Each pizza is hand-spun, so be patient and enjoy an antipasti plate or salad while you wait. At Apizza Scholls, pizza isn't fast food, but after you try it you'll never want to have a "fast" pizza again. Apizza Scholls is located at 4741 SE Hawthorne Blvd., at the black awning next to JaCiva Bakery, in Portland, Oregon. You can call (503) 233-1286 or check out their website at www.apizzascholls.com.

Nonna Emilia Ristorante Italiano

In 1978, Stephen Ceccanti opened Nonna Emilia Ristorante Italiano, which he named in honor of his grandmother (nonna is Italian for grandmother). For over 25 years, Stephen has been serving family-style authentic Italian cuisine from a historic wooden building in Aloha. The loving influence of Stephen's grandmother is imbued in the ambiance, the food and the friendly family warmth that envelops you at Nonna Emilia. Stephen's grandmother learned to cook in her family's café in Florence Italy. She and her husband Ernie immigrated to the United States in 1921 and in 1927 they opened "The Monte Carlo," one of the first Italian restaurants in Portland, Oregon. In the family tradition, Nonna Emilia passed her grandmother's recipes from "The Old Country" down to Stephen, who oversees the kitchen today. It is this rich history and family tradition that creates the remarkable flavors which saturate Nonna Emilia's food. The extensive menu offers everything from pasta, chicken and veal dishes to pizza, calzones and fabulous desserts. The wine list features Italian, Northwest and California vintages. On weekend nights a strolling accordionist completes the Italian dining experience. In 2004, the combination of fabulous food, friendly service and family traditions resulted in citysearch.com selecting Nonna Emilia's to receive the "#1 Italian Food in Portland" award. Take-out food, banquets, a cocktail lounge and catering are also available and the lunch buffet features the same award winning dishes that are served at dinner. Nonna Emilia is located at 17210 SW Shaw, Aloha, Oregon. For reservations, call (503) 649-2232; for take-out call (503) 649-8531. For more information visit their website, www.nonnaemilias.com.

Elephant's Delicatessen

Since 1978, Elephant's Delicatessen has had a reputation for food of the highest quality and taste. Elaine Tanzer and Anne and Scott Weaver and their staff incorporated this quality into a catering menu that is varied and unique and always beautifully presented. Their Northwest store makes twenty varieties of fresh baked breads and specializes in everything from elaborate receptions to boxed lunches for business and community events and same day catering for last minute parties or dinners. Elephant's is more than a store, it is a group of people who are in the business of making life better. They want to improve the quality of life for everyone around them, not only with the goods and services they offer, but with the way they treat each other. They feel that if they treat each person with the respect and attention they deserve, the world will be a better place. You will have fun shopping in their store. The visual and sensory experience is a treat in itself. Enjoy lush, bountiful displays and scintillating demonstrations. Elephant's offers homemade soups, sandwiches and pastries. Try their famous Tomato Orange Soup and Chicken Enchiladas Verde. Everything is made from scratch without preservatives or other harmful chemicals. To insure freshness and quality, they use local and seasonal goods. Elephant's stocks a tremendous selection of cheeses and wines and they will create gourmet gift baskets and food-to-go for your romantic picnic. You name it; they will do their best to create your request and always with their kind and thoughtful service. Elephant's Uptown is located at 115 NW 22nd Avenue. Flying Elephants is located at 812 SW Park. You can reach them by dialing (503) 546-3166 and you will find Flying Elephants Kruse Way at 5885 SW Meadows Way in Lake Oswego. Their phone number is (503) 620-2444). For further information you can access their website at www.ElephantsDeli.com. Elephant's may also be reached at (503) 224-3955.

Genoa

Genoa was originally opened in 1971 by Michael Vidor, at the suggestion of his brother-in-law, famed restaurateur, Warner LeRoy. Vidor sought to bring to the city of Portland the distinctive cuisine of Northern Italy. Thirty-three years later, Genoa is still doing just that from the comfort of a building that is now on the National Register of Historic Places. Currently owned by Kerry Debuse, who originally worked there as a waiter, Genoa offers true Italian cuisine, and specializes in a traditional seven-course Italian dinner put together by Head Chef, Jerry Huising. By combining regional Italian recipes with Northwest elements, handmade fresh pasta, and local and organic ingredients, Genoa offers patrons a superb dining experience. The menu is changed every three weeks, and the servers go above and beyond the norm to make your dining experience pleasant. Though certain changes have occurred over the years, (such as smaller portions so diners can make it through all seven courses) and the use of more olive oil instead of butter and cream so that the meal is not too rich, Genoa still maintains its dedication to providing only the best. Genoa is a perfect place to go for special occasions. When in Portland, be sure to visit Genoa, a masterpiece of Italian cuisine. Genoa is located at 2832 SE Belmont Street in Portland, Oregon 97214. For reservations call (503) 238-1464. You can also visit their website at www.genoarestaurant.com.

Cameo Cafe

When you are in the Northwest 23rd Shopping District be sure to visit the Cameo Café. Owners, Charlie and Sue Gee Lehn, bring award winning breakfasts, lunches and dinners to this trendy part of town. If you join them for breakfast, you might want to try the Acre Pancake. As the name implies, Acre Pancakes are enormous pancakes ordered by the acre. Even though they are of ample size they still retain the warm, pillowy goodness we all come to expect from great pancakes. But if an acre of pancake is too much for you, you might want to try their award winning malted Belgium waffles, crispy on the outside and light and airy on the inside. These are just two of the many fine offerings available to you for breakfast. For lunch and dinner there are menu items that originate in France, Italy and the Mediterranean and because Sue Gee was born in Korea, all the offerings have a distinct Asian influence. Although the Cameo Café does get busy, you can rest assured you will find plenty of seating in their five dining rooms. This is a great place for get-togethers due to the ample space but also because of the casual family style dining environment and affordable prices. So, if you're looking for a fun, tasty and affordable restaurant, drop in at the Cameo Café. They're located at 2340 Northwest 23rd Place, which is at the corner of Westover Street, in Portland. You can reach them at (503) 221-6542 or visit their website at www.cameo.com.

Skyline Restaurant

The "best burgers in Portland", that's what the Skyline Restaurant has been promising and serving up on their trademark caraway seed buns since the early 1930s. The diner's classic Art Deco lines and blazing neon have made it a beloved Portland landmark. Current Owner, Michelle Nelson, is well-qualified to maintain the Skyline's legacy. Michelle began working there as a waitress, serving the unique tables and booths and the counter, learning the business from the ground up. When she bought the Restaurant, she knew all of the recipes, she'd learned how to run a successful operation, and she was dedicated to keeping the place the way it was. Sadly, some traditions couldn't be maintained. Carhop services were discontinued in the mid 1970s. But the wonderful burgers, homemade chili, clam chowder and split pea soups are still served, the dressings for the salad are still made fresh, and there are still thirty flavors of milk shakes made with soft ice cream. Homemade pies are another perennial favorite. Open seven days a week, the atmosphere is family-friendly and warm with seasonal holiday lights, children's drawings on the walls, and the traditional lunch counter and family-sized booths along the windows. Memorabilia from past years reminds customers of the Skyline's history as they enjoy the wonderful present of a true Oregon Treasure. The Skyline Restaurant is located at 1313 NW Skyline Boulevard in Portland, Oregon. To learn more about this great place, call (503) 292-6727.

Nick's Italian Café

A fabulous Italian dish created with seasonal offerings and local wines in mind is what has made Nick's Italian Café a top destination in the Willamette Valley for over twenty-five years. Evening meals consist of a delectable five course prix fix feast that may include appetizers of melon and pears with Proscuitto or steamed Manila clams marinated in lemon with garlic and parsley followed by minestrone soup, a salad of mixed greens and Gorgonzola and Dungeness crab and pine nut lasagna. Main entrée options may include such savory treats as highly acclaimed Salt-Grilled Salmon or Rabbit braised in Oregon Pinot Gris with a Rosemary Gorgonzola Polenta or Baby Lamb Chops marinated in sage and garlic. Topping off this fine meal is a choice of Creme Brulee, lemon ice cream, gin and tonic ice, tortes, and Tiramisu. All choices are available a'la carte. All menu options change daily. The pastas are always made fresh on site using recipes taught to Nick from his grandmother and father. The special minestrone is a family treasure passed down through the generations. In the late 1970's Nick found his inspired recipes aligned well with the pioneering wine makers of the Willamette Valley. Recently Nick has been joined by Chef Jeremy Buck, fresh from one year in Italy. Soon Nick's Café would be synonymous with Oregon's growing wine industry. Inasmuch as they supported him he supports them with his commitment to crafting dishes with Oregon wines in mind. You can find Nick's Italian Café at 521 East 3rd Street in McMinnville. You can reach the Café at (503) 434-4471 or check out their website at www.nicksitaliancafe.com.

Golden Valley Brewery

As you step into the bar, it is hard to miss the Grand Old Hoyt Hotel Bar that was salvaged when half of the hotel was partially destroyed by fire in Portland, Oregon. The bar is solid Honduran mahogany and is 27 feet long with the back reaching 14 feet high. The stained glass and mirrors are also original. Peter and Celia Kircher founded Golden Valley to revive traditions from years gone by when the good things in life were to enjoy good food with friends and family. That atmosphere has been recaptured in the Old Mission-style renovation of a 1921 warehouse building, in the brewing of handcrafted beers and in the fine quality of the freshest handmade cuisine. The skilled kitchen staff creates sauces, smoked meats and sausages, and they bake fantastic brownies and cobblers. Using homemade products and working daily with fresh ingredients, they create the finest in local cuisine. From the bar or your table, watch the brewery in action as the brewers create some of their famous lagers and ales.

The banquet room can accommodate up to 80 persons for special events and corporate dinner functions. In 2004, the Kirchers began raising premium Angus beef cattle and feeding them with spent grain from the brewery. With a taste and tenderness found nowhere else in the Willamette Valley, it is sure to be the next big hit for Golden Valley. From friendly dining with friends over a burger and brew, to more gracious dining with Saffron Salmon, Roasted Garlic Rib Steaks, or Vegetarian Portobello Mushrooms and a glass of wine, you will know you have found an Oregon Treasure in the Golden Valley Brewery and Restaurant. Enjoy a meal and brew at 980 E. Fourth Street in Historic Downtown McMinnville, Oregon. Contact them at (503) 472-BREW (2739) or on the Internet at www.goldenvalleybrewery.com.

Los Báez
Mexican Restaurant

Angel Báez is living the American dream. That is how the Statesman Journal described the owner of Los Báez Mexican Restaurant a couple of years ago. It was Báez' personal dream to own a Mexican restaurant in the United States. Oregon has benefited from that dream now that Báez and his family have expanded from a single restaurant to four eateries between Salem and Roseburg. Come in to the original Los Báez at 2920 Commercial Street SE in Salem, started in 1973. You can experience the terrific food that has made these restaurants so popular. Or go to their eatery at 1292 Lancaster Road. They serve authentic, delicious Mexican food. The popularity of Los Báez' homemade flour tortillas and table salsa has crossed international borders. Besides treats like sopapillas, chiles rellenos, sizzling fajitas, and deep-fried ice cream, Los Báez also has some specialty "healthy menu" items like low carbohydrate tortillas used in the Low-Carb/Low-Fat Wrap. There are many choices on the menu for vegetarians, as well, including Guacamole Tostadas and the "Veggie Wally," a veggie version of their famous Wally Burrito. The Báez family comes from Michoacan, one of the most picturesque states in central Mexico, "where cooking is an art." They follow the region's delicious traditions. The oldest and best Mexican restaurant in Salem and the Willamette Valley, Los Báez serves imported and domestic wines and beers, including great Mexican beers. They are open daily for lunch and dinner, closing only on Christmas and New Years. They will also gladly do off-site catering in the Salem area and beyond. Their gracious staff will welcome you to enjoy truly great Mexican food and atmosphere at any location of Los Báez. If you are on your way south, be sure to try the Roseburg location at 1347 Stephens Road. In Salem, call (503) 363-3109.

Jonathan's Oyster Bar

Since 1979, Jonathan's Oyster Bar has been serving up a delicious array of seafood delights under the discerning eye of Owner, John Cunningham. While Jonathan's is actually two places in one, the Seafood Grill on State Street and the Long Bar Café on the Liberty side, they are connected by a single hallway and both serve the same menu items prepared by one kitchen.

Bedecked in opulent amounts of nautical memorabilia, including surfboards, boats and a wall-mounted marlin, Jonathan's landmark location has long been attracting those seeking splendidly prepared seafood, salads and carnivore-pleasing entrees. With special emphasis on Southwest, Cajun cooking and a full bar offering top shelf liquor, beer and wine, Jonathan's is truly a pearl of a restaurant. Jonathan's Oyster Bar and Long Bar Café are located at 445 State Street in Salem, Oregon 97301. To contact this Salem landmark, call (503) 362-7219.

Rudy's at Salem Golf Course

Here's the deal at Rudy's at the Salem Golf Course in Salem, Oregon. "We want you to relax, hang out and enjoy yourself." They say so right on the menu, along with their theme "It's a done deal!" The building the restaurant is housed in is an exact reproduction of the Rosedown Plantation, one of the few pre-Civil War manors not destroyed in the war between the states. Rudy's prides itself in its premium corn-fed, aged beef. The staff cuts all steaks on site, daily. Soups are made from scratch, and Owner, John Rudishauser proudly declares them "some of the best soups in town." The salad dressings? Made right there at Rudy's, of course, as are the sauces and desserts. The idea, says Rudishauser, is start with great food. For example, corn-fed Midwest beef steaks aged six to eight weeks, cut and prepared in-house. Here is a sample of recent offerings on the Entrees menu: Top sirloin, thick and juicy, offered in four different cuts, including the "awesome" baseball cut; Roast Prime Rib, roasted with rock salt and spices, then trimmed to be super juicy and flavorful, and creamy horseradish on the side; Charbroiled Rack of Lamb, a 12-ounce New Zealand rack of lamb served with mint jelly; Dungeness Crab Cakes, fresh cakes dusted in panko flakes and cooked until golden brown, served with red pepper cream sauce; Salmon Filet, a beautiful filet touched off with Rudy's own lobster sauce; and Cajun Chicken Linguine, tender chunks of broiled Cajun chicken breast tossed in a light cream sauce with mushrooms, onions, and linguine noodles. Among the Clubhouse favorites is Rudy's Chicken Sandwich, a teriyaki chicken breast topped with crisp hickory smoked bacon and double Pepper Jack cheese. Ask about the private banquet room with a tree-covered patio overlooking the golf club. It is set up to handle parties, weddings, meetings, or whatever event you'd like, for up to 150 people. Rudy's is located at the Salem Golf Club, 2025 Golf Course Road South, off of South River Road. Call (503) 399-0449.

Bistro Maison

Chef, Jean-Jacques Chatelard, and his wife, Deborah, bring to McMinnville an authentic French bistro dining experience. Designed with care and attention, Bistro Maison utilizes the best locally produced items and taps into an extensive selection of fine local wines. The intimate ambiance of Bistro Maison's house, built in the 1890's, and the attached garden patio add further charm to your special lunch or dinner. Epicures will find great pleasure in the local wines and weekly specials created with seasonal availability and quality as leading inspirations. Saffron rich bouillabaisse, escargot, coq au vin, fondue and cassoulet are readily recognized staples of the bistro experience but at Bistro Maison these staples take on a new flair under the skill of Jean-Jacques. Consider his special Pate D' Maison with cornichons and sweet shallot confit or take a gastronomic tour with the Fromage Et Charcuterie assortment of cheeses, meats, pate, cornichons, and baguette. The mussels have drawn many accolades and of particular interest is the Moules A La Crème De Pernod. Weekly specials include Pot Au Feu, Choucroute Garnie, Bouillabaisse Fruits De Mer, Couscous and Cassoulet. On the last Wednesday of each month the very popular BYOBB (Bring Your Own Best Bottle) Wine Cellar Dinner is hosted at Bistro Maison. Every month there are cooking classes offered covering a range of French favorites. Bistro Maison is located 729 East 3rd Street in McMinnville. Call for reservations at (503) 474-1888 or visit their website at www.bistromaison.com.

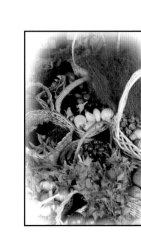

j. james restaurant

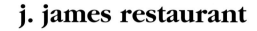

Combine the best of the Northwest with the best of France, and you have the j. james restaurant. Winner of the AAA 3 diamond award. Salem is lucky that former resident Jeff James returned to his hometown to create a restaurant that "brings life to Salem's dining scene!" according to the Oregonian. Before becoming Chef and Owner of his own restaurant, Jeff built up an impressive cooking résumé. First culinary school, then the tutelage of Rob Pounding at the Salishan Lodge on the Oregon Coast. Then work as sous chef at the historic Columbia Gorge Hotel in Hood River. He returned to the Salishan as executive sous chef for the next five years. Prior to opening his own restaurants in Salem, Oregon and Mazama, Washington, he completed an intensive culinary course in France. He was the executive chef at Sun Mountain Lodge for several years – a destination ski resort in Washington, where his cuisine accumulated numerous prestigious awards and earned raves from magazines, as well as recognition from the prestigious James Beard Foundation. After he cooked for guests at The James Beard House, he was commended in their newsletter for working "culinary miracles with the finest local produce." As an integral part of the community, the j. james restaurant boasts the 2002 award for New Business of the Year from the Chamber of Commerce. Also an award for outstanding community partner from Marion-Polk County Food Share. Here are a few of the items from the menu at j. james restaurant: White Cheddar & Goat Cheese Tart with spicy onion jam & citrus reduction; Grilled Black Mission figs wrapped in prosciutto stuffed with Spanish blue cheese, roast red peppers; Crab Cakes and balsamic reduction; plus a daily Risotto with the market's freshest ingredients. And those are just the starters! To see the full menu, go to www.jjamesrestaurant.com. If you ever need a great place for a meeting or family get together, you can click on their "banquet" link to read about the services and facilities that the staff at j. james is proud to offer. And when you come in, be sure to try their great Crème Brulee. j. james restaurant is conveniently located at 325 High Street SE, Salem. For information or to make reservations, call (503) 362-0888.

Court Street Dairy Lunch

Where do people in the know in Salem go when they want the best lunch in town? Since 1929, the answer has been Court Street Dairy Lunch! Started by Dairyman, Glen Morris and now owned by Kathy Puentes and Marlene Miller, the restaurant has an unbroken tradition of enjoyable, hearty food at a price you can afford. Salem's oldest continuously operating restaurant, Court Street Dairy Lunch has changed very little over the years. Two things that have stayed the same are their great food and their support and involvement in the community. They also were recognized in the National Register's Who's Who in Executives & Professionals for 2004 & 2005. As you sit down in a booth or at the counter for breakfast or lunch, you may feel like you've traveled back in time. The food is made from scratch, and there are only a handful of concessions to modern sensibilities. You can now get a Vegetarian Garden Burger or an omelet if you're not in the mood for meat. Or you can dig into a stack of their famous hot cakes, made from the Dairy Lunch's special recipe. As you might expect from an institution founded by a dairyman, the restaurant is renowned for its milkshakes. You won't want to pass up their sundaes or malts either! The Dairy Lunch offers free refills on coffee and soda, a policy you'll be grateful for when you find out why they call their coffee the world's finest. This is fast food the way it was meant to be, daily proof that you can serve food quickly without sacrificing quality and service. They also have gift cards for any amount towards food at the restaurant. The Court Street Dairy Lunch serves breakfast and lunch Monday through Friday. It's located at 347 Court Street, Salem. For more information, call (503) 363-6433. Don't miss it the next time you're in Salem. You may just find yourself planning return trips to go there again.

Alessandro's

Listed in Best Places, rated Three Diamonds by AAA, and awarded Three Stars by Mobile Travel Guide, Alessandro's is listed in four travel guides in Italy and has been featured in Sunset, New York Times, Bon Appetit, and many other national publications. Although some recipes have been altered to the American palate, Chef, Mickael Azizi's use of only the freshest and highest quality foods follows Italian tradition. Ingredients like oils, vinegars and Porcini mushrooms are imported from Italy. You can look at their menu at www.alessandros120.com. They are known for their salmon baked with dill, delicious veal dishes and superb desserts. Lunch in particular has a terrific assortment of vegetarian choices. This emphasis on quality and the finest Italian traditions comes from the founder's philosophy and training. Alessandro's Restaurant was originated in 1972 by the late Alessandro Fasani, a native of Rome who was trained in Italy and Switzerland. The restaurant in Salem is in a historic building, dating from 1870, and features interiors designed by Alessandro's wife, Jane. The design reflects the spirit of Italy with colors, textures and artwork that are typical of the restaurants found in the hill towns of Rome. Come in and experience for yourself the wonderful food and charming ambiance. The wine list offers wines from Washington, Oregon and Northern California as well as from all the regions of Italy. Many of the labels are current vintages from vineyards that Alessandro's Restaurant has featured for almost three decades. They are located at 120 Commercial Street NE in downtown Salem (between Court and State streets). You'll find a map on their website. You can also call Alessandro's at (503) 370-9951 or (866) 225-7985 for reservations. They are open for lunch and dinner Monday through Friday, and on Saturday for dinner only.

Taylor's Fountain & Gifts

In the 1940s, soda fountains were a fixture on Main Streets across the nation. In Independence, Oregon, the Main Street still boasts a vintage 1940s soda fountain where you can still buy strawberry sodas, hot fudge sundaes, milkshakes, malts and lunches, made just like they used to be. Started as a drug store, Taylor's Fountain & Gifts is now a first-rate Historic Landmark, which has had the same owners since 1945. They describe it as "part restaurant, part gift shop, part museum." It has been featured in Sunset Magazine and Bon Appetite. This living museum of soda fountain culture is run by Marjorie Taylor and her daughter, Billie Kay Herrell. The building, built in 1884, is a monument in its own right. This Historic Landmark features 1940s-era equipment and furnishings, including the original soda fountain, and one of the largest collections of Coca-Cola memorabilia in the nation. It goes all the way back to 1903. Independence is a small, rural town, just 12 miles southwest of Salem, and Taylor's Fountain and Gifts has become one of the local landmarks. The Store is located at the corner of Main and Monmouth Streets, in a town where life still strolls by at a leisurely pace. The Soda Fountain's specialties reflect this old-fashioned style with hard ice cream and whole milk, used to flavor its milkshakes, sundaes, and sodas. There are 14 wonderful flavors to choose from. And in keeping with the old fashioned way of doing things, they don't use any preservatives or additives. Taylor's Fountain & Gifts is open seven days a week and the friendly folks who work there are looking forward to welcoming you to a nostalgic step into the pleasures of the past. Call (503) 838-1124.

Michael's Landing

Fine dining in a historic setting distinguishes Michael's Landing as a delightful Corvallis institution since 1982. The building housing the restaurant has a colorful past. It was a train depot originally located at Ninth and Washington, and was moved to Sixth and Monroe by teams of mules in 1917. At the time it was a process that took three weeks. Home to Southern Pacific and later the Corvallis Police Department, the Depot was almost demolished in 1979, but concerned citizens rescued it from the wrecker's ball, and in 1982 it was moved to its present location at 603 Northwest Second Avenue. Under the management of Owner, Dan Bell, the beloved building now draws visitors from across the country. Fittingly for its historical character, the Restaurant features authentic regional cuisine such as Wild Northwest Salmon, Fresh Pacific Oysters and Alaskan Halibut, but seafood is just one of the specialties here. The lunch and dinner menus also feature contemporary dishes with an ethnic flair, like Wok-Fried Cashew Chicken and Portabella Mushroom Burgers. Steak lovers can try the Blackened Prime Rib, and vegetarians will enjoy selections such as the Roasted Vegetable Wrap served with sweet potato French fries. There's truly something for every taste here. In addition to fine dining, Michael's Landing also offers a fine view of the Willamette River, making it an especially popular spot for Sunday brunch. Diners can sit back with a complimentary glass of orange juice or champagne and try delightful offerings such as the Newport Omelet, a true Oregon delicacy made from local farm eggs, Dungeness crab, and Bay shrimp, topped with Hollandaise sauce. Fine dining is best with fine wines, and Michael's Landing offers an extensive wine list including many Oregon selections. Catering is available for off-site brunches, lunches, receptions, and full-service parties from thirty to three hundred, and the staff will be happy to customize a menu for any event. To make reservations (and they are recommended), call (541) 751-6141. For more information, visit their website at www.michaelslanding.com. It's a delightful treat for anyone who loves really great food!

The Dundee Bistro & Ponzi Wine Bar

Located in the tiny town of Dundee, The Dundee Bistro and Ponzi Wine Bar offer the finest in regional cuisine and Oregon wines. With impeccable service and over 70 wines from throughout the state, this is a wining and dining experience you won't soon forget. The Bistro prepares fresh, seasonal cuisine showcasing ingredients from local farms and ranches. Award-winning Chef, Jason Smith, changes his menu daily, and selects organic ingredients whenever possible. The cuisine is top rate, served in a casual and friendly atmosphere. Diners may select a courtyard table in warmer months, or seating near the fireplace in the winter. There are more than 14 wines by the glass, presented and poured at the table. Second-generation winemaker, Luisa Ponzi directs The Dundee Bistro's wine program, which was honored with a Wine Spectator Award of Excellence. A full bar is available, with classic cocktails, microbrews and Italian coffees.

The Ponzi Family has pioneered winemaking in the Northern Willamette Valley since 1970. In 1999 they realized a vision of establishing a fine dining restaurant to complement the many wineries in the area, and opened the doors to a culinary center housing The Dundee Bistro, Ponzi Wine Bar, and Your Northwest, a specialty boutique selling regional food and crafts. The Dundee Bistro is open daily. The restaurant seats 80 and full service off-site catering is also available. The Bistro is located at 100 SW 7th Street in Dundee, Oregon. From Portland, go south on Highway 99W through Newberg. The Dundee Bistro and Ponzi Wine Bar are found on the right hand side of Highway 99W at the center of Dundee. The Dundee Bistro phone number is (503) 554-1650. The Ponzi Wine Bar can be reached at (503) 554-1500.

French Bear

What would you expect to find at a place called the French Bear? If your first guess was "the best restaurant in downtown Newberg," You're right on the money! Located in the historic Union Block Building, the French Bear has quickly achieved a reputation as the place to go for "real food in a casual setting." When owner Holly Kinne worked as a caterer, she often heard her customers mention their disappointment at Newberg's lack of a first-class restaurant, and she decided to do something about it. The French Bear, dedicated to comfort and good food, is the result. People come from all over for daily specials at the Bear, lining up for paella on Tuesdays and succulent barbecue every Friday. Seasonal specialties such as huckleberry French toast are also major draws, but any day is a good day to eat here. As befits a restaurant in the heart of Oregon's prime winemaking region, the French Bear also offers a splendid selection of locally-produced wines and superb Pinot Noir made by Holly's own "McKinlay Vineyards." If you're touring the local wineries, get a box lunch so you can take the Bear with you. Holly also makes picnic lunches for people who want to enjoy the natural beauties of the Willamette Valley. The French Bear is an active participant in community activities, including Newberg's First Friday Art Walk. You'd think that running such a great restaurant would be more than enough work, but Holly still provides off-site catering as well. Whether you go to the Bear or the Bear comes to you, you'll be delighted by the friendly, professional service and the exquisite food. The French Bear is a true treasure of Yamhill Country and is located at 107 South College, just one block south of Highway 99 W, in Newberg. For reservations or to arrange for catering, call (503) 538-2609.

Best Little Roadhouse

"More Than Just Great Food." That's the motto at the Best Little Roadhouse, and they live up to it too. Their food is pretty great as well. Some of the Best Little Roadhouse's specialties are Baby Back Ribs, Whisky River Salmon, and Smoked Tri-Tip. All steaks are grilled over a mesquite wood fire, and if you would like one of their homemade sauces on your steak, you can choose from red wine demi-glace, peppercorn, or wild mushroom sauce. Don't forget to try the homemade yeast rolls served up with honey butter, and wonderful baked sweet potatoes with brown sugar and cinnamon. And when you check out their menu, you will find their special dessert, the "Outrageous, I'm Scream'n Outrageous, Fudge Brownie." The Best Little Roadhouse promises you "delicious food, a fun family atmosphere, and miniature golf … served up with enthusiasm and style." They go on to ask, "When is the last time you enjoyed 18 holes of golf just after enjoying dessert? Everyone loves their miniature golf course. Bring the whole family, club or group." They are open daily for lunch and dinner, and groups are welcome, whether for school or business. The patio dining is very appealing. Once there you are able to enjoy the outdoors while sitting by a fireplace. With delicious daily specials, a full range of top-shelf liquor, and friendly service, this is a wonderful restaurant for everyone. The Best Little Roadhouse was voted the "Best New Restaurant" by the Statesman-Journal. Come in and see for yourself how they earned that distinction. You can visit the Best Little Roadhouse at 1145 Commercial Street in SE Salem, Oregon 97302. Their telephone number is (503) 365-7225.Visit their colorful website at www.bestlittleroadhouse.com to see pictures of their smiling staff and some of their dishes.

White's Restaurant

Before "the other guys" were serving skillets or scrambles, there was Don's Big Mess. Bacon, sausage, ham, onions, green peppers, mushrooms, tomatoes and hash browns are grilled together and smothered with sausage gravy, then topped with an egg or two. Are you salivating yet? There's only one place to get Don's Big Mess. It's at White's Restaurant in Salem, Oregon, established in 1936. It is now owned by Don Uselman, hand-picked in 1995 by Bob White to take over the long-standing family business because of Don's obvious pleasure in making every customer who walks in the door feel welcome. Here are some of the other specialties favored by regular customers at White's Restaurant. French Toast, two slices of crunchy French toast served with two slices of honey cured bacon or two sausage links and two eggs. Homemade biscuits and gravy. There are omelets, ranging from standards like Denvers and Vegetarians to the Build Your Own. Maynard's Meatloaf (served Thursdays only). The Turkey Club Sandwich with sliced turkey, crisp bacon, melted Swiss cheese, lettuce, tomato and mayo on grilled sourdough. Another favorite is the Roasted Pork Sandwich. It has slow-roasted pork served with grilled onion and a zesty sauce on a hoagie roll. White's Fatso Burger is a full pound of ground beef, four slices of cheese, mayo, pickles, lettuce, onions, and tomatoes piled on a six-inch bun. If a full pound of beef is a bit much today, go for the Whoopee! Burger with a mere half pound of beef, plus ham, bacon, tomatoes, pickles, egg, onions, Swiss and American cheese and special sauce. For dessert, try the warm apple crisp, it's "to die for" in the words of a recent customer. White's Restaurant is located at 1138 Commercial Street SE, Salem, Oregon 97302. For questions, call (503) 363-0297.

Wild Pear Catering and Wild Pear Restaurant

The Wild Pear Catering and Delicatessen and Wild Pear Restaurant are quickly becoming known as two of the best places to eat in Salem. In 2000, owners and sisters, Cecilia and Jessica Ritter, breathed new life into the neglected 1900 Roberts General Store, opening Wild Pear Catering and Fine Foods. Within a few years, the sisters had a loyal lunch and catering clientele and countless requests to provide a more full-service menu. Heeding these requests, they introduced a dinner service and wine bar, Karl's Place, in June of 2003. However, customer demand was still so great that they opened a second location in 2004, the Wild Pear Downtown, in the 1880 Adolph Block Building on State Street in Downtown Salem. Together the two sisters create flavorful, seasonal menus with an emphasis on fresh local ingredients that reflects the bounty of the Northwest. Serving a delicious gourmet breakfast, lunch and dinner at the restaurant and an upscale deli, bakery and catering menu at their downtown spot, both locations are a must visit while in Salem. Wild Pear Catering and Delicatessen is located at 372 State Street in Salem, Oregon 97301 and can be reached at (503) 378-7515. The Wild Pear Restaurant is at 3635 River Road South in Salem, Oregon 97302. Their phone number is (503) 589-4532.

The Acorn Tree & Junction City Cafe

The Acorn Tree and Junction City Café have captured the hearts and loyalty of the locals and are definitely worth a visit if you are passing anywhere near Junction City, Oregon. They are on your way to the coast or Eugene. As one visitor described it, "This is my favorite place to come to for lunch and shopping!" The Acorn Tree is a 2-story building with flowers, antiques, gifts, home accents and a bookstore. The Book Loft carries a wide range of categories, both used and new releases. Their flowers include a "Sunny Day" assortment, with yellow lilies and big, brilliant Gerber daisies in a blue glass vase. It's just one of the many bright and charming arrangements at the Acorn Tree's flower shop. If you have something special in mind they would love to create it for you. If you can't come in to see it for yourself, you can order a bouquet from their website, www.junctioncity.com (click on the acorn icon). To make it really personal, they have a large variety of greeting cards, message balloons and even delicious truffles from Euphoria Chocolate. The Acorn Tree is also home to the Junction City Café, serving lattes, homemade soups, and an extensive menu including their famous Chicken Almond Salad. On a nice day you can sit outside. The Acorn Tree is located at 264 W. 6th Street in Junction City, Oregon. For more information, call (541) 998-8031 or (800) 886-8031.

Gilberto's Mexican Restaurant

If you love authentic Mexican food, this is it. Owner Gilberto Duarte doesn't just combine exotic and traditional family recipes, he also brings four generations of the Duarte family together to create them for you. You'll probably never see the special copper pots they use to prepare your meal and you won't ever know all of the "secret" ingredients in Gilberto's great Aunt's mole sauce, but you will probably want to ask for more. The tortillas are always made from scratch and are freshly grilled. The nachos are the best in the western hemisphere and even the rice and refried beans taste superior. Gilberto's extensive lunch and dinner menus include appetizers, low-carb meals, chicken steaks and seafood, all at affordable prices. Even if you're from Mexico City you'll admire the quality, tradition and love that the Duarte family pours into every dish they prepare. Gilberto's Mexican Restaurant is located at 1347 NE Stephens in Roseburg, Oregon. For more information about their menu, call (541) 673-4973.

Rodeo Steak House

As you enter this distinctive eatery, you'll see the inviting decor of saddles, tack and buckets of peanuts everywhere. Rodeo Steak House is the perfect fun place to take the whole family for a casual, yet fine dining experience. Their hamburgers are a favorite with the younger crowd, but the prime rib or the Roy Rogers sirloin are the top choices for more sophisticated diners. For those who prefer seafood, the mesquite grilled shrimp or big gulf shrimp are both served to perfection. For lunch, the steak sandwich is a longtime favorite. Along with a full bar and wine list, the Rodeo Steak House has a specialty drink, called Strawberry Lemon-aid and it's served in a quart mason jar. That's enough to share with the whole family! Don't forget to finish off with the Oregon blueberry cobbler. A scoop of ice cream will make this perfect dessert even more unforgettable. To experience the Rodeo Steak House for yourself, go west off of Interstate-5 at The Garden Valley exit in Roseburg or call (541) 440-3760 for more information.

Pedotti's Italian Restaurant

Whenever you get the craving for real Italian food, Pedotti's Italian Restaurant should be your destination. Owner and Chef, David Pedotti and his wife create homemade specialties seven days a week in this deliciously-aromatic atmosphere. Lasagna, manicotti, ministrone, calzone, ravioli, homemade pizza and baked sub sandwiches are among the favorites of their loyal customers. Portions here are always generous, so you'll never go away hungry, but Pedotti's also offers slightly smaller portions for their Early Bird Specials. With daily lunch and dinner specials, the Pedotti's have made it affordable to bring the entire family along for a wonderful dining experience. They specialize in serving local Oregon wines, Italian sodas, Micro-Brew beers and much more. To enjoy a truly traditional Italian meal, come to Pedotti's Italian Restaurant, located at 1332 W Central Avenue, Sutherlin, Oregon. If you'd like more information about other authentic dishes they serve or you are interested in having them cater a special event for you call (541) 459-3773.

Nilknarf's Bar & Grill

Everyone will have fun at Nilknarf's family diner and sports bar. You can enjoy the big screen TV while savoring homemade salads, sandwiches and the best burgers west of the Mississippi. The Franklins (spelled backwards it's Nilknarf) serve the hamburgers and sandwiches on delicious hoagie rolls with homemade french fries. In the sports bar you'll find smiling faces from age twenty-one on up. It's there that you can cheer on your friends in a friendly pool tournament or watch your favorite team on Monday Night Football. For dinner, savor the prime rib or steak and shrimp beside the blazing fireplace. Both dinners are local favorites and reasonably priced, along with the bacon cheeseburger. No matter what age you are, Nilknarf's Bar and Grill is a great place for the entire family. Located at 1023 NE Stephens in Roseburg, Oregon. Reach them by phone at (541) 957-5300. Sunday through Thursday Nilknarfs is open from 11:00 a.m. to midnight. Friday and Saturday they're open 11:00 a.m. to 2:00 a.m.

Waldron's Tom Tom Restaurant & Lounge

In 1962 Waldron's Tom Tom Restaurant was established in Roseburg and since that time two generations of the Waldron family have been serving up flavorful, Oregon Country Fare to their very happy customers. Ken and Aimee Waldron began the tradition and now their son, John, and their daughter-in-law, Debi, continue creating delicious, homemade foods that people will write home about. Quality is not just a word to this family. The meats they serve are all cut and smoked in-house and the Tom Tom's soups are all made from scratch with the finest ingredients available. The Waldron family is proud of their Oregon heritage and to prove it they feature many local and regional Oregon products. There are also local wines, beers and a full service bar available. For breakfast try the Horse Blanket Hot Cakes, for lunch the Bronco Burger is a favorite, but if you're there for dinner, the New York or Porterhouse Steak is a must. The secret family recipe for the Waldron's meat loaf is a local favorite that keeps customers coming back year after year. The Waldron family also makes fresh pies, cinnamon rolls and homemade cakes daily, so be sure to save some room for dessert. To try Waldron's Tom Tom Restaurant & Lounge take Garden Valley exit 125 at Roseburg. Go west and take the first turn by the Chevron station, following the drive one block back, just past the motel. 780 NW Garden Valley Center, Roseburg, Oregon 97470 (541) 672-3741.

Beef & Brew

A distinctive building design and a warm, helpful staff are all part of the ingredients that make for an exceptional night out on the town. Beef & Brew specializes in steak and delectable seafood along with a full service bar. You can get cozy near the roaring fire in the central fireplace and then order a hamburger made from the highest quality meats which you can add all your own favorite fixings to at the burger bar. For a more intimate dinner you can share a booth in the lounge. Chef Steve Cunningham recommends the tender, oven roasted prime rib or the captain's platter with cod, prawns, oysters and scallops. Steak lovers with varying appetites will love the twenty-four ounce porterhouse served with a potato baked to perfection. There's also a delicious filet wrapped in bacon with broccoli. No matter what you choose from Beef & Brew's menu, you're sure to enjoy your meal. Come to Chef Steve Cunningham's Beef & Brew located at 2060 Stewart Parkway in Roseburg, Oregon. To call for directions or reservations dial (541) 673-8030.

Gogi's Restaurant

Tucked away at the foot of Britt Gardens in historic Jacksonville, you'll find Gogi's Restaurant featuring first class cuisine exquisitely prepared by renowned Chef/Owner, William Prahl. Chef Bill and his wife, Joyce have brought the fine dining experience of quality, selection and service known in the finest restaurants in San Francisco, New York or Paris to the quaint romantic town of Jacksonville. Bill's passion for using the freshest ingredients for preparing each meal will excite your senses and keep you coming back again and again. His intensely flavorful and creative cooking has earned him a reputation of being one of Oregon's most influential chefs. First tease your palate with an Enticing Appetizer followed by the signature Grilled Romaine Salad, a creation of Bill's which is highly recommended. The menu changes seasonally, although you can always find favorites such as the Pan Roasted Rack of Lamb, Mushroom Crusted Ahi Tuna, or the delicious Duck Breast. There is a good selection of wines to complement your meal as well as a full bar. Whether you're dreaming about a romantic dinner for two or a casual place to dine, locals have deemed Gogi's a favorite you'll want to visit. For reservations, call (541) 899-8699. Gogi's is located at 235 W. Main Street in Jacksonville, Oregon 97530. For more information, go to their website at www.gogis.net.

Rosario's Italian Restaurant

When Laura and Mike Hogan took over the ownership of Rosario's Italian Restaurant, they brought something special to it, authentic recipes and an unyielding commitment to excellence. Together Mike and Laura have made Rosario's a place that's more than just a cut above the rest. During the years they lived in the Bay Area, Mike worked in the hi-tech industry and Laura was an RN, but they dreamed of someday having their own restaurant. When they moved back to Medford three years ago to be near family, the opportunity to run Rosario's seemed like the natural fulfillment of that dream. Laura is Italian and when she needs a new recipe she gets it from her family back in Italy. Hospitality is another Italian tradition embodied in Rosario's, where anybody and everybody is welcome to stop by and try the deli sandwiches, pasta dishes, calzones, salads, antipasto and unbeatable wood-fired pizzas. Tiramisu and other unique Italian desserts top off the menu, and everything from the bread to the sauces is made fresh, from scratch. At Rosario's Italian Restaurant nothing comes from a box or a can. With food this good, you won't believe how reasonable the prices are, but you will definitely want to come back again. Rosario's is located at 2221 West Main Street in Medford, Oregon. There is ample patio seating during the summer months and catering is also available. For more information, call Laura and Mike at (541) 773-2230.

Callahan's Restaurant and Lodge

If you've traveled all the way from LA on Interstate 5, you'll be glad to find true Oregon ambience at exit 6, in the Siskiyou Mountain Range just 6 miles inside the state line. For over 50 years, locals have driven up the mountain to wine and dine at this exceptional restaurant with its incredible setting and views, or even to spend the night at the beautiful lodge. Open for breakfast, lunch or dinner, the Italian fare is as fresh as the snow on nearby Mt. Ashland. For dinner, choose from many authentic recipes in the three or five courses, including hearty specialty dishes like Veal Scaloppini, juicy steaks or seafood. There's even tasteful acoustic entertainment every night of the week. The mid-day menu includes salads, sandwiches, and similar versions of many of the delicious dinner entrees. All complemented by a full bar and a great selection of premium Northwest wines. If Callahan's 26-foot high native stone fireplace just inside the door doesn't inspire you to spend the night, take a look at the cozy downstairs rooms or upstairs luxury suites, furnished with wood burning fireplaces and whirlpools jetted for two. Both are affordable and include a gourmet breakfast from the regular menu. Try the Smoked Salmon Hash or Smoked Salmon Benedict and you'll definitely be glad you chose to stay. For reservations and a premier Oregon experience, phone (800) 286-0507. Callahan's Restaurant and Lodge is located at 7100 Old Highway 99 South in Ashland, Oregon 97520. You can also view their incredible website at www.callahanslodge.com.

The Black Sheep Pub & Restaurant

Ashland's The Black Sheep Pub & Restaurant is much more than a place to eat. It's a beloved institution among residents and visitors alike, especially theatergoers. You'll trundle upstairs into the cavernous second-floor to find the British-themed restaurant, filled with memorabilia (that bright red telephone box in the corner is an authentic antique shipped over from England). Then you can enjoy authentic traditional specialties such as leek and potato soup, fish & chips, steak & kidney pie, or bangers & mash (sausages and mashed potatoes). Of course, you can also order dishes like grilled salmon with lemon dill butter and duck breast with raspberry balsamic sauce. Vegetarians can also delight in a variety of treats including Grilled Szechwan Tofu and delicious Vegetarian Shepherd's Pie. For dessert, the Sherry Trifle is superb. The British theme includes elevenses and tea (including crumpets!) and the Pub serves Guinness on tap as well as some of Ashland's finest microbrews. As you enjoy your lunch or dinner, you can take in the grand view from the picture window. It's then that you'll understand why everyone comes back more than once. The Black Sheep is located at 51 North Main Street on the Plaza, just a few steps away from the Oregon Shakespeare Festival. It is open daily till 1am. Non-smoking is until 11pm. Reservations are recommended for parties of seven or more, especially in summer when competition for seating among theatergoers can get intense. Call (541) 482-6414 or see their website at www.theblacksheep.com The Black Sheep is "Where You Belong"!

Omar's Restaurant

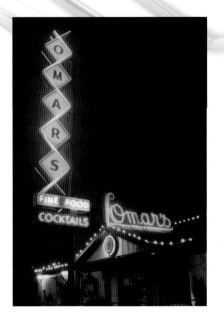

Welcome to a Southern Oregon Icon. This famously friendly 1950's style roadhouse has kept locals coming back for over fifty years. Specializing in delicious yet affordable food they have become a staple with the locals as well as the professors at nearby Southern Oregon University. Omar's offers fresh seafood, steak and a full bar. The steak is truly aged to perfection and surpasses what you dream a great steak should taste like. Order the New York Steak and ask Proprietors, Don Mercer or Bruce Dwight, to choose a special wine for you and you will be delightfully surprised. Omar's is always filled with local and international wines along with real drinks for real people on real budgets. A local newspaper rated Omar's Alaskan Halibut as the very best prepared fish in the entire Rogue Valley. Ask for Coupe Denmark, a dessert Bruce created and gives free to patrons who celebrate their birthdays or anniversaries at Omar's. Located at 1380 Siskiyou Blvd., Omar's opens at 5:00 pm seven days a week. Call (541) 482-1281.

Monet Restaurant & Garden

Monet, a real French restaurant, is owned and operated by Chef Pierre Verger and his wife, Dale. When the Restaurant is open, they are there. Pierre in the kitchen and Dale in the dining room. Pierre is originally from the Rhone Valley in France. He began his training in his hometown of Tain l'Hermitage and continued at the renowned Plaza Athenee in Paris. Dale and Pierre moved to Ashland in 1991 to open Monet. The Restaurant, named after the famous French impressionist, is decorated using the colors of Monet's palette. Serene, classical music complements the décor. The garden, with outside dining available during the outdoor play season, was designed to include many of the same plants as Monet's garden. The result is a peaceful, romantic setting where you can enjoy contemporary, authentic French cuisine presented artistically and served by their friendly staff. Choose appetizers and salad or a full meal. The garden provides Pierre with herbs and flowers to use. His food is a visual as well as a culinary treat. Feast on it first with your eyes before you even take a taste. Monet is an experience you will not want to rush through. Monet is located at 36 S. 2nd Street in downtown Ashland. For reservations or to learn more, dial (541) 482-1339 or check their website at www.mind.net/monet.

Café Dejeuner

Just a few blocks from downtown Medford on a lovely, tree-lined street, you'll find Café Dejeuner, where Owner/Chef, Terry Swenson and his wife Louise have been serving lunch since 1998 ("dejeuner" of course, means lunch in French). The Café recently added dinner to its menu as well. Terry, who began his cooking career at age 17, brings thirteen years experience as a Chef at the Rogue Valley Country Club to Café Dejeuner. His skill is on display in delicious dishes such as Flash-seared Ahi, Filet Mignon with green peppercorns and sun-dried tomatoes, and Pistachio-encrusted Rack of Lamb served with a Rosemary-Shiraz reduction. The Café boasts an impressive assortment of wines from around the world, including selections from local wineries such as Weisinger's of Ashland. And the desserts are true works of art, always made fresh from scratch. Located in a quaint, revamped building that was formerly a private residence, Café Dejeuner provides a quiet, intimate ambience with its candle-lit dining room; also patio dining is available during the summer months. The house is an appropriate setting for a true family business. Terry's daughter, Kylie, a promising young artist, provided some of the art that adorns the dining room walls. Café Dejeuner is located at 1108 East Main Street in Medford, Oregon. The dining room has only ten tables, so reservations are a must. For an outstanding dining experience, call (541) 857-1290.

Amuse Restaurant

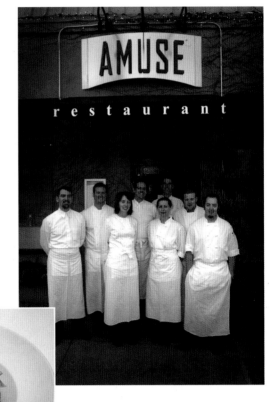

In Ashland, husband and wife chef/owners Erik Brown and Jamie North prepare a Northwest/French menu using organic, seasonal meat and produce at the Amuse Restaurant. Amuse serves dinner in an elegant and contemporary atmosphere. The carefully selected wine list focuses on a wide array of excellent Oregon and California wines with smaller wineries included. The wait staff is highly knowledgeable and dedicated to providing the most professional yet warm, unobtrusive service. Erik and Jamie prepare all items on the menu in-house, including their own sausages, breads, and desserts. Menu items are prepared from local, organic ingredients. The dining room seats 40 patrons inside, and weather permitting, another 35 can be seated on the patio. So make a reservation and try a meal like this: For a first course, Belgian Endive Salad with Bosc pears, Roquefort, walnuts and date vinagrette. As a main course: Pan Roasted

Game Hen with fingerlings, Italian kale and celery root remoulade. Add a cheese such as Rogue Creamery "Crater Lake Blue" with quince paste and Lavender Blossom Honey. For dessert: Scharffen Berger Bittersweet Chocolate Truffle Cake with coffee and ice cream. Erik and Jamie serve it all to you with a passion that is an all-consuming love affair with food and each other. Amuse Restaurant is located just a few blocks from the plaza at 15 N. First Street in Ashland, Oregon 97520. Days and hours of operation change seasonally. Call (541) 488-9000 for current information. Reservations are not required but are recommended. Visit the Website at www.amuserestaurant.com where you can view the current menu, check hours of operation and make reservations or buy gift certificates.

Arbor House Restaurant

Since 1979, the Arbor House Restaurant in Talent has been delighting residents and visitors in the Rogue Valley. Known for both great gourmet food and warm, friendly service, the Arbor House takes its name from the vine-covered arbor that highlights its lovely woodland setting. Outdoor dining with a view of the Japanese garden and fishpond is an added pleasure during the summer months. The Arbor House has been a family-run business since Patrick and Kitty Calhoun opened it in 1979. Now run by their youngest son Joel and daughter Leah, the Restaurant offers specialties like Scampi Alla Griglia (sautéed shrimp in garlic butter), Jambalaya, and a variety of curries – you can order them mild, medium, spicy, or hot. Every night features a fresh fish or seafood special. Beef lovers can choose from Filet Mignon, New York Strip Steak, T-Bone or Rib Eye, and there are many vegetarian entrees available as well. Fine beers and wines, including many local vintages, complement the meal. Remember, by pacing your meal properly, you will leave just enough room for one of the Arbor House Restaurant's wonderful dessert selections. Perhaps you'll choose the mouthwatering Strawberry Shortcake. The Arbor House is located at 103 West Wagner in Talent. Reservations are recommended. To reach them, call (541) 535-6817.

Chateaulin Restaurant

This well-loved restaurant is located next door to the Oregon Shakespeare Festival Theatres, in Ashland, Oregon. Chateaulin Restaurant Français has been regarded as one of the Pacific Northwest's premier restaurants since it opened more than thirty years ago, and recalls a small, cheerful restaurant in Paris or New York – elegant, yet simple. The mood is relaxed, charming and romantic, with white tablecloths, crystal, deep burgundy carpet, lace curtains, fin-de-siecle etched glass partitions, and polished wood. The small but carefully chosen menu changes frequently and is best described as a blend of contemporary and traditional French cuisine. David Taub is the Chef de Cuisine and Co-Owner. He is a graduate of the Culinary Institute of America in Hyde Park, NY. The Manager, Jason Doss, is his partner, and they share a passion: to prepare the freshest, best ingredients in a simple, colorful, uncluttered style with efficient and friendly service. Some of the highlights are the salmon (only wild, line-caught), or the fish flown in weekly from Hawaii. They feature Anderson Ranch Rack of Lamb, and their signature dessert is Chocolate Raspberry Roulade. They have a very popular Prix Fixe Dinner, which changes weekly and includes three-courses, with two courses of specially chosen wine, for only $32.50. Visit their website to read their full, mouth-watering menu, and read the glowing critics' reviews. "In the late hours, Chateaulin becomes more like a neighborhood bar where good conversation mingles easily with the warmth of strong coffee, delectable desserts, tasty appetizers, exceptional wine, and cocktails until after midnight." Chateaulin's wine list is award-winning, and features hundreds of domestic and imported selections, as well as many hard to find boutique wines from Oregon, Washington, and California. If you wish to purchase a bottle of wine you enjoyed with dinner, you can walk next door to the adjacent Chateaulin Wine and Gourmet Shop where an array of treats is available. Chateaulin Restaurant Français is located at 50 East Main Street, on the Plaza in Ashland, Oregon. For information or to make reservations, call (541) 482-2264 and remember, reservations are recommended.

The Bella Union

Since 1988, Proprietor, Jerry Hayes has much to be proud of. The Bella Union Restaurant & Saloon, located in historic Jacksonville, Oregon has garnered a multitude of awards. The Bella remains a first choice for an intimate lunch, dinner or savory Sunday brunch. Once you taste their delicious fare, you'll become a Bella regular too. Enjoy fresh, flavorful cuisine creatively prepared by Executive Chef, Tom Bates. Savor the delicious pizza or the authentic pasta made fresh daily along with delectable homemade desserts and breads. Choose from more than a dozen lunch and dinner specials created daily, and enjoy an extraordinary selection of wines served up by the glass or bottle. Select from four unique indoor dining areas or be seated on the outdoor deck in the shade of the 600 square foot canopy of wisteria. The attentive staff will pamper you as you experience the great food and informal atmosphere that has Bella regulars claiming, "It's more than just a great place to eat." Stop by and experience for yourself all the delights of the Bella Union Restaurant and Saloon in historic Jacksonville. Food to die for at a price that won't kill you. Open seven days a week for lunch and dinner, The Bella Union is located at 170 West California Street in downtown Jacksonville. For more information, call (541) 899-1770.

Jacksonville Inn Restaurant

To appreciate the Jacksonville Inn Restaurant located in Jacksonville, Oregon, you may want to start with the critical acclaim they've received. First there is the fact that Medford Mail-Tribune readers recently voted it the "Best Restaurant" and "Most Romantic Spot" in the Rogue Valley. Then consider that the Mobil and AAA tour guides rate it at three stars, and the Star Academy Award of the Restaurant Industry gives it five stars! Frequently featured on CNN and "The Learning Channel," Pacific Northwest Magazine and the Oregon Magazine have recognized it as one of Oregon's best restaurants. The Wine Spectator bestowed an award on the Restaurant for its comprehensive wine list (over 2,000 wines!). Are you getting hungry? Come on in then and try the superb international cuisine prepared by the Jacksonville Inn Restaurant's master chefs. You can select; Fresh Oregon Salmon or Razor Clams, lamb, beef, Prime Rib, Stuffed Hazelnut Chicken, Northern Velvet Venison, and "Healthy for your Heart" choices, just a few of the delectable menu selections. Fresh herbs and spices, many of which are organically grown in the garden at the Inn, are used by the chefs to prepare your meal. End your meal with a choice from the tempting dessert tray, with its array of sumptuous desserts from the onsite bakery. You can enjoy it all in the formal dining room with its five-course Table d'Hote, or have a more casual experience in the bistro or lovely patio garden setting. The Restaurant is located in the Jacksonville Inn at 175 E. California Street in Jacksonville, Oregon 97530. Jacksonville is located in the Rogue River Valley, just five miles west of the city of Medford. For reservations or for information, call (541) 899-1900 or toll-free at (800) 321-9344. You may also visit their lovely website at www.jacksonvilleinn.com. See their separate listing in this book for the Jacksonville Inn.

Wild River Brewing & Pizza Company

First established in 1975 by Jerry and Bertha Miller, as Miller's Shady Oaks Pizza Deli in Cave Junction, the restaurant then expanded to Brookings Harbor in 1980 where son Darrel, and his wife Becky, managed the Restaurant. However, with an intense interest in brewing quality beers, the family eventually ventured into the brewing world, establishing the Steelhead Brewery in 1990. A need for more space landed them in Grants Pass, where they were able to install old-world wood-fired ovens and a 15 BBL brewhouse with five fermenting tanks, four bright beer tanks and a bottling line capable of turning out 1800 BBL per year.

Renaming their business the Wild River Brewing & Pizza Company in 1994, the Millers still serve gourmet pizza and pasta dishes. In addition, their pub also has a Public House, ideal for receptions, meetings, conferences and other large group functions. Wild River Brewing & Pizza Company is a great spot to enjoy great food and great beer in a comfortable, relaxed environment. You'll find Wild River Brewing and Pizza Company located at 595 NE E. Street in Grants Pass, Oregon. To contact them, call (541) 471-7487 or visit their website at www.wildriverbrewing.com for a list of their other locations.

Lithia Fountain & Grill

Downtown Ashland is rich in history, and the Lithia Fountain & Grill, located in the historic Swedenburg Building, is a perfect place to turn back the hands of time. You can enjoy a richly nostalgic experience of old-fashioned fun at the Fountain & Grill. The marble fountain here is the first soda fountain ever installed in Ashland. It's beautifully restored and in fine working condition after 95 years of service! Lithia Fountain is the only place in Ashland where you can get a root beer float made with draft root beer. It's an experience not to be missed. This is a place the whole family can enjoy, with antique pinball machines and a toy chest for the kids, beer and wine for mom and dad (including Guinness on tap), and delicious food for all. The unbeatable homemade soups offered by Owner, Lori Forrest, keep people coming back time and again. Other choice offerings include Natural Beef Burgers with fresh Tillamook cheese from the Oregon coast, and there are many vegetarian selections as well. Free puppet shows featuring Arnold the Lion puppet entertain children, and on the first Monday of every month there's fun for adults with the live Comedy Showcase at 9 pm. The Lithia Fountain & Grill is located at 303 East Main Street in Ashland. They are open seven days a week for lunch and dinner. For inquiries, call (541) 488-0179.

Retirement
Centers

Willamette View

Did you know that of all the retirement communities in the U.S., a mere 10 to 15 percent win accreditation from the Continuing Care Accreditation Commission? To be accredited, a retirement community must meet high standards in every aspect of its operation and have a clearly defined mission that guides its work. What this means to you, if you're looking for such a community, is that it is a sound investment and will be there for you for the long term. One such standout community is Willamette View in Portland, Oregon. Accredited and nonprofit, Willamette View is a continuing care community offering campus-style living for people 55 and older. It is situated on 27 park-like acres overlooking the Willamette River, eight miles south of downtown Portland, across the river from Lake Oswego. Willamette View, opened in 1955, offers five levels of residential options: independent living, personal care, assisted living, skilled nursing, and a state-endorsed Alzheimer's unit. More than 550 residents take advantage of the services and care here. Willamette View also has a licensed home-health agency, serving people in their own homes in the community, and contracts with various agencies for their nursing and health care staffing needs. For residents, over 150 activities are available. There are three libraries, two wood shops, a computer lab, fitness center, indoor swimming pool, putting green, tennis court, personal gardening spaces, art studios, and Clackamas Community College classes taught onsite. Willamette View currently offers single-story homes and apartments for residents living independently, personal care apartments for supportive living, and licensed assisted-living apartments. In addition, there is an Alzheimer's unit and licensed and certified skilled-nursing beds. Willamette View is located at 12705 SE River Rd., Portland, OR 97222. Call (503) 654-6581 or (800) 446-0670 toll-free. Visit the web site at www.willametteview.org.

SpringRidge at Charbonneau

For fourteen years, SpringRidge at Charbonneau has justifiably styled itself as "The Northwest's Most Distinctive Retirement Community." There's a conscious pride that you'll sense the minute you cross the threshold. You'll feel it in the handsome surroundings, the manicured garden courtyards, and the rich architectural detailing reminiscent of a French country manor. Nestled on an impeccable 10-acre parcel of natural beauty and serenity that only Charbonneau can offer, this charming community offers everything you could possibly want. "We've taken an uncommon approach to retirement living." SpringRidge at Charbonneau's approach to retirement living blends understated elegance with personalized service and supportive health and well-being programs. SpringRidge offers 10 different models of one and two bedroom apartments set amidst lush outdoor courtyards and verandas. Instead of a dining hall, SpringRidge offers the Charbonneau Room Restaurant, with crisp linen tablecloths, fine china, and gourmet meals. A full range of social, cultural, and recreational activities promote personal growth and physical, mental, and emotional well being. What is there to do? Perhaps an energizing health and fitness session at the private, enclosed pool and spa, followed by a relaxing visit to the adjoining sauna. You can play golf or tennis, or take a shopping excursion to Washington Square or Portland. In the evening, you might attend a lecture, play some bridge, or join the Charbonneau Book Club for an intellectually stimulating session with friends new and old. Located in one of Oregon's most desirable residential communities, the 477-acre master-planned community of Charbonneau features a 27-hole golf course, tennis courts, and scenic walking paths. SpringRidge residents enjoy all of the benefits of a social membership at the Charbonneau Country Club. SpringRidge at Charbonneau is located at 32200 Southwest French Prairie Road in Wilsonville. Look online at www.ahomeforseniors.com/springridge_at_charbonneau.htm for more information, or call (503) 694-2700.

Terwilliger Plaza

Terwilliger Plaza is a nationally accredited Continuing Care Retirement Community with a fine reputation for providing seniors with outstanding services and amenities in a beautiful urban setting. Today Terwilliger Plaza continues as a not-for-profit, self-governing organization with a membership that draws from a broad range of backgrounds. Although it first opened in 1962, the original 12-story building has been beautifully renovated to include the Terrace, an enhanced assisted living community, parking garage, restaurant style dining, large auditorium, fitness and wellness center, deli/grocery store, beauty salon, rooftop garden, high speed Internet access and much more! At Terwilliger Plaza, you can be as social as you like or enjoy the privacy and comfort of your own apartment. With a variety of floor plans, you will have much to choose from when selecting the one that is perfect for you. Additionally, the many services included in your monthly fee will give you more time to do the things you love best. You'll enjoy living in a retirement community that offers both independent lifestyle options and the security of onsite health care services for the future. You are invited to come for a visit and experience the wonderful lifestyle awaiting you . Terwilliger Plaza is conveniently located at 2545 SW Terwilliger Boulevard in Portland, Oregon 97201. For information call (503) 299-4716 or phone toll free (800) 875-4211. You can also visit their website at www.terwilligerplaza.com.

NorthWest Place

NorthWest Place represents a distinctive and exciting retirement lifestyle. Its many attractions are designed for active seniors. One of the highlights is their exciting location near 23rd Avenue in Portland. There you will find plenty of opportunities for shopping, dining, entertainment, and even healthcare, all just a couple of blocks from your front porch. Managed by the Senior Retirement Group (SRG), NorthWest Place encourages healthy, active, independent living, where residents enjoy a full life while expanding their horizons and making their own decisions. The full range of social, cultural, and recreational activities at Northwest Place promotes your personal growth and they are designed with physical, mental, and emotional stimulation in mind. A one-time entrance fee plus an all-inclusive monthly service fee covers a variety of programs and services. They include a complimentary breakfast and choice of lunch or dinner daily in the gracious dining room, weekly housekeeping services, and all utilities (except telephone), including individual heating and air conditioning, water, sewer, and cable television. Each one- or two-bedroom apartment has an oven, range, full-size refrigerator, garbage disposal, microwave, and dishwasher, as well as a washer/dryer. Add scheduled transportation, a full calendar of social, recreational and cultural programs, and a 24-hour emergency response system, and you can see why people look forward to living at NorthWest Place! To arrange for your visit at NorthWest Place located at 2420 NW Marshall Street in Portland, Oregon, call (503) 221-2075. For more information about NorthWest Place and the SRG's other retirement communities in Oregon, California, and Arizona, visit their informative website, www.srgseniorliving.com.

Cascade Manor

Located in the south hills of Eugene, in one of the city's nicest residential neighborhoods, Cascade Manor is perfectly situated to offer the best in senior living. The beautiful five-acre campus is close to all the cultural, educational, and recreational opportunities Eugene offers. Eugene itself is conveniently situated mid-state between Portland and Medford and offers almost everything a larger metropolitan offers without the hassles of big-city living. As Lane County's first and only continuing care retirement community (CCRC), residents enjoy peace of mind, now and into the future. With three levels of care right on campus, residents have the security of knowing that if their health status changes over time, they'll find Residential Living (designed for people who need a little help with daily activities), nursing care provided in an on site Health Care Center, and compassionate In-Home Care. Equally important is the comprehensive Wellness Program, which is designed to help residents maintain health, wellness, and independence.

But most importantly, Cascade Manor offers residents a lively environment where social and recreational opportunities abound. Residents enjoy the varied calendar of on-campus programs and activities, as well as the scheduled outings to theatres, museums, restaurants, shopping, and more. And now, this already fine community is undergoing a major renovation and expansion that will take it to another level of excellence. The expansion includes adding brand-new Garden Apartments in a variety of styles and beautiful outdoor courtyards complete with their own creek, ponds, and waterfalls. Cascade Manor is also renovating its existing building and adding a number of fine amenities including a state-of-the-art Fitness Center and an indoor pool and spa. To learn more about this unique community call (800) 248-2398.

Willamette Valley backroad

Linus Oakes
Retirement Center

Linus Oakes offers the safety and security of living independently with the reassurance that there will always be someone nearby should you need assistance. Within walking distance of Mercy Medical Center and located among the rolling hills of Southern Oregon, Linus Oakes was created as a haven of comfort, peace and security. Linus Oakes is an integral part of Mercy HealthCare, a ministry of healing established by the Sisters of Mercy in 1909. Linus Oakes provides residents with all the amenities enjoyed in small town life including many social, cultural, religious and educational opportunities. Golfing, gardening, fishing or simply taking leisurely walks in a beautiful setting are sure to appease the naturalist in all of us. With a centrally-located main lodge, Linus Oakes encompasses 123 cottages and apartments in 17 separate buildings. Transportation is routinely provided for excursions and live entertainment occurs on a regular basis. Recently, the "Oregon Companion Dog of the Year" title was awarded to a pet living at Linus Oakes, so as you can see, important "family members" are welcome too. Like Dorothy said, "There's no place like home," and that's exactly what the caring staff at Linus Oakes creates... a home you'll love. Linus Oakes Retirement Center is located at 2665 Van Pelt Blvd., Roseburg, Oregon 97470. For more inofrmation call (541) 677-4800 or toll-free (800) 237-9294. See their website at www.mercyrose.org/loakes.

Riverview Terrace

As you enter Riverview Terrace's lobby you will see one of the most stunning areas imaginable. At first the gorgeous fireplace captures your attention, then you'll notice the huge saltwater fish tanks which are displayed throughout the room. They are filled with exotic, colorful fish from all around the world. Riverview Terrace is managed by Omega Management Group and the dedicated, hands-on General Manager is George Boisacq. This is not your ordinary retirement community. The caring staff at Riverview Terrace guarantees unparalleled resident service, along with affordable elegance, personal care and sumptuous meals complete with a riverside view. Each apartment is equipped with state-of-the-art 24-hour emergency communication systems and 24-hour professional security to ensure your peace of mind. Riverview Terrace is located at 1970 W Harvard, Roseburg, Oregon or you can reach them at (541)672-2500.

Rogue Valley Manor

Rogue Valley Manor, one of the top Continuing Care Retirement Communities (CCRCs) in the nation, offers the very best in retirement living. The Manor is the only CCRC in Southern Oregon, having won several awards throughout its 40-year history. The gorgeous 750-acre campus sits atop Manor Hill in Medford and provides spectacular views of the Rogue Valley and Cascade Mountains. Residents enjoy a vibrant lifestyle filled with activity and the companionship of other interesting people. Virtually every service and amenity you can think of is found on this campus. Everything from two banks, a travel agency, a computer learning center, two fitness centers, an indoor pool and spa, woodworking and lapidary shops, a pharmacy, a boutique, a barber/beauty salon and more. And, with more than 30 special interest groups on campus, there's something for everyone to enjoy, like ceramics, painting, music and

theatre groups, hiking, water volleyball, exercise classes, volunteering, and day trips to name a few. Most importantly, as a CCRC, the Manor offers an extensive continuum of care, so residents have the security of knowing health care is available, should the need arise. Services include assistance with daily living, special care for memory loss and skilled nursing care. In addition, the Manor is one of the few CCRCs on the West Coast to offer residents its own on site Medical Clinic along with the services of a full-time medical staff. And the Rogue Valley Manor is fully accredited by the Continuing Care Accreditation Commission. Residents also enjoy exploring the rich cultural offerings of Ashland and historic Jacksonville (both just minutes away), and broadening their knowledge in one of several senior programs at Southern Oregon University. With opportunities like these, its no wonder people from across the nation choose to retire at the extraordinary Rogue Valley Manor. The Manor is located at 1200 Mira Mar Avenue in Medford. For more information, call (541) 857-7214 or toll free (800) 848-7868. See their website at www.retirement.org/rvm.

Horton Plaza

Since 1995 Horton Plaza has been Southern Oregon's premier retirement community. Located in Medford, Horton Plaza's residents are able to enjoy Southern Oregon's pristine surroundings, mild climate and strong community values. Owners, Ann and Larry Horton, proudly offer seniors the extraordinary lifestyle that comes with living in a full-service senior community living facility. With spacious studios, one bedroom and two bedroom apartments available, all featuring abundant storage, well-equipped kitchenettes and bay windows, Horton Plaza will delight residents with all of its first-class amenities. Indulge yourself in their elegant, full-service dining room, where three delicious restaurant style meals are served daily. A private dining room is also available for entertaining family or other special occasions. Curl up with a book in the Library, receive a little pampering at the Beauty Salon, enjoy a gourmet cooking class in the Community Kitchen, participate in an invigorating exercise class or take a leisurely stroll through the lush Oriental Courtyard. Whatever your pleasure, Horton Plaza and its location in the heart of the Pacific Northwest provides the very best in resort-style living for the active senior. Horton Plaza is located at 1122 Spring Street in Medford, Oregon 97504. To learn more about how Horton Plaza can make you feel at home, call (541) 770-1122 or (800) 844-4058. Visit their website at www.hortonplza.com.

Mountain Meadows Community

Discover the active retirement lifestyle of Mountain Meadows Community in beautiful Ashland, Oregon. Live independently in a charming Craftsman-style detached home or condominium, knowing that the equity in your investment belongs to you. Nestled on a scenic hillside, this 30-acre campus includes walking paths, a community garden, clubhouse, dining room, library, and fitness center with exercise pool. Just one mile away, explore the exciting theater, restaurants, shopping and university in downtown Ashland. Then come home to watch the sun set behind verdant hills in the comfort of your own living room. Orchestrate any level of service you wish, from care in your own home to residency in assisted living nearby. Mountain Meadows Community has been recognized with numerous awards including the Best Small Active Retirement Community in America by the National Council on Senior Housing, one of the 100 Best Master Planned Communities in America by Where to Retire Magazine, and the Gold Nugget Grand Award for Best Senior Housing in the West by the Pacific Coast Builder's Conference. You really can have it all at Mountain Meadows, 857 Mountain Meadows Drive in Ashland, Oregon 97520. To inquire about this wonderful living opportunity, call (800) 337-1301 or (541) 482-1300, www.mtmeadows.com.

Mountain View Retirement Residence

Retire with both independence and peace of mind in a beautiful apartment or cottage with no leases or buy-in fees. At Mountain View Retirement Residence, all the services you need are included in the monthly rent, so you can relax and enjoy the lifestyle you so richly deserve. Let the chef present all your meals in the elegant dining room or use your own convenient kitchenette. Relax with your family in one of the tasteful and comfortable common areas or meet with other residents either casually or in a variety of fitness and activity programs. Enjoy day trips and excursions in exciting Ashland for convenient shopping and world-class entertainment. Mountain View Assisted Living, located within the same facility, offers an individually crafted plan that will meet whatever personal services you need or prefer. Mountain View Retirement Residence is located at 548 N. Main St. in Ashland, Oregon. Call (541) 482-3292 for more information about carefree retirement living.

Wineries

Cathedral Ridge Winery

Cathedral Ridge Winery is located in the recently designated viticulture region of Hood River in the Columbia River Gorge. As providers of a full selection of fine wines they take great pride in sharing their award winning creations with you. The Tasting Room is open every day from 11am until 5pm. If you are adventurous with your palate, are familiar with the selection at Cathedral Ridge Winery, or would simply like to have your wine delivered regularly, then try out the Cathedral Ridge Wine and Food Club. There isn't any membership fee, just fill out a simple form with your selection of just wine or wine and gourmet foods. With the Wine and Food Club you will be guaranteed to receive all of the Cathedral Ridge wines when they are first released and you can choose a package to be delivered to you once a month or seven times a year. Regular selections of wine include Halbtrocken, a very rare blend of several different wines, a toasty vanilla Chardonnay, a full bodied Pinot Gris, crisp and clean white Riesling, a rare Riesling Blush, a Pinot Noir, Merlot and a few Cabernets. Banked by views of Mt. Adams and Mt. Hood, the Winery's seven acres of sweeping vineyards and lush garden landscapes are perfect for special events, receptions and weddings. Let them know what you would like to do and they will help you plan it. Cathedral Ridge Winery can be found at 4200 Post Canyon Drive in Hood River, just off of the first Hood River exit. You can reach them at (541) 386-2882, or check out their website at www.cathedralridgewinery.com.

Cooper Mountain Vineyards

Cooper Mountain Vineyards rests along the gentle slopes of an ancient volcano west of Beaverton. With four vineyard sites covering 123 acres, the Winery produces just over 15,000 cases of premium wine annually. It is within these vineyard sites that Cooper Mountain retains an increasingly important distinction among vintners. Under the direction of Owner and visionary, Dr. Robert Gross, these vineyards are certified organic and Biodynamic. For the lay person this simply means that the use of chemical pesticides and fertilizers have been eliminated in favor of herb and mineral preparations. For the connoisseur this brings wines of distinction, wines that reflect their unique terroir. When you sample Cooper Mountain's wines you are supporting a new direction in fine wine, one that

has gone from the fringes of alternative farming to now entering mainstream consciousness. These practices utilize compost preparations that include yarrow, chamomile, nettle, oak bark, dandelion and a host of other natural compounds all brought together in recipes developed to enhance the soil and improve the natural ecosystem. Still controversial, Biodynamic viticulture is gaining acceptance industry wide, in part due to the early efforts of Cooper Mountain Vineyards and their stunning wines. Tasting Room hours are Noon until 5:00pm daily but is closed in January and on major holidays. Wines offered include Pinot Noir, Chardonnay, Pinot Gris, and Pinot Blanc. Special reserves and premium blends are also available. Cooper Mountain Tasting Room is located at 9480 SW Grabhorn Road in Beaverton, Oregon. You can reach them at (503) 649-0027. For more information on biodynamic or Cooper Mountain Vineyards, check out their website at www.coopermountainwine.com.

Oak Knoll Winery

From milking parlor to main wine cellar, the Oak Knoll Winery facility has changed dramatically from its early days as a dairy. It is an independent, family-owned winery with two main goals: to continue producing while always seeking to improve some of the best wines in Oregon and to consistently offer some of the best wine values in America. The Oak Knoll Winery story began in 1970, when Ronald and Marjorie Vuylsteke founded the first winery in Washington County. Both native Oregonians, Ron was an electronics engineer in the early 1960's when a bumper crop of blackberries at the family home led to a gallon of outstanding blackberry wine, and the family winemaking heritage was born. The Oak Knoll Winery is a family owned and operated business, with Marj and the children being involved since the very first crush. They did everything from unloading flatbed trucks filled with berries to hand labeling the bottles. Today, all five of the Vuylsteke sons and a nephew have followed Ron and Marj's footsteps, and have become knowledgeable wine professionals as well. The longevity of Oak Knoll Winery can be attributed to its having produced some of the finest wines anywhere. A wine connoisseur from The Wine Advocate commented on "the high quality of your pinot noirs and chardonnays." Oak Knoll also produces a delightful, Burgundian-balanced Chardonnay; a slightly sweet, Spatlese-styled Riesling; and a native-American varietal, Niagara. Besides a sterling reputation for fine dry table wines, Oak Knoll Winery is one of the premier producers of superior quality Raspberry wine in the world. This special dessert berry wine is the only fruit wine still made at Oak Knoll. Nearly one pound of fruit is used for each half bottle, and fine wine shops and restaurants seek it out for its "concentrated depth of flavor and ability to match exquisitely with a wide range of desserts." The Oak Knoll Winery is located eighteen miles west of downtown Portland, in the beautiful countryside near Hillsboro. Oak Knoll is located at 29700 SW Burkhalter Road. For more information, call (503) 648-8198, or for toll-free, dial (800) OAK KNOL You can also arrange to take a private or group tour by appointment.

Hip Chicks do Wine

Found amongst the artistic dwellings and industrial factories near Reed College is the unexpected winery of Hip Chicks do Wine. A unique urban micro winery designed with the Gen X crowd in mind, Hip Chicks do Wine is also a boutique winery that hand crafts their wine in very small batches with grapes from several Oregon Appellations. They believe that this is the key to their wines with full, well-rounded fruit flavors. Producing only around 2,500 cases annually this small winery produces truly inspired wines while experimenting with new processes each year. They use a half-ton basket press to gently extract the best quality juices from fruity full-bodied Pinot Noirs, Chardonnays, Reislings, Gewurtzraminers and Merlots. Special treatment of the different grapes in small bins, French oak barrels or stainless steel tubs according to what is best for that particular wine style is only possible due to the small batches created here. These wines are intended to be enjoyed when purchased without any need to cellar. Tasting Room hours are Tuesday through Sunday from 11am until 6pm. Wines offered include Shardoneaux, Vin Nombril, Pinot Noir and Riot Girl Rose. Check out their apparel, gifts and accessories as well. Hip Chicks do Wine Tasting Room is located 4510 SE 23rd Avenue in Portland, near 26th and Holgate. You can reach them at (503) 753-6374. For more information or to purchase wine and goods, check out their website at www.hipchicksdowine.com.

Oregon Wines on Broadway

At Oregon Wines on Broadway you can sample Portland's best selection of Pacific Northwest wines. If you are too busy to visit the wine country, you can come in and try the Northwest's best by the taste, the glass or the bottle. They have Tastings on the first and third Thursday of each month from 5-8 p.m., featuring a different wine maker each time. They also usually pour new releases. The Tasting includes food and three wines for $12. And a schedule of which wine makers will be there is posted on Oregon Wines on Broadway's website at www.oregonwinesonbroadway.com. They also offer membership in their Northwest Wine Collector's Club, which offers "selections from the lush Pinot Noirs of Oregon's Willamette Valley, to Washington's rich Red Mountain Cabernets, and the dense ripe fruit of Walla Walla's incredible Merlots, Syrahs and blends." When you join, you receive two or three bottles of these magnificent wines delivered to your home each month. With your shipment you'll also receive wine maker's notes and information about the wines. Oregon Wines on Broadway ship nationally, offer local wine delivery, as well as custom gift baskets, and they have travel boxes for airplane carry-on. "Come in and enjoy wines produced and grown locally, we will help you get them home." Their website has a full list of the wines they have at any particular time. When we looked, Oregon Wines on Broadway had 278 wines listed. Check out their website, and then come in to enjoy one of their terrific wine tastings. Oregon Wines on Broadway is located at 515 SW Broadway, in Portland, Oregon. For more information, call (503) 228-4655 .

Kramer Vineyards

Visiting family-owned and operated Kramer Vineyards is a welcoming experience for all who venture to this small vineyard just outside the town of Gaston, Oregon. Keith and Trudy Kramer's dream came true when they planted their vineyard in 1984 and harvested Kramer Vineyards' first batch of wine in 1989. On their 20 acres of land, they now produce high quality Pinot Noir, Pinot Gris, Müller-Thurgau, Dijon Chardonnay, and a special wine, Carmine, otherwise known as Big Red. Although they have won numerous awards and accolades over the years, including a gold medal at the 2003 Oregon State Fair for a Pinot Noir, the Kramers ultimate goal is to produce wines that are enjoyed by their customers and do justice to the fruits. The Vineyard includes a tasting room where at least ten fine wines are available each day and are poured by a friendly staff. The deck outside their tasting room boasts an outstanding view of the valley below and is a popular dining spot for visitors who think ahead to a picnic lunch. During the months of July and August, the Kramers host multi-course dinners "under the stars." Special events are held on Mother's Day, Father's Day, Fourth of July, and Labor Day Weekend. This is truly a hands-on vineyard, where the owners want guests to understand all aspects of producing hand-crafted wines. Visitors always feel welcome and are invited to experience the harvest by "punching down the pinot," (tasting freshly squeezed juice or wine and touring the winery and observing their equipment). The accommodating staff is helpful, the Kramer's Labrador Retriever and big tabby cat casually escort visitors as they tour the Tasting Room and grounds, plus the Kramers are always nearby to share information and visit with those who want to learn more about the winemaking process. Kramer Vineyards is truly an Oregon Treasure you'll want to visit. They are located at 26830 NW Olson Road, in Gaston, Oregon. For more information visit their website at www.kramerwine.com or call them at (503)662-4545.

Mt. Hood over Portland

Duck Pond Cellars

Beautiful landscaping lines the driveway to the Duck Pond Cellars tasting room. Meticulously landscaped grounds surround the outdoor patio where you may sip wine and enjoy a picnic beside the pond. Duck Pond Cellars, the largest family-owned winery in Oregon, was founded in 1993 by Doug and Joann Fries. They, their children and families extend their expertise and warm hospitality toward every guest's enjoyment. Each step, from tending the soil to distributing to worldwide merchants shelves, members of the family have given their all to ensure that Duck Pond wines deliver the highest possible quality for their price. With distribution to over 45 states in this country and six foreign nations, the Duck Pond label from Oregon is getting well-deserved attention. Chardonnay is the number one seller, followed by Pinot Noir. Enjoy these and many other wines in the Tasting Room where the warm, friendly and knowledgeable staff help to make your wine tasting experience memorable. Both complimentary and nominally priced tastings and tours are available daily, 10am until 5pm, May through October. Times change to 11am until 5pm, November through April. Duck Pond Cellars is closed for Thanksgiving, Christmas, New Year's Day, and Easter only. Groups from two to forty people are welcome on informative tours that interest novices to wine connoisseurs alike. Many people just stop by for tasting, but Duck Pond Cellars can also accommodate groups, clubs, families and bus tours just out enjoying the countryside. Visit Duck Pond Cellars at 23145 Highway 99 West in Dundee, Oregon. You can also reach them at (800) 437-3213 or check out their website at www.duckpondcellars.com.

Honeywood Winery

It seems like an obvious choice that founders Ron Honeyman and John Wood would come up with the name, Honeywood, for their winery. But actually, they didn't want to do something so self evident. It was a quotation that changed their minds. It was a line from a play that goes, "smooth as honey… aged in wood… the drink of the good natured man." This sentiment suited their philosophy beautifully, and they have created an enduring establishment out of it. Since 1934 Honeywood Winery has been located in Salem in the heart of Oregon's fertile Willamette Valley. It's just minutes away from some of the world's finest vineyards, cane berry fields and fruit orchards. This abundance of nature is the starting place for Honeywood's products. The Winery is famous for its premium fruit wines and specialty wines, as well as varietal wines. This, the oldest producing winery in Oregon has become known for wines like Olallieberry Supreme (produced from a hybrid Oregon blackberry), Tropical Sunset ("a delicate wine, drier than most fruit wines, with the juice of fully ripe pineapples, guavas, and apricots balanced with a blend of quality white wine"), and Triple Berry (a specialty wine with flavors of marionberry, raspberry, and strawberry added). Come in to visit at 1350 Hines Street SE, in Salem, where the delicious traditions of Honeywood Winery continue. They have a great gift shop with books and kitchen items as well as their wines and other food items. You can also go to their website at www.HoneywoodWinery.com. There are more than forty luscious gift packs you can order online, as well as plenty of history about the Winery. Or you can call (503) 362-4111.

Erath Vineyards

Dick Erath started his wine career as a home winemaker in San Francisco, falling in love with Pinot Noir when he tasted some old French Burgundies. That was 37 years ago, and he is now one of the original wine pioneers of Oregon. You can visit Erath Vineyards and see the stunning setting of his award-winning winery. You can also read about Erath's passion for wine in "The Boys Up North - Dick Erath and the Early Oregon Winemakers" by Paul Pintarich, published by The Wyatt Group, a recounting of the early days of Pinot Noir in Oregon. (You can purchase it on the very helpful and informative Erath website at www.erath.com). In the 1960s, Erath traveled up and down the west coast in search of an ideal place to grow Pinot Noir. Determined to make elegant, food-friendly Pinot Noir, he finally found what he was looking for in the then-unproven northern Willamette Valley of Oregon. He made extensive studies of the soil and climate, and was convinced that this was the place where he could make his dream of world-class, affordable Pinot Noir a reality. In 1969 he planted a vineyard in Yamhill County and in 1972 he produced his first Pinot Noir and Riesling wines. Today, Erath produces around 40,000 cases of wine per year of Pinot Noir, Pinot Gris, Pinot Blanc, and smaller amounts of Riesling, Gewürztraminer and Dolcetto. Erath's cellar-quality wines, produced in extremely limited quantities of 100 to 500 cases each, rank with some of the finest Pinot Noirs in the world. They are only bottled when they display the hallmarks of their pedigree and "terroir." Dick Erath invites you to come visit and see first-hand Erath's 115 acres of grapes in the Dundee Hills of Oregon's Willamette Valley. Taste for yourself what makes his wines distinctive. You can reach the Erath Vineyards at (503) 538-3318, or toll-free at (800) 539-9463.

Anne Amie Vineyards

Anne Amie is a new wine label from Oregon's Willamette Valley, producing wines that reflect the passions of Owner, Robert Pamplin, and Winemaker, Scott Huffman. "Our single-vineyard designate Pinot Noirs represent our finest expression of the variety." Their passion is to produce memorable wines from low-yield vineyards with minimal processing, "wines with a sense of elegance." Dr. Pamplin purchased the Chateau Benoit Winery in 1999, and the Winery was officially renamed in May 2004 after his two daughters. When you visit the Anne Amie winery on a panoramic hilltop in Yamhill County, you will find a European-style tasting room, an open terrace with tables, and a Mediterranean garden – as well as spectacular views and warm hospitality. They offer a complimentary wine tasting daily of several wines, and the Vineyard Designate Pinot Noirs are available to taste for a fee. Small lots of other Anne Amie wines are available exclusively here as well as unique gift and gourmet food items. To capture the quality and distinction of the Vineyard Designate program, winemaker Huffman started with four sites that met specific requirements ; (optimal aspect, exposure, soil type and plant density): Doe Ridge, La Colina, Yamhill Springs, and Laurel, all in Yamhill County. Huffman also oversaw the planting of two Pinot Noir sites west of Newberg. These sites boast breathtaking views of the valley below and Mount Hood to the northeast, and promise to make great contributions to the Anne Amie Vineyard Designate Pinot Noirs in years to come. Information about their wines, wine making style and vineyards is found on Anne Amie's website. Some of the fascinating details include the limits on yields (well below Oregon's average) that are employed to concentrate the character of the grapes, 100% gravity flow for Pinot Noir vinification, and a comprehensive oak barrel program comprised solely of French oak barrels. One of their vineyards, Hawk's View, is a working study of organic viticulture. It shows a commitment to sustainable practices and best practices for obtaining exceptional fruit naturally. As well as welcoming visitors, the Winery is available for events and has its own Vineyard Club. For more information, call (800) 248-4835, or visit their website, wwww.anneamie.com.

Domaine Serene

Atop the prestigious Dundee hills of Oregon sit the Domaine Serene vineyards where the red volcanic soil and the ideal climate combine to create a place to grow world renowned Pinot Noir and Chardonnay grapes. "Pinot Noir knows everything that happens to it—and it remembers," says Grace Evenstad. She and her husband, Ken, have been proprietors of Domaine Serene for 14 years. Ken designed a state-of-the-art, gravity flow winemaking facility where Tony Rynder, winemaker, creates award-winning wines. In fact, in June 2004 at a blind tasting of Domaine Serene wines against the world's most expensive and celebrated Burgundy producer, Domaine de la Romanee-Conti, Domaine Serene ranked first and second in vintages from 1998, 1999, and 2000. Ratings were on aroma, taste and preference. The Domaine Serene wines, priced at $75 per bottle, ranked first and second against wines priced to $595. July 2004 Wines & Spirits Magazine named Domaine Serene "Estate Winery of the Year" in their annual buying guide which is released in October 2004. This is the winery's second consecutive year to receive this prestigious award which places them among the 100 top wineries of the world. All the fruit is estate-grown with an insistence on extremely low yields to maximize the quality. Domaine Serene's vineyards are sustainably farmed without the use of chemical insecticides. The Tasting Room is open on Saturdays only, tours are conducted by appointment. Visit Domaine Serene at 6555 N.E. Hilltop Lane, in Dayton, Oregon. You may contact them by phone at (503) 864-4600 and access their website at www.domaineserene.com.

Kristin Hill Winery

Located in the heart of the Yamhill County wine country, one mile north of Amity, you will find a truly unique winery owned and operated by the warm and friendly Linda and Eric Aberg. The lovely late 1800's home accented by an absolutely stunning Camperdown Elm Tree, which is thought to be at least as old as the home, lets you know that you have arrived. Giant Sequoias, Ponderosa pines and Port Orford cedars flank the property and provide interest to the grounds. Bring along a picnic lunch, find a complementary sparkling wine to match, and enjoy a restful meal in their constantly blooming garden with twenty acres of vineyard views. Sparkling wines are their specialty with their first vintage in 1990. Jennifer Falls, a blend of Pinot Noir and Chardonnay, is their signature wine. Jordan's Joy is an inspired salmon colored Pinot Noir. The cranberry colored, cherry sweetened Fizzy Lizzie is wonderfully unique and all are worth trying. Seek out the Generic Eric Blush, Spice is Nice Gewurztraminer, Pinot Gris, Chardonnay, Pinot Noir, Muller Thurgau and Port red wines. Kristin Hill Winery is located at the Southern end of Yamhill county at 3330 SE Amity Dayton Highway in Amity. For more information, give them a call at (503) 835-0850.

King Estate Winery

The King Estate winery combines breathtakingly beautiful grounds with high quality wines to create an unforgettable experience for visitors. The spectacular 1000-acre mountain estate includes 250 acres of vineyards. This majestic state-of-the-art Winery encompasses 110,000 square feet and is one of Oregon's largest. Modeled after a European Chateau, the Winery is an impressive sight indeed. Also located at this beautiful site are orchards, gardens, and a traditional cottage. Visitors will appreciate both the sight and sweet aroma of the 3,000 lavender plants that adorn the hillsides. The organic garden produces fresh herbs, berries, vegetables, and fruits which the culinary team uses to create masterpieces. The Winery has developed two cookbooks and has also sponsored a nationally televised PBS cooking series, New American Cuisine. Tours are given daily. The popular tasting room is often full on weekends with a line of people waiting to enter to taste the delicious Pinot Noir, Pinot Gris, and Chardonnay produced by the King Estate Winery. In response to this high demand, the Winery is building a new visitor center that will feature wine tasting, food, and a place for visitors to sit back, relax, and learn about wine. Located southwest of Eugene, the Winery is owned by the King family. Ed King Jr. and his son, Ed King III first began planting the vineyards in 1991. The Winery was built in 1992 and can now produce 400,000 gallons of wine a year. In the fall of 2004, Ed King Jr. and his son, Ed King III, were recognized by Wine and Spirits magazine as two of the "50 Most Influential Winemakers in the World." The King family employs organic growing practices, and in 2002 was certified by the Oregon Tilth Certified Organic Association. All grapes are hand farmed, with labor intensive practices including hand crop thinning and harvesting. The King Estate Winery is located at 80854 Territorial Road in Eugene, Oregon. For more information, phone (800) 884-4441 or visit their website at www.kingestate.com

Elk Cove Vineyards

As you approach the Elk Cove Vineyards' tasting room, you pass wonderful vineyards surrounded by roses, terraces and scenic views of the North Willamette Valley in Oregon. As Robert Parker of The Wine Advocate wrote: "For the pure beauty of its setting, no winery in Oregon can match the breathtaking views from Elk Cove's splendid wine tasting room." Staffed with friendly and knowledgeable hosts, the Tasting Room is warm and inviting. When Pat and Joe Campbell found their secluded property in 1973, they knew that this was the place to build on their dreams of producing fine wines. Magnificent Roosevelt Elk roamed the estate and added to the majesty of this wonderful place. The Campbells have been handcrafting wines for more than 30 years. Their son, Adam, grew up on the vineyard, and joined his father in winemaking in 1989. Adam has been the full-time winemaker since 1999. Adam loves the interesting mixture of agriculture and artistry in winemaking. The philosophy at Elk Cove is to allow the grapes to naturally express their best qualities and then to handcraft the wines. All of their Pinot Noirs are aged in the finest quality French oak barrels, and moved from tank to barrel only by gravity or inert gas pressure to protect the inherent qualities of the fruit. Elk Cove is also known for their Pinot Gris and late harvest Rieslings. The Winery is a picturesque place for weddings, corporate functions, winemaker dinners, and delicious afternoons tasting wine. Guided tours are available by appointment. The tasting room is open daily from 10am until 5pm and is closed only on Thanksgiving, Christmas and New Year's Day. Visit Elk Cove Vineyard at 27751 N.W. Olson Road, in Gaston, Oregon. You may contact them by phone at (503) 985-7760 or on the Internet at www.elkcove.com.

Cuneo Cellars

Established in 1993 with an exclusive focus on showing how red grapes express themselves in the Pacific Northwest, Cuneo Cellars creates wines that offer a passionate expression of European grape varieties with a uniquely Pacific Northwest sensibility. Under the guidance of Co-Owner and Winemaker, Gino Cuneo, the Winery has pioneered the introduction of Italian varietals to complement its Burgundy, Bordeaux, and Rhone-style red wines. They have won praise from authorities such as Northwest Palate magazine, which writes that Cuneo Cellars has the "most distinguished of all Italian varietals tasted from the Northwest." Whether they're trying a Nebbiolo or Brunello, Pinot Noir or Syrah, or even a suave Bordeaux-style blend of Cabernet Sauvignon and Merlot, red wine aficionados will find lots to love at Cuneo Cellars. Conveniently located on Highway 47 in the heart of Oregon Pinot Noir country, Cuneo Cellars offers visitors the opportunity to take part in a variety of activities. You can relax under the spacious skies on the Winery's patio, play a game of bocce ball on the traditional-style courts, and sample the best of Italian condiments and foods as you sip samples of Cuneo Cellar wines. The strategic location of Cuneo Cellars in Carlton, Oregon means it is situated midway between the warm-climate growing regions of eastern Washington and southern Oregon. To get the best grapes from these regions, the Northwest's best, Cuneo Cellars, only work with premier vineyards in order to grow and make great wines of structure and complexity, as you'll experience through their flavor and intensity, balance and length. Wine lovers are sure to enjoy the relaxed atmosphere and varied wines of Cuneo Cellars located at 750 West Lincoln Street in Carlton, Oregon. Cuneo Cellars can be contacted by calling (503) 852-0002. For more information, see their website at www.cuneocellars.com.

Oregon Wine Tasting Room & Bellevue Market

Are you on your way to the Oregon Coast and need a basket of wine and cheese to make the day memorable? Or perhaps you're on your way home, and want to sample the best wines that Oregon has to offer. Either way, the place to stop is the Oregon Wine Tasting Room and Bellevue Market on Hwy.18, 7.5 miles SW of McMinnville at the Bellevue Junction. Widely regarded as the number one wine-tasting room in the state, wine tasting manager Patrick McElligott and market manager Theresa Putman invite you to sample tastings from all five Oregon wine appellations. McElligott is considered one of Oregon's true wine experts. In addition to the wine, the store offers gourmet Oregon cheese, chocolates from a local monastery, locally made bakery goods, fine candies, espresso, ice cream, jellies, sauces, shortbreads, and more. The building, with its high-beam ceilings and concrete floor, has been in existence since the 1920's. It has served as a gasoline service station, meat market, and general store, before being transformed for its present use. The management and staff are happy to put together food, wine, and other essentials for your picnic.

The number-one red wine seller at the Oregon Wine Tasting Room and Bellevue Market is Oregon Pinot Noir. Pinot Gris is the number-one selling white wine, with Sparkling Muscat a close second. The fastest-growing grape for white wine is Viognier; Syrah has that distinction among the reds. At any one time, the tasting room features 70 to 80 or more Oregon winerie, thereby earning it the recognition as Oregon's number one tasting room. The Oregon Wine Tasting Room and Bellevue Market are co-located at 19690 SW Highway 18, McMinnville, OR 97128. Take 99W to Hwy18 past McMinnville then go 7.5 miles to the Bellevue Junction. Call (503) 843-3787 for the wine tasting room; (503) 843-2947 for the market.

LaVelle Vineyards

The beautiful manicured grounds of LaVelle Vineyards are as pleasing to the eye as their high quality wines are to the palate. Located on a secluded hillside 15 miles west of Eugene, Oregon, this 16-acre estate produces distinctive Pinot Noir, Pinot Gris, Riesling, sparkling wines, and a limited amount of Marechal Foch and Gamay Noir. First planted in 1972, LaVelle Vineyards was originally named Forgeron Winery and is the oldest winery in the Southern Willamette Valley. Doug LaVelle purchased the Winery in 1994, and the LaVelle Winery and popular Tasting Room opened in 1996. The spacious, welcoming Tasting Room exudes Old World charm with its many antiques. Every other month they offer a Murder Mystery Dinner Theater. They also have one of the largest wine clubs in the area, with private club parties and wine discounts. During the summer months, visitors are welcome to the vineyards seven days a week. LaVelle Winery presents a Full Moon party in summer. During Labor Day and Memorial Day weekends, live music and wine tasting take place. LaVelle Wine Bar & Bistro was opened in the historic 5th Street Public Market in Eugene to further serve their many customers. The Tasting Room is open daily and serves the same quality wines as those found at the vineyards, as well as delicious lunches. On Wednesday, Thursday, Friday and Saturday nights, the lights are lowered as the room is transformed into an upscale wine and piano bar, complete with talented musician, Gus Russell. A mouth-watering fondue buffet with cheese and chocolate is served along with gourmet bistro fare. Doug invites everyone to visit LaVelle Vineyards to sample their distinctive wines and experience the intimacy of the small winery. LaVelle Vineyards is open daily May through September, and on weekends October through April, at 89697 Sheffler Road, Elmira, Oregon. For more information, phone (541) 935-9406. LaVelle Wine Bar and Bistro is located at 296 E. 5th Avenue in Eugene, Oregon 97401. You can reach this location by calling (541) 338-9875.

Tyee Wine Cellars

In the Chinook trading jargon of the early Northwest, Tyee meant "chief" or "the best," a fitting name for a winery committed to producing varietal wines of the highest quality. The scenic and historic Buchanan Family Century Farm, in the heart of Oregon's Willamette Valley, is home to Tyee Wine Cellars. It was founded in 1985 by two couples, longtime local farmers David and Margy Buchanan, and Barney Watson and Nola Mosier. Tyee's labels feature Northwest Indian art and legends including raven, salmon, Dungeness crab, great horned owl and Canada goose strikingly rendered by Oregon artist, James Jordan. Tyee has a special relationship to the Willamette Valley. In 1999, the Buchanans converted 246 acres of their farm into a Wetland Reserve. Their commitment to sustainable agriculture was recognized by the Oregon Wildlife Society, who presented them with a Private Landowner Stewardship award. The Vineyard and Winery are certified under the Salmon Safe eco label. Tyee specializes in limited releases of Pinot noir, Pinot gris, Pinot blanc, Gewurztraminer, and Chardonnay, using grapes from their own Beaver Creek Vineyard as well as selections from neighboring Willamette Valley growers. Barney Watson, Tyee's winemaker, has an advanced degree in Enology and Viticulture from the University of California at Davis and worked as enologist at Oregon State University. He received a Lifetime Achievement award from the Oregon Winegrowers Association, citing his "fundamental role in bringing credibility to Oregon wines on the world stage." Tyee's Tasting Room is open to the public from noon until 5pm on weekends, April through December, and daily during the summer (June 15 through Labor Day) but visitors may also arrange an appointment. During the spring, summer and fall, plan a picnic or hike along their Beaver Pond Loop Interpretive Trail. Tyee also hosts exciting and interesting special events. To learn more, visit their website at www.tyeewine.com, or call (541) 753-8754 for questions.

Melrose Vineyards

When planning a wedding, reception, or corporate social event - indoor or outdoor - consider the spacious, pristine grounds of Melrose Vineyards located in Roseburg. Whatever your needs, the catering staff offers some of the best culinary delights to be found. Pair the great cuisine with their award winning wines and the result is an unforgettable event. The Vineyard is located on a bench of the South Umpqua River on an early French settlement. The spectacular views are a local favorite, as is the large tasting room housed in a beautifully restored 100 year old barn, complete with a gift boutique and friendly staff. The tasting room is only 5 minutes off I-5 and open daily from 11am to 5pm. Take Exit 125 and travel west on Garden Valley Blvd., to Melrose Road. Turn left on Melrose and right on Melqua, by the Melrose Store. Melrose Vineyards is located at 885 Melqua Road, in Roseburg, Oregon 97470. Call (541) 672-6080 or visit their website at www.melrosevineyards.com.

Troon Vineyard

Located just outside of Grants Pass, Troon Vineyard is a boutique winery in the heart of the Applegate Valley. Founder, Dick Troon first planted the Vineyard in 1972, and twenty years later produced roughly 1500 cases of his first wine. When Mr. Troon decided to retire, current owners, the Martin Family jumped at the chance to buy the Vineyard. Since purchasing it in August of 2003, Vintner, Chris Martin, and Winemaker, Herb Quady, have worked to expand both its size and production. The 11,000-square-foot expansion project is scheduled for completion in the summer of 2005 and will include adding an architecturally stunning new winery and tasting room as well as the planting of additional acreage. They hope to eventually expand production to 5,000 cases. One of the oldest vineyards in Southern Oregon, Troon produces world-class wines, including Alice's Rose, Jeanie in the Bottle (blush wine), Chardonnay, Cabernet Sauvignon, Zinfandel, River Guide Red and Druid's Fluid (their most popular blend). Soak up the grandeur of Troon Vineyard's 100-acre estate with 25 acres of grape-growing vineyards in their magnificent tasting room and winery. You can also enjoy the delicious pairings of food and wine their visiting chefs offer up. Troon Vineyard is located at 1475 Kubli Road in Grants Pass, Oregon 97527. To learn more about their wines, call (541) 846-9900, or you can visit their website at www.troonvineyard.com.

Bridgeview Vineyards

Cave Junction is home to Bridgeview Vineyards, a winery that stands out among the many superb Oregon wineries. Declared Oregon Winery of the Year in 2004 by Wine Press Northwest, Bridgeview is dedicated to reasonably-priced wines of extraordinary quality. And Bridgeview continually delights wine connoisseurs with its award-winning favorites, such as the Pinot Noir that took Best of Show at the Oregon State Fair in 2002. People thought Bob and Lelo Kerivan were crazy when they first started planting grapes on a 75-acre plot in 1986. The naysayers told them the rows of vines were too close together and too heavily pruned. But ignoring the criticism, the Kerivans proved that they knew exactly what they were

doing. They based their techniques on centuries-old practices common in Germany, where Lelo was raised. Now the Kerivans, with Lelo's son, René Eichmann, produce a dazzling selection of reds and whites, highlighted by their signature Blue Moon line. Prices range from $7 to $40. Bob says they have made a $100 bottle of wine, but "we just haven't found anyone silly enough to buy it!" Bridgeview's Wine Tasting Room is a popular stop in Josephine County. It receives 100,000 visitors a year thanks to the nearby proximity of the Oregon Caves and other local attractions. The word about Bridgeview is spreading far and wide. Private tours are available upon request. Located at 4210 Holland Loop Rd., Cave Junction, OR. Call toll-free, (877) 273-4843 or for more information, visit their website at www.bridgeviewwine.com.

Woolridge Creek Vineyard

At Wooldridge Creek Vineyard and Winery in Grants Pass, Oregon, Owners, Ted and Mary Warrick and Winemakers, Kara Olmo and Greg Paneitz invite you to stop in and experience an intimate family vineyard and winery. Wooldridge Creek is located in the heart of the Applegate River Valley. The Winery and vineyards are situated on a beautiful rolling hillside that overlooks the majestic valley in the distance. The vineyards were first planted in the 1970's and today consist of nine different varietals including Bordeaux: Cabernet Sauvignon, Merlot and Cabernet Franc, and Rhone: Syrah and Viognier. Wooldridge Creek's goal is to offer boutique wines that are approachable, just like the people you will meet during your visit here. Expect to learn about the history of the vineyards, about food that pairs well with the wines, and hear colorful local tales (be sure to ask about the local bears). You can contact Wooldridge Creek Winery by phone at (541) 846-6310 or visit their website at www.wcwinery.com. The tasting room is located at 818 Slagle Creek Rd., Grants Pass, OR 97527.

Weisinger's of Ashland

No trip to Ashland is complete without a visit to Weisinger's, the wonderful family-owned winery just a short drive from downtown. The Weisinger family welcomes you to their Tasting Room where you can sample their superb wines. Stop by the Gift Shop for wine accessories and gourmet treats and feel free to ask for recommendations for local restaurants or other information you might want to know about Ashland. The Weisingers know the area better than almost anyone, and they are always happy to help. The Winery was founded in 1988 by John Weisinger, a former Presbyterian minister and enthusiastic amateur winemaker since the age of 15, who turned his hobby into a vocation. Today, John and his son, Eric, who is the winemaker, are partners in this family run business that utilizes locally grown fruit, as well as their Estate vineyard, to produce ultra-premium wine. One of their most famous wines is the Petite Pompadour, an elegant blend of Bordeaux varietals from one of their Estate Vineyards, the Pompadour Vineyard, named after nearby Pompadour Bluff. Among their white wines, the Chardonnay and the Estate-grown dry Gewurztraminer are especially good, but you'll want to try as many as you can. The tasting room is located at 3150 Siskiyou Boulevard, about a mile south of downtown Ashland. Open daily May through September, and Wednesday through Sunday from October through April. Call toll-free, (800) 551-WINE (9463) or visit their website, www.weisingers.com, for more information, which includes their Calendar of Events. It features information about their elegant Winemaker's Dinners, the Annual Grape Stomp Competition, their Spring and Fall Case Sales events, and so much more.

Paschal Winery & Vineyard

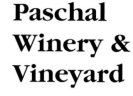

A few minutes from Ashland, the hilltop Paschal Winery and Vineyard overlooks world-famous pear orchards and the Cascade-Siskiyou mountain ranges. Here in the Eastern Rogue Valley Appellation, Owners, Roy and Jill Paschal, and award-winning Winemaker, Joe Dobbes, ply their craft to create the elegant aromas, balance and complexity that are the signature of Paschal wines. And there is a wide selection. White wines include Pinot Gris, Chardonnay, Pinot Blanc, and Viognier. Reds include Syrah, Merlot, Cabernet Sauvignon, Pinot Noir, and many more. Additionally, Paschal is starting to produce Italian style wines including Tempranillo, Dolcetto, and Sangiovese. While at the Tasting Room, enjoy the lovely views of the Vineyard and surrounding area. Let the extremely knowledgeable tasting room staff keep you informed as you sample the wines along with a selection of local cheeses and tortas. Ask if you are there at the right time to try some of the Dobbes Family Estate wines. The Paschal Winery and Vineyard is located at 1122 Suncrest Road in Talent, Oregon 97540. From I-5, take exit 21 and follow the signs for two miles to the Winery. If you visit and can't stand the thought of leaving, ask about the vacation villa available for lease. Call toll-free (800) 446-6050 or visit their website at www.paschalwinery.com.

Eden Valley Orchards & EdenVale Winery

Eden Valley Orchards, in Medford, Oregon was established in1885 by early fruit grower, Joseph H. Stewart, and expanded between 1899 and 1932 by Colonel Gordon Voorhies. This time period marked the first planting of a commercial pear orchard, and its subsequent expansion into a leading industry for the area. After revitalizing the lands once used for pear planting, current Owners, Tim and Anne Root, continue its unique tradition as a destination facility for wine lovers, promoting sustainable agriculture, historical preservation and agricultural education in the heart of Southern Oregon's wine country. Tour the Voorhies Mansion and gardens, a hallmark of the area's hospitality and an ideal place for meetings, wine tastings and weddings. Visit the Rogue Valley Wine Center's Wine Tasting Room & Market to sample their award-winning EdenVale wines, as well as other boutique Southern Oregon wines. Lastly, take a tour of the EdenVale Winery and experience the tremendous amount of effort that goes into producing a top-quality wine. Eden Valley Orchards will delight its visitors with its history, exquisite wines and gorgeous location with spectacular views.

Make sure to visit the next time you're in Southern Oregon. Eden Valley Orchards is located at 2310 Voorhies Road in Medford, Oregon 97501. For more information, call (866) 512-2955 or visit their website at www.edenvalleyorchards.com.

Index

Index

Index

Index